CW01390298

PANIC

PANIC

DAVID MARR

**TERROR! INVASION! DISORDER!
DRUGS! KIDS! BLACKS! BOATS!**

Black Inc.

Published by Black Inc.,
an imprint of Schwartz Media Pty Ltd
37–39 Langridge Street
Collingwood VIC 3066 Australia
email: enquiries@blackincbooks.com
http://www.blackincbooks.com

Copyright © David Marr 2011

ALL RIGHTS RESERVED.
No part of this publication may be reproduced, stored in a retrieval system, or
transmitted in any form by any means electronic, mechanical, photocopying,
recording or otherwise without the prior consent of the publishers.

The National Library of Australia Cataloguing-in-Publication entry:

Marr, David.

Panic / David Marr.

ISBN: 9781863955515 (pbk.)

National characteristics, Australian. Australia--Social conditions
--21st century. Australia--Economic conditions--21st century.

994.07

Printed in Australia by Griffin Press. The paper this book is printed on is certified
against the Forest Stewardship Council® Standards. Griffin Press holds FSC chain
of custody certification SGS-COC-005088. FSC promotes environmentally
responsible, socially beneficial and economically viable management of the
world's forests.

FSC
www.fsc.org
MIX
Paper from
responsible sources
FSC® C009448

Contents

1. FEAR ITSELF

Panic, power and politics in a happy nation. OCTOBER 2011.   1.

2. BEYOND THE PALE WITH PAULINE

One Nation hits the road. MAY 1997.   10.

3. PRIMAL FEAR

Race, politics and respectable Australians. MAY 1997.   16.

4. PICTURES FROM *WIK*

Waging war on native title. DECEMBER 1997.   25.

5. THE FAITHFUL GATHER

John Howard decides who comes to this country. OCTOBER 2001.   32.

6. ON THE NOSE

Letting the drug dogs loose. DECEMBER 2001.   35.

7. THE SHAPE OF THE ARGUMENT

The scary agenda of the Left. SEPTEMBER 2004.   38.

8. SAVING THE NATION

Al-Kateb condemned to everlasting detention. OCTOBER 2004.   49.

9. THE HERO OF CRONULLA

Alan Jones and the business of race riot. DECEMBER 2005.   60.

10. PICK AND STICK

Defending the hero broadcaster. DECEMBER 2006.   64.

11. A DAWN SWEEP THROUGH SYDNEY
Demonstrators today, terrorists tomorrow. MARCH 2007.   71.

12. COWBOYS AND INDIANS
The needless ordeal of Mohamed Haneef. JULY 2007.   84.

13. SCENES FROM A CITY UNDER SIEGE
Sydney battens down for APEC. SEPTEMBER 2007.   106.

14. HOME FREE
Al-Kateb gets his papers. OCTOBER 2007.   113.

15. TRUST ME
The great American mistake of 1791. APRIL 2008.   120.

16. NAKED AS THE DAY
Bill Henson and his terrifying photographs. MAY 2008.   123.

17. THE WASH-UP
Children, art and virtue. DECEMBER 2008.   144.

18. ONE HOT NIGHT FORTY YEARS AGO
Stonewall and the politics of hate. JUNE 2009.   150.

19. TIME ON THE ISLAND
Our refugee prison far, far away. SEPTEMBER 2009.   158.

20. ABBOTT RISING
An underestimated man takes charge. DECEMBER 2009.   177.

21. CAT AND MOUSE
Error, death and the destruction of SIEV 36. FEBRUARY 2010.   180.

22. MY LOVE OF DRUGS
The lost politics of reform. NOVEMBER 2010.   195.

23. BELLING THE CAT
Naming and shaming the enemies of rights. DECEMBER 2010.　　210.

24. THE DARK MATERIALS
Old fears and the toxic politics of the boats. OCTOBER 2011.　　224.

Notes　　251.

Rae de Teliga
Wise friend

1.

FEAR ITSELF

We are in a panic again. This golden country, so prosperous, so intelligent, so safe and orderly, is afraid of refugees arriving in fishing boats. This is the great Australian fear, one that never really goes away: the fear of being overrun by dusky fleets sailing down from the north. Every time refugee boats appear on the horizon in any numbers, we panic. Facts then count for little. Hearts are hardened. Terrible things are done in the name of protecting the nation. Though this is not the first wave of boats and won't be the last, the politics are more rancorous than ever.

Panic has been with us from the start. It's so Australian. Panic over the Chinese was the midwife of Federation and we have been swept by panics ever since. We were terrified of saboteurs in World War One, Wobblies and Reds in the 1920s, anarchy in the Depression, and Communists all over again after World War Two. Drugs, crime and queers have provoked panic forever, it seems, though lately the thousand-year fear of homosexuals has faded away. So has the old Protestant terror of Catholics. What were they all about? It's a mark of panics that once they die down they seem, looking back, unconvincing and even comic. We used to panic about the novels of D.H. Lawrence and the films of Pasolini. Christians still fight the good fight against smut but unless the victims seem somehow to be children – very much a panic of our time – public alarm has almost entirely died.

It came to me when I was reporting the mad uproar over Bill Henson's photographs a couple of years ago that I've been writing about panics all my career: how they are whipped up, do their worst and disappear leaving only wreckage behind. Perhaps I'm alert to the subject because I'm gay. When I was growing up, preachers, police, politicians and the press were still keeping panic alive about people like me. It has left me despising panic merchants, particularly those Tory fear-mongers who represent themselves as guardians of decency. The politicians I most admire are those who hold their nerve in the face of irrational fear on the rampage. I've come to believe the fundamental contest in Australian politics is not so much between Right and Left as panic and calm.

Labor drove the early fear of the Chinese, and Labor has been up to its neck at times in panics about Blacks and Reds, poofs and dirty books. Labor can't claim to be always on the side of calm. This is an issue that goes deeper than division between the parties. It's about the odd willingness of Australia's leaders to beat up on the nation's fears. They coarsen politics. They narrow our sympathies. They make careers for themselves in this peaceful and good-hearted country by managing, from time to time, to make us afraid. The last fifteen years have seen this country in states of exaggerated alarm over native title, Muslim preachers, Muslim rapists, drugs, terrorists both foreign and home grown, demonstrators in the streets and pictures of naked children on gallery walls. But we end the decade as we began in a full-scale panic over refugees coming here – as they reach countries all over the world – uninvited in little boats.

I was a kid journalist in 1975. My heart was with Whitlam even as I watched his government fall to pieces. His defeat was inevitable but his opponents wanted him out at once. To that end a mighty panic was beaten up in the press, in parliament and at the big end of town. By October 1975, a deeply conservative paper like the *Sydney*

Morning Herald was unashamedly calling on its front page for the overthrow of a government:

> It is in the plainest interest of national self-preservation to get rid of a management which has reduced a rich and fortunate country to the verge of economic and social disintegration.

Fantasies of vice-regal power were being promoted everywhere. Lawyers who knew better were calling for the urgent disregard of the constitution. In the midst of that hysteria Whitlam was dismissed by the governor-general. Two lessons were there to be learnt about the politics of panic: how willing conservative politicians in this country are to toy with disorder, and how popular that can be. Whitlam's fall was endorsed overwhelmingly at the ballot box. But who except a few Liberal Party hacks and monarchists are left willing to defend 1975?

Big political careers have been built in this country on little more than a talent for whipping up fear. Billy Hughes was an absolute master of the art. He blamed Fenians and their Catholic supporters for blocking conscription in 1916 and opened a religious fissure in Australian society that would not heal for half a century. And in the last years of World War One he set off perhaps the greatest panic ever to sweep the country. Ships had begun mysteriously disappearing along the coast of New South Wales. Hughes knew a German raider was responsible but, with no warships to hunt it down and a great clamour for action at home, he furiously blamed German saboteurs at work on land. *The Wolf,* a riveting account of the raider's work, details the witch hunts and arrests that followed. Newspapers backed Hughes to the hilt, screaming for the internment of anyone even remotely touched by a German connection. It was pure panic:

Thousands of Australians of German extraction were fired from their jobs and spied on by neighbours, and more than four thousand of them imprisoned in rural concentration camps, often on mere suspicion of disloyalty. More than two and a half thousand companies were identified as suspicious or shut down completely, and up to ten thousand letters a week were intercepted by the censor. The names of dozens of Australian towns – Bismarck, Blumberg, Heidelberg, Germanton – were changed to remove all traces of their origins as German immigrant communities. Even the Australian army general John Monash – later hailed as one of the most brilliant military tacticians of the First World War – was subject to hostility and rumour because his parents were German-speaking Poles.

The authors Richard Guilliatt and Peter Hohnen observe laconically: "In the entire course of the First World War, not a single case of German espionage within Australia would be substantiated."

In war and peace, panics must have something at their heart that matters. They can't be whipped up out of nothing. Panics are reasonable fears twisted out of all recognition. A decent face has to be put on the passions aroused. Appearances count. Language matters. Skilled panic merchants find ways of suggesting, however vaguely, that the survival of the nation is at stake – not always the integrity of its territory but its heart, its health, its spirit, its way of life. Such desperate times require tough laws and strong leadership. Panic is a rallying cry for power.

The fall of the Berlin Wall was a low moment for panic-mongers. Communism had been a great gift to panic in this country, keeping the right people in power for a long, long time. There was much to fear in and after World War Two from Communist espionage, treason and industrial mayhem. But fear of the Red Menace was kept alive in this country long after the party was spent. Cold War warriors still had troops to command into the 1980s but the game was up when the wall came down. Energetic attempts in the Howard years to ignite fear about the agenda of the Left – particularly entrenched in the "taxpayer-funded" ABC, universities and museums – caused angst in the commentariat but failed to move the public. The Red Menace was utterly exhausted. In the end, Communism even betrayed its detractors.

Race took its place. Nearly all the panics that gust through our politics start somewhere abroad. We share them with the world. But the source and focus of Australia's disquiet about race is peculiarly our own. It goes back to the beginning: back beyond Federation, even beyond the gold rushes. The discovery of native title by the High Court in 1992 let loose across the country wild fears and old hatreds that had not died down when the judges delivered a second shock in 1996: first *Mabo* and then *Wik*. Pauline Hanson surfed both waves of panic to a series of political victories that briefly turned her One Nation Party into a third force in national politics. John Howard dealt in the same panics, implacably opposed to *Mabo* and determined to cut *Wik* to the core. By the time Australia calmed down over native title in the late 1990s, he was more firmly entrenched in power than ever and the redhead from Ipswich was a spent force. When it came to playing the panic game, one was a professional and the other an amateur.

Australians aren't much impressed by great abstractions like justice and liberty. We are an orderly, practical people. We trust our politicians. We expect them to look after us. When they call for fresh powers to meet fresh dangers we nearly always agree to their demands. The warnings of lawyers and the civil liberties brigade don't have much traction. On the statute books of this country are ferocious laws barely used and mostly forgotten once the fears that provoked them die down. They are the scar tissue of panics passed.

September 11 and the London bombings in 2005 provoked John Howard to introduce – and Labor to support – a radical regime of secret detention without charge or trial; house arrest and control orders without charge; detention of witnesses for questioning; covert surveillance of non-suspects; blocking the access of lawyers to evidence; criminalising anti-war protest and extending the reach of already shadowy sedition laws. Kent Roach of the University of Toronto recently remarked: "Australia has exceeded the United Kingdom, the United States, and Canada in the sheer number of new anti-terrorism laws that it has enacted since September 11, 2001."

This assault on fundamental principles provoked opposition from the legal profession, human rights and civil liberties bodies and the now familiar – if still incongruous – alliance of Gough Whitlam and Malcolm Fraser. But at that time, with fears running high, Australians embraced the gutting of old protections and old principles in order, or so it seemed, to save the country from terrorism. Yet using those laws can be dangerous for their backers. Injustices we can't grasp in the abstract are clear enough to Australians in practice. We didn't need any convincing that the jailing of the Gold Coast doctor Mohamed Haneef was wrong. Very wrong indeed. It helped unseat a police commissioner and was another blow to the already ragged reputation of the prime minister.

In the face of panic, the courts in this country have a mixed record. When the mob is restless and the shock jocks are howling for action, judges are supposed to stay aloof, focus on the facts and be guided by principle alone. But judges aren't immune from irrational fears. The noise of the mob too often reaches the courtroom. It didn't in 1951 when, at the height of post-war alarm over the Red

Menace, the High Court struck down Bob Menzies's Communist Party Dissolution Act designed to give – without any supervision by the courts – power to Coalition ministers to seize the party's property and imprison its members. Menzies, who always touted himself as a great defender of liberty and the rule of law, then tried to acquire the power by referendum. What followed was the rare sight of the Labor Party standing up to the mob and beating fear at the ballot box. For once, panic met its match.

For a long time the High Court gave its seal of approval to the cruel and unusual measures Australia put in place to punish and deter refugees arriving in this country by boat. The court signed off on mandatory detention in the early 1990s and so there grew up in this country a parallel prison system for refugees, as often as not stuffed with children. Had the judges brought calm to this issue then, governments of all stripes would be looking back now with profound gratitude. The court folded and the camps in the desert are with us still. But the mood of the court has shifted. Late in 2010, with fears of the boats running high, the court came to the unanimous conclusion that everyone detained in the system had to be treated fairly and according to law. In August 2011, the court made a decision as radical and as simple: any asylum seekers we send away to another country for processing must have the same rights up there they would have had down here. We have obligations, said the judges. We can't just dump these people and run. This might have been a moment for taking stock, for calming down. Instead the court's decision provoked political uproar with the Opposition driving and the government driven by this defining panic.

The fears of the most fearful Australians cannot be ignored in a democracy. They must be decently addressed. Perhaps what gives Australian politics its particular flavour is the willingness of both Labor and the Coalition to indulge fears they haven't the courage or the will to contest. They come and go. Old fears recycled work their magic over and over again. We don't seem to learn. Yet most Australians are not fearful. According to the polls we are on the whole optimistic, open and accepting. Even so, at every election since the mid-1990s – Kevin Rudd's victory in 2007 being the only exception – the mandate of the fearful has decided who governs Australia.

Radio, television and newspapers are so often the friends of panic. There's a cynical old saying that the purpose of the tabloid press is to maintain a perpetual state of false alarm. My years at *Media Watch* were largely spent investigating those alarms and becoming, in the process, enthralled by the leading panic merchants of the media: Piers Akerman, young Andrew Bolt and the indestructible Alan Jones. Radio is the perfect medium for whipping up panic: the voice without the face brings fear so efficiently to the breakfast table. For these shock jocks and newspaper columnists, the Labor Party and shadowy forces out on the Left are to blame for all the catastrophes closing in on Australia. There is another adage about the tabloids I once put to Bob Carr: that their purpose is to persuade the working class to vote Tory. He replied, "I think it is incontrovertible."

Jones was an old interest of mine. Watching that monster of rectitude in the witness box at the cash-for-comment inquiry proved one of the most amusing assignments of my career. He couldn't for the life of him remember what was going through his head when he signed secret contracts worth millions of dollars to plug goods, services and causes on 2UE. "I can't get into the mindset," he said, twisting his fingers to his brow as if performing *bewilderment* in a serious game of charades. "I can't, I can't get into the mindset." But his followers did not desert him after this humiliation. He survived with ratings intact. Ditto his self-belief. Jones would go on to become one of the most energetic panic-mongers of our time, his rages against

Muslims defended by John Howard even in their violent aftermath.

Politicians who deal in panic wear out their welcome. The grubby business of terrifying the electorate over and over again takes its toll. Howard was the most professional politician I expect to see at work in my lifetime, and nothing was more professional than his manipulation of Australia's fears. He took the art further than any prime minister since Billy Hughes. He brought the fanning of race fear back into mainstream politics. But a decade of this left him – as it left Hughes – rather shop worn. So many scares had come and gone, failing to deliver on their bleak promises. His last days in office caught the disenchantment perfectly. Sydney was locked down for a gathering of world leaders: crowds were corralled behind high wire fences; demonstrators were arrested in droves; police strutted about in brand new riot gear; water-cannon were at the ready – and into this great security panic drove a team of comedians in Arab dress in a car flying the Canadian flag. Howard looked foolish. Australia laughed all the way to the polls. Panic can't take a joke.

Under different leaders we soldier on, the same country we've always been: a wonderful place but a bit gullible at times. We trust our leaders but that trust is not always repaid. As Australia grows inexorably more prosperous and progressive and relaxed, the forces of reaction have to work a little harder to frighten us from time to time – just enough to make it difficult to imagine how much better life might be if we were ruled more often than not by good sense, order and calm.

Here are a few dozen dispatches from the republic of panic, stories of fear and fear-mongering under three prime ministers. Some chart panic on the rise and others pick through the wreckage left behind, but all grew out of my wish to honour the victims of these ugly episodes: the people damaged and a damaged country.

2.

BEYOND THE PALE WITH PAULINE
MAY 1997

"Here I am," she called, and with a girlish wave Pauline Hanson planted her gold shoes on the stage of Ulverstone's Leven Theatre and the audience on the last stop of her Apple Island tour rose to give her a standing ovation.

From the evidence of the past few days, these ovations are about the extent of her people's generosity. They are not the rednecks they are imagined to be. Ulverstone might be the epicentre of suicide, unemployment and dashed dreams on the "Paradise Coast" of Tasmania, but these folk are doing OK – perhaps not as well as they once did, but OK – and they are planning to share none of their prosperity with blacks, Asians or the world.

Hanson shines in this assembly. There is no one who looks remotely like her in the room – pale, precise, immaculately turned out, alert. She is a hardworking woman who's looked after herself. One of her lines is: "If there is a little bit of grease still on me, not washed off from the fish shop, you'll understand." Even from the back row we can see there's not so much as a speck of lint on that perfectly ironed jungle-green jersey suit. "I've just sold the shop," she says. "March 8 was my last day. Part of my life that's finished. This part has started."

Hanson's face is so very familiar from television now – the fine powdered skin, coral lips and dark smudged eyes – but in the flesh there's something uncomfortable about that look: Irish above and Japanese below, kabuki with red hair. She might be a sister to the protestor wandering a couple of nights before through the Hobart demonstrations dressed as "Poona Li Hung", the multiracial lesbian and part machine that One Nation claims may rule Australia in 2005.

We must be frank about this: none of us would be waiting in Ulverstone's little theatre if this were a man. Pauline Hanson is a woman seen to have had the guts to stand up to the big parties and tell the truth in the face of "political correctness". Men respect her for showing courage they know they lack. It's sexy and so is she. Her first swing through the rest of Australia since last month's formation of One Nation has provoked both jeering and wolf whistles. "If I didn't think they'd arrest me, I'd kiss yer," called a follower in Launceston, a proposition she answered with a flash of teeth and quickly crinkled eyes.

Sex is oddly in the air because Hanson's host on the island is Chester Somerville, a chocolate seller from Hobart whose last-ditch stand to keep sodomy a crime in Tasmania ended in utter defeat ten days ago. But the horrors of sodomy are not mentioned at any of the meetings nor – a year after the massacre at Port Arthur – is One Nation's pledge to give gun lovers back their semi-automatic weapons.

She still hadn't spoken. The preliminaries ground on. Very patiently the Ulverstone crowd was waiting for Somerville to finish with Voltaire. This was a great day for Voltaire: Hanson was citing Voltaire at lunchtime and the prime minister was on the radio all day quoting Voltaire with a brass band in the background. As Somerville pledged himself and Pauline and the Concerned Voters Association to die for the right of us all to speak, the sound of shouting was coming through the theatre walls. The absolutely silent vigil of an hour before – with candles burning, in the Tasmanian way – had broken down into noisy confusion and chanting but it was nothing to the utter bedlam of Hobart two nights earlier.

That lasted twelve minutes by the clock at City Hall. Somerville, a suit-proud man with a sad face, called on Tasmanians to show the world what peaceful people they are: "This is an opportunity to sell our State …" But the place was already half full of chanting demonstrators: "Pauline Hanson has to go. Hey hey. Ho ho." A stout woman with three Air Force badges on her lapel explained the situation to me. "White Abos bussed in all week from Woop Woop," she said pointing to the trouble makers. Camera crews with their lights flaring headed through the chaos for the Nazi saluters. There was no fighting, but Somerville was pacing a stage now crowded with plainclothes police. His supporters were hopelessly chanting "We want Pauline" against a roar of "Piss off Pauline". In a brief lull he closed the meeting: "Democracy has been denied." He was personally liable for any damage, he explained to me when I reached the stage. So he pulled the plug.

"These are just kids," I said. "They're not dangerous, are they?"

"I don't think so."

But that was that for Hobart. Hanson called it "anarchy" at her press conference later, but it was just a very rowdy demo of a kind we haven't seen since the Vietnam days. Nor was it, as she said, provoked by the major parties. That's Hanson the blamer talking: for every setback there is always someone or something to blame. But what Hanson showed that night in Hobart is that she's not a rabble rouser – a cause of rabble, perhaps, but not a rouser. She could have come out onto the stage and provoked astonishing pictures – and all of it would have played her way. But she didn't. For her a good meeting is one where she's heard, but she also knows there's a useful message when she's not. Hence Voltaire.

Tasmania heard Pauline Hanson at last in Launceston's Albert Hall. More chairs had to be found for the lunchtime crowd of about 2000. These people seemed not so different from the demonstrators outside, but whiter, much older – and a lot of them, a local journalist said, "have lost guns".

"Can you hear me?" she asks after the second standing ovation subsided. They roar back. But what an odd manner she has: she doesn't work to lift their spirits or muster their enthusiasm. She lays out her complaints and lays them out cold. She isn't exciting. Her voice is as uncomfortable in the flesh as on television. And she doesn't breathe: what often sounds like Hanson on the verge of tears is in fact an unpractised speaker running out of breath.

Those who say she has no policies are flinching from the obvious: that she is a white woman speaking up for old White Australia. Nothing seems to come so directly from her heart as the reiterated: "I don't want to be Asianised." But her essential theme is money and these purse-proud people respond to the twin prospect of saving money and taking Australia back to some half-forgotten image of itself: white and peaceful where they might again rule the roost. Menzies is the most-dropped name, and Hanson is giving Menzies's rhetoric of the "forgotten people" another go: "You are not the forgotten people as far as I am concerned."

Always she is talking about saving money: by cutting aid to blacks, foreigners, immigrants and single mothers. The cornerstone of the One Nation Party is stopping all immigration at once, to make jobs for Australians and save money. Money, money, money. When people say "Pauline has got something" this is what they're essentially responding to: the prospect of money saved and perhaps directed their way.

Race is the chilli in the mix. She denies being a racist and this crowd would deny being racist, too. But she had a great ovation in Launceston every time she brought money and race together. And when she listed the suburbs of Australia – Cabramatta, Surfers Paradise, Richmond etc. – where "we" now feel foreigners in our own country, the people of this very white town gave her all their attention. When she pledges to get the UN off Australia's back, the applause goes way off the meter.

She is strangely uncomfortable in the face of all this. Of course, she likes it but she doesn't surf applause as good speakers do. It dies around her. She's always starting from scratch. Yet she doesn't lose the crowd: there's a kind of protective embrace that keeps her going even when she has the look in her eyes of someone not at all sure of the direction. It's the "poor chook" factor with Hanson: she's widely seen not to be very bright, but still people listen.

Which gets us to Ulverstone. At last all the formalities were done and she began, not reading her script but speaking a text she knew by heart. This was Pauline Hanson the mother speaking: the mother who had raised children on her own, stood on her own two feet, run a business and found herself in parliament because she was determined to be her own person. "Let me assure you there is no puppet pulling Pauline Hanson's strings. What you see is what you get." This is militant motherhood. And when she attacks special programs of assistance to Aborigines, she attacks them as a mother: "If you treat one child different from the rest, it creates resentment."

But for this audience she was also a frail woman: surprised to find herself a national figure, much blamed, still getting lost in the corridors of parliament and struggling – but giving herself six years – to learn the "protocol". She was at her most persuasive here: not stumbling through figures on Asianisation or putting a nearly incoherent argument about tax, but presenting this image of her steely frailty.

They gave her three cheers and bought every single $5 poster available of her wrapped in the flag rather like the queen in her Garter robes, the great star on her shoulder, staring into the far distance. As she autographed them – with a very big P for Pauline – I noticed her scarlet fingernails are plastic. For most of her fans she had only a curt yes or no, but she was a very long time leaving. Then a bulky detective at each elbow ran her through the straggling remains of the mob to her car. It was a nearly faultless operation: the car was moving before she hit the seat. The rest of the demonstrators reached the street to see her tail-lights disappearing into the night. Paul from City Hall said, "She'd better get used it, it's going to be like this every time."

1997 TO 2001

The violence at her meetings died away as Australia grew used to Pauline Hanson. The Ipswich firebrand was transforming conservative politics, robbing the Coalition parties of voters and bringing down two premiers: the Nationals' Rob Borbidge in Queensland and the Liberals' Richard Court in Western Australia. This woman was dangerous. Beating up on boat people would become her signature strategy but her early success came from driving the panic over native title. In a way that it hadn't been for half a century, race was back at the centre of Australian politics.

3.

PRIMAL FEAR MAY 1997

Noel Pearson spoke and the room was very, very still. He was not pleading, nor was he bothering much to charm, but a couple of hundred Sydney lawyers crowded into the New South Wales Supreme Court were listening to him with something like relief. He was speaking a language they understood. QCs forgot to fidget. Old Sir Harry Gibbs, last but one chief justice of the High Court, sat forward in his seat. This was as close as some of these men and women had ever been to a black Australian.

Pearson's voice is pure North Queensland softened by the Lutheran cadence of St Peter's College, Brisbane, then ironed out by the years he spent at Sydney University Law School. Pearson spoke of his time in that legal factory, where one day he discovered in one of the underground lavatories graffiti that read "True land rights by '88". And underneath in another hand, "But can fauna own land?"

Experts on the subtleties of racism in this country believe that racism in its primal form – the notion that Aborigines are a lower order of life, more another species than another race – has all but died out except in pockets of far distant Queensland. Pearson spoke of old aunts and uncles at Hope Vale up on Cape York who not so long ago quizzed a visiting anthropologist about the "scientific" theory they'd grown up with all their lives: that they were not entirely human. "How was it regarded these days?" Well, traces survive in the clever graffiti of a university in the middle of the city of Sydney. Pearson wasn't moaning about this. He was making the point that terra nullius sprang from that same notion: an assumption that the original inhabitants of the continent were not quite human. "We occupied the land, but we were fauna."

Pearson chuckled but the banks of spectators were silent. We were assembled under the ermined portraits of dead chief justices to open Law Week with an eccentric public discussion about the constitution. Pearson was the only reason for the crowd: a stocky young man, a black from the north still a few formalities short of qualifying as a solicitor. This was not a bad turnout for an articled clerk. He sat there, at ease with his own authority, chuckling away at the little shock he'd delivered this crowd by reminding them how persistent, how close to home white racism is – just over the road at the Law School.

Pearson was at the table because he has *Mabo* and *Wik* at his back. The law that once bound and excluded blacks is now the ground on which Aboriginal Australia is choosing to fight. Lawyers are winning victories which even sympathetic white politicians have baulked at pursuing. And it's being a black lawyer that brings Pearson face to face with attorneys-general, chief justices, QCs. He would be talking next day to most of them again when he addressed the NSW Law Society. He talks, they listen. They may profoundly disagree with him, but Pearson is bringing white Australia news from the other side in a language it can comprehend.

Mabo is getting hard to talk about: the word is wearing out. But Pearson has a true campaigner's knack of softening up an audience to listen once again to a message they've heard a hundred times before. He concedes that *Mabo* has produced "impatience, anger, arguments, misgivings" in white Australia, yet he sees the High

Court's decision as the best basis we have for reconciliation. "I can see it," he said, holding out his hands, dead level, in the general direction of Sir Harry Gibbs. "I can see it – just down the track."

Poor Dame Leonie Kramer. She too was on the panel to talk about the constitution, but may not have turned her mind to how *Mabo* and *Wik* have transformed the oldest debate in this country: the place and rights of those who were here first. She was putting the conservatives' familiar case, that a bill of rights might lead to an unfortunate "litigation mentality" in Australia. Pearson replied in a devastating aside: "I'm rather a fan of litigation myself."

Racism is so subtle that no white Australian can really claim to be untouched by that mix of shame, boredom and fear that has marked white response to black from the start. When we read of terrible things done to Aborigines now and in the past, we try to claim that this was the work of others and in other times. It doesn't work. Today's statistics on black disease, imprisonment, literacy and housing are damning in themselves, but it's our unexpected, fugitive responses that really give us whites away.

Did you (like me) jump out of your skin at the sight of the old black standing in the rain in Peter Weir's film *The Last Wave*? It was a fright straight out of childhood. Where did I learn about black bogeymen who take little white children away? Probably in the playground at Gordon Public. I'm still carrying that baggage somewhere on my person and know I'm not alone in that: Weir, a maestro of fear, knew exactly what he was doing when he put that silent black figure out in the storm.

The other night, an artist who works all the time with Aborigines confessed that when he was a little boy growing up in Sydney in the early 1960s he had felt "secretly grateful" to know they were dying out. He knew this was really the Aborigines' country and knew that terrible things had been done to them and "it would be so much easier if they were not around." Where all this came from he doesn't know, but it seeped into his life.

Sydney's Geographic Names Board has utterly failed to persuade developers to give new suburbs Aboriginal names. The Wahroongas and Killaras of today are Winston Hills and Chipping Norton. We could be back in the Home Counties but these names sell and Aboriginal names don't. In the past few years, the board has only been able to persuade a corner of Five Dock to rename itself Wareemba and a slice of Baulkham Hills to become Maroota. That's about that except for the chance that one of the stations on the new line to Mascot may one day be called Eora. Really, it's too embarrassing to pursue: Eora is the indigenous name for the territory lying under the Sydney CBD.*

Black stories turn away white audiences. The two stories that have mattered most this year – and are yoked together – are the rise of Pauline Hanson and the High Court's decision that the native title of the Wik people survives underneath pastoral leases on Cape York. But when *Four Corners* opened the year with a big story on *Wik*, its ratings halved from the 20 per cent of viewers it sees as its regular crowd to about 8 per cent. Nevertheless, *Four Corners* went ahead with a show about life on the Redfern "block". That got 16 per cent. John Budd, executive producer of *Four Corners*, told me: "The strength of the audience surprised me."

There were several conferences to discuss illustrations for this story when it first appeared in the *Sydney Morning Herald*. The paper was keen to run my argument – that the return of race makes sense of so much of the politics of this country – but we were facing the old worry that black faces deter white readers. Someone came up with the idea of using a black garden gnome: a

---

* It never happened.

kitsch image of Aboriginal Australia, as fake as our worst fears, but still seen occasionally in suburbs where people say of Pauline Hanson, "Yes, but she's got something."

I first heard that line the day Hanson made her debut on the *Midday Show*. I was at an aunt's house in Sydney and half a dozen of her friends were talking about the Queenslander over their whiskies. This was very early days, of course, but none would concede the obvious: she was a racist. These are good people, perhaps never very keen to absorb the facts of Aboriginal Australia, but ten years ago they would have seen Hanson for what she was. Why not now?

The sight of so many supporters outside Hanson's meetings in Tasmania posed the same question: how can they not see, or not particularly care, what she is preaching? What has happened? So many in crowds volunteered when they saw my reporter's notepad: "She's not a racist, you know."

Hanson doesn't talk race in the old biological terms these people grew up with, smearing blacks as fauna and lower orders. She uses the new racial jargon of equality and self-help. "I am not a racist. None of my remarks in their proper context could be fairly regarded as racist. I am not opposed to any person or group because of their race, colour or national or ethnic origin … but I am opposed to, and so are the vast majority of Australians, discrimination in favour, as well as against, any person or group. I want equal treatment for all Australians."

Then she belittles Aboriginal need – argues, indeed, that they are privileged – and puts dispossession and discrimination a long way back in the past. Time is an essential part of Hanson's appeal: the 200 years she puts between us and the subtle guilt revived in Australia by *Mabo*. "I am fed up with being told, 'This is our land.' Well, where the hell do I go? I was born here and so were my parents and children. I will work beside anyone and they will be my equal but I draw the line when told I must pay and continue paying for something that happened over 200 years ago."

Exasperation with *Mabo* and *Wik*, a sense that we've all gone too far, a feeling that these decisions contradict every expectation of how race works in this country, seem to explain the public blindness to Hanson's racism: this is where the line must be drawn. That has changed the map of race in modern Australia, and the map of politics. *Mabo* and *Wik* stand equally behind Noel Pearson, Pauline Hanson and John Howard.

Only racism can finally explain our national response to *Mabo*. That some day Aboriginal communities may have title to Crown lands they already occupy hardly warrants the outpourings of rage since the decision was announced on 3 June 1992. But it goes much deeper than land. *Mabo* was the moment when the courts turned face-about: instead of expressing racism through terra nullius, they began modestly to oppose. The law changed sides, though the judges didn't order stolen land to be handed back – as is happening nowadays in New Zealand and South Africa – but said what was left might belong to Aborigines.

Those who found the result impossible, a violation of the proper order of things, were arguing neither from law nor history. Race makes sense of their gut rejection, first of *Mabo* and then of the court's modest conclusion in *Wik* that black communities which have never lost their connection with lands now leased by pastoralists to run cattle may continue to enjoy access to these lands – so long as they don't hinder pastoralists as they go about their work.

The hammering the High Court has been getting since for "inventing" new laws is starting to take on the pattern of a racist backlash – supported by most of the governments of the Commonwealth – to decisions that challenge white Australia's sense of its natural place in the system. In the course of this controversy, the difficulties whites now face owning and using land in the bush have been spectacularly exaggerated. Indeed, the challenge of the *Wik* decision to pastoralists' "certainty" is emerging as one of the great beat-ups in the history of relations between the races in Australia.

The prime minister's Ten-Point Plan – the forced transfer of Aboriginal property rights to pastoralists – can be contemplated calmly only by those unworried by its essentially racial logic, which Howard stood and defended to the Akubras and tweed assembled in Longreach. They wanted the logic pressed to its conclusion: complete extinction of native title rights. Would they – would Howard – want this if whites held those rights? For all the prime minister's wish to locate in the unexamined past our wrongs to Aboriginal Australia, we are planning in the 1990s to take from black to give to white roughly as we always have on this continent. It was always the Australian way.

Aboriginal paintings were never more in demand than when the Coalition moved into the Parliament House suites just vacated by Paul Keating's defeated ministers in 1996. The stores were ransacked for desert masterpieces. Ochre and dots was the new government's look. But the ministers had fought their way there with a campaign slogan, "For All of Us", that whispered the same egalitarian racism that Pauline Hanson was later to preach openly: the idea that minorities (blacks, foreigners, unionists etc.) were taking too much from government, that it was time for ordinary (white) Australians to be the centre of attention again. And once in power, this was the ministry that made immediate moves against what John Howard called "the Aboriginal industry".

Race has taken its place at the main table. The 1967 referendum wasn't the moment we put all this behind us. Australians are hugely generous when called on to make big gestures that cost nothing –

and no referendum has ever been carried with such unanimity as this was to bring black Australians into the Federation. But what followed – land rights, black health, justice for Aborigines – cost white Australia money and a little land. These programs were contested all the way. The politics was tough. Yet for much of the thirty years since the referendum, a decent compact operated in Canberra not to take party-political advantage of the persistent racism that both sides of politics know is out there. All their polling tells them this. We're celebrating the anniversary of the referendum with that old compact in tatters. The Howard government boasts this achievement as the end of "political correctness".

Once having let race out of the bag in which it has been contained (more or less) for the past 20 years, Howard faces the daily more difficult task of keeping the mainstream happy while finessing issues out at the fringe. Noel Pearson calls this "wedge politics" and attacked these "ruthless tactics" in another powerful speech last week – this time delivered at the presentation of the NSW Law Society's media awards.

> Whilst elections in the Northern Territory have routinely generated and exploited white paranoia and racism in relation to Aboriginal people and land rights to secure Country Liberal Party victories, I cannot think of an election in which Aboriginal affairs, and particularly questions of Aboriginal privilege and comparative white disadvantage, have featured at all in a national election campaign. It was a big part of the undercurrent of the last campaign – particularly in regional Australia – and in my view it was deliberately so.

It was a rousing speech gently delivered. Pearson ended, as he always does these days, by invoking *Mabo* as "the foundation of truth" without which a national structure can't endure. "We forsake *Mabo* and we will be bereft of our one chance at national coherence: an opportunity to come to terms with the past, take its prescriptions in the present and therefore map out the future."

During the ovation that followed, the Sydney QC Rick Burbidge leant over to the *Four Corners* reporter Liz Jackson and wondered aloud if Pearson had written the speech himself. Jackson was shocked: "The speech was so clearly from the heart. It was so personal." The exchange was reported next day in the *Financial Review*. Burbidge has now assured the *Herald* that he was not sceptical because Pearson is an Aborigine. Burbidge is aware of speakers who speak from drafts and notes prepared by others. He is anxious to make this clear: "I'd have asked it if it was the governor-general making the speech."

4.

PICTURES FROM *WIK*

John Howard's Ten-Point Plan to roll back *Mabo* and *Wik* reached parliament in September 1997. The fear of blacks then sweeping the country had been whipped up for a purpose: to persuade the Senate it was better to pass the plan than risk a dirty, destructive election fought over Aborigines and native title. An alliance of all the Opposition parties plus the independent Tasmanian senator Brian Harradine could defeat Howard's legislation. A man of high Catholic principle, Harradine had to judge how far to push the government on a number of key issues. One was Canberra's plan to suspend the Racial Discrimination Act and expose native title rights to attack by hostile state governments.

BACKYARDS IN PERIL 4 DECEMBER 1997

These senators should know better: Eric Abetz, BA, LLB (Tas.), Amanda Vanstone, BA, LLB (Adel.), Nick Minchin, BEc, LLB (ANU). Their colleagues may be thrashing around in the dark, but these three know native title claims cannot succeed on freehold land.

They are lawyers. Lawyers know how to read a High Court judgment. They know the basis of *Mabo* is that white freehold extinguishes native title. They know the High Court described the history of Aboriginal dispossession as conquest, not by guns, but by the spread of white freehold across the continent. They know that if native title was really claimable on freehold land, the prime minister would have been holding up on television a map of the Commonwealth that was black from shore to shore.

But they have been part of the government's high-octane scare campaign built round clever legal fudging of the possibility that blacks might, by whim of the High Court, make a successful claim on a freehold backyard. Yesterday, Amanda Vanstone took the Senate through the great occasions on which the High Court has changed its mind. The message was: you can't trust the judges to hold firm on extinguishment, and the court that gave us *Wik* and *Mabo* is just waiting for the chance …

Senior lawyers across Australia are deploring the scare campaign. They are not succinct by nature, but a couple of days ago a group of them – including Ian Barker QC, a former solicitor-general of the Northern Territory – wrote a letter to this paper that read, in full: "To suggest that native title can possibly attach to freehold land is simply a lie." The letter was read in the Senate yesterday, in a bad-tempered patch of what's been, for such a passionate debate, remarkably calm.

John Herron, minister for Aboriginal and Torres Strait Islander affairs, had a hard time explaining how other ministers could hold fears for backyards when *Rebutting the Myths* – a Commonwealth publication with his face and endorsement on page five – should list as a myth "My backyard isn't safe from an Aboriginal claim" and give an official reassurance that on freehold land "a native title claim cannot succeed". Herron, a leading surgeon, replied: "That quote is quite consistent with the statement from the Prime Minister, me and Senator Minchin that no case has gone before the High Court to test the High Court's decision. That is the fact. The fact is that there has been no case."

For the government, *Mabo* and *Wik* don't count.

Herron seemed to know he was on toast and took it well. The non-lawyers have been able to go down the backyard track without much personal pain. But it hurts the lawyers to go through this. Amanda Vanstone gave a volcanic performance in the Senate earlier in the week defending her version of the freehold scare – both admitting backyards were safe but warning of dangers to freehold everywhere.

And yesterday Nick Minchin lost it as he defended himself against "the scurrilous accusations" and "deliberate misrepresentation" of his position on backyards. There was lots of complex stuff in his answer that had nothing to do with people sitting under their Hills hoists in the suburbs. And there wasn't the simple statement that would end this scare – if the government wants it ended – before it does any more damage: freehold backyards are absolutely safe.

Maybe later in the week. Maybe not.

HARRADINE'S SANDWICH 6 DECEMBER 1997

After lunch yesterday, the pale senator sat for a moment at his seat, steadying himself perhaps, before walking over to Nick Minchin. From the gallery we couldn't, of course, hear the few words Brian Harradine said before stepping away. Senator Minchin shook his head.

Minchin is a man almost devoid of gesture. In all the hours of close debate this week as he defended this immensely complex bill from three-way and sometimes four-way attack from the Greens, Democrats, Labor and Senator Harradine, Senator Minchin hardly ever raised his voice. He struck no poses. At this point he looked very, very still.

He had seemed to have another victory almost in the bag. Before lunch Senator Harradine wasn't going to have anything to do with the Opposition's plan to put the bill under the protective umbrella of the Racial Discrimination Act. He denounced the idea as "a lawyer's picnic" and told Labor angrily to "face up to the real world".

Senator Harradine left the chamber. Waiting outside the door was one of the invisible senior advisers to the Opposition, John Basten SC. "Senator, you've made a terrible mistake," he said. "This will send the wrong message to all of Australia." Over lunch – a sandwich – the lawyers worked on Senator Harradine. They told him this: the totality of the bill had a much better chance of surviving a High Court challenge if it declared itself within the principles of the Racial Discrimination Act. Senator Harradine was convinced.

Nothing had changed in his demeanour when he re-entered the Senate. The gruelling work of the past few days hardly seems to have touched him. After delivering the news to Senator Minchin, Senator Harradine sat with Labor's Barney Cooney, a man of Senator Harradine's generation, a barrister who gets to the quick of complex legal issues. Senator Harradine admires him. A weak patch of sunlight fell on the two old men as they spoke. Senator Harradine's big hands were working. They nodded. Senator Harradine returned to his seat to await the moment.

"I have been giving this further thought," he began. Ron Castan QC, the hitherto invisible most senior adviser to the government's opponents, was sitting with Senator Harradine's team – John McCarthy QC and Jeff Kildea – at the back of the Senate. Castan was slumped forward in what seemed an attitude of prayer.

"Much of the power under this act is going to devolve to the States and that's a matter I've been concerned about," Senator Harradine began. Before lunch he'd said what was needed to protect the Aboriginal people was a vigorous Federal minister, and an alert public in the States to "ensure the political message gets across". John McCarthy was now praying as Senator Harradine took his time.

Everyone all week had taken their time. It had meant a long debate – longer spent amending than passing the Native Title Act in the first place – but this was parliament working. The senators were out to persuade one another, debate was repetitive but lucid – particularly as Senator Harradine drove his colleagues to translate complexity into real English – and the result of nearly every important vote was unknown until it was taken.

Only up in the galleries was parliament not working: hard as it was for everyone else with piles of paper in front of them, it was impossible for the public upstairs to follow the amendments and counter-amendments. But they sat waiting for bursts of rhetoric, or vital votes. Early in the week there was a bit of a showing by graziers. They didn't last long. The Aborigines, of course, were the stayers.

Senator Harradine now laid it out: "Unless we have the act constrained subject to the Racial Discrimination Act we may indeed be giving the wrong messages to the whole of Australia and all Australians – not only indigenous Australians but also those likely to require the provisions of this act to resolve problems in a sensible and orderly fashion." Then came the moment of pure Harradine. With his hands in a gesture of atonement he said: "I do apologise to the Senate and I indicate now that I am supporting the amendment proposed by the Opposition."

This was a very big loss for the government. Senator Minchin rose, cool as ever. "I don't know what Senator Harradine had for lunch," he said. "I retain my respect for Brian Harradine but he was right before lunch and wrong after lunch." They took the vote. The gallery applauded. Senator Minchin showed nothing. Senator

Harradine looked immensely pleased. After that, the vote that sent the bill back to the House of Representatives was an anti-climax – except for the sight of the Nationals' Senator Ron Boswell, weeping.

SAVE THE BEES 6 DECEMBER 1997

As of yesterday, Hindu temples are safe from native title claim. At least in Queensland. So are monorails, coral art displays, club-houses for the Grand Lodge of the Royal Antediluvian Order of Buffaloes, ski clubs (in Queensland!), kangaroo pet-food depots and pottery clubs.

These are just a few details of the States' "shopping lists" contained in a fat schedule at the back of the bill which is a measure, in its way, of how little success anyone has had out in the bush explaining – if anyone, Labor or government, really tried to explain – what *Mabo* and *Wik* mean.

Of course, under *Wik* you can keep on doing what you're given a lease to do – native title or not – but the States have served Canberra with a list of leases to be made absolutely "safe" while those leases run: no Antediluvian Buffalo will ever have to co-exist with an Aborigine on his little plot of land. They shall not pass …

Queensland's list runs for three tightly packed pages, in alphabetical order from "abattoir" to "youth hall". There are crocodile farms, croquet pitches and knackeries. Safe from Aboriginal claim after yesterday's vote in the Senate will be Queensland's rugby league clubs. Rugby union does not seem so protected by law – perhaps those blokes can look after themselves.

The West's list is even more detailed. It includes an artificial limb factory, stacks of firewood, anything to do with pearling, a whaling factory (something going on here Canberra should know about?), a dog kennel and a tourist facility associated with emus.

The miners put in their own list in the West. Every single facility that could be in any way associated with a mine is listed in detail. This includes a dog pound and a red mud pond.

Up in the Territory, they've given the Salvation Army a guernsey.

New South Wales guarantees, as do all States, that there will be no co-existence on golf courses, archery ranges, CWA rooms and Scout halls. But we have added a few specials that do honour to the State. From now on, no native title claims can succeed on land leased for the purposes of a night soil depot.

But perhaps the "bee farms" are beyond a joke. Does the Carr government really believe we live in a world where bees and blacks can't co-exist in the same stretch of bush?

JULY 1998

After the longest debate in the history of the national parliament, the much-amended Native Title Amendment Act was passed. With that, the panic over native title was allowed to die. It has never revived. The election that October was fought not over race but tax. Howard won the GST election only narrowly. The anxieties of the nation now shifted to refugees who were beginning to arrive by sea in numbers Australia had never seen before: over 4000 in 1999 and nearly 3000 the following year. The detention centres in remote Australia were bursting with Afghans who had fled the Taliban and Iraqis on the run from Saddam Hussein. Panic stoked by One Nation was spreading across Australia as more boats than ever continued to arrive in the election year of 2001.

5.

THE FAITHFUL GATHER

In late August 2001, John Howard refused to allow a Norwegian freighter called the *Tampa* to disembark at Christmas Island 433 asylum seekers rescued from a boat broken down in the Indian Ocean. There followed a diplomatic brawl with Norway and Indonesia, a stand off with the United Nations, the deployment of the navy and the SAS and millions paid to the bankrupt little nation of Nauru to house these refugees thousands of miles from Australia. It was all hugely popular.

OCTOBER 2001

A good recital hall makes applause sound great. Sydney's City Recital Hall is perfectly tuned to let an audience bask in the sound of its own clapping. It took the Liberal Party backroom boys – professional even in this – to realise what's good for Bach and Boccherini will work to launch an election campaign. The hall offers tight security, no windows for yobbos to bash as they did in Parramatta last time and, despite the empty seats in the gods, great rolling breakers of applause.

For Philip Ruddock, the protector of Australia's borders, this meant a tumult of whistling, stamping and clapping. The needle went right off the dial, not once but twice. The first time John Howard praised him, the minister stood and took a bow. The second time he kept modestly in his seat, inclined his head and mouthed "thank you very much" at a beaming prime minister on stage.

Wherever the *Tampa* tactics lead Australia in the years to come, those of us in the City Recital Hall yesterday will remember the sight and the sound of a white, prosperous audience baying for border protection. They know it's the winning ticket and John Howard has found it for them. He is a genius of sorts: he looks this country in the face and sees us not as we wish we were, not as one day we might be, but exactly as we are. The political assessment is ruthlessly realistic. Only the language is coy. But who has ever admitted to playing the race card?

Staring straight into the barrel of the television cameras he declared the big theme of the 2001 election was national security which called for more than "a proper response to terrorism" and a far-sighted defence policy. "It is also about having an uncompromising view about the fundamental right of this country to protect its borders. It's about this nation saying to the world we are a generous open-hearted people … We have a proud record of welcoming people from 140 different nations. But we will decide who comes to this country and the circumstances in which they come."

As the applause rolled on, Howard gripped each side of the lectern hard, straining upwards a little as if trying to catch the light. He is very good at reading applause. He knows when to smile, when to gesture in triumph and when, as now, to stay resolutely grim. Still they clapped. All the old premiers of New South Wales brought out for the occasion; the shattered ranks of the Liberal Left which once rolled Howard for suggesting a faint shadow of the *Tampa* policy; most of the cabinet; a squad of sitting members and senators; Liberal contenders for hopeless seats which are now suddenly winnable; and the Howard family, wife, children and brothers, superbly turned out in the front row.

Up in the second tier, Channel 9's Laurie Oakes and the ABC's Jim Middleton were standing with their backs to the stage. This looked, at first, like an Aboriginal gesture of disapproval which other journalists weren't brave enough to join. Then it became clear they were waiting to do their pieces to camera when Howard finished. He spoke for over an hour. Howard is not as funny, young and dangerous as his deputy Peter Costello. He doesn't let himself use laughter. But this was a very effective Howard performance, on song right to the finish. "I believe my instincts, my energy, my experience, my successes to date, and my sheer commitment to the land I love, best equip me for the job."

There was a standing ovation. He took what bushmen call a dingo's breakfast – a sip of water and a quick look around – then plunged into the applauding crowd. The recital hall rang with a sound very like victory.

6.

ON THE NOSE 22 DECEMBER 2001

No sniffer dogs came through the premier Bob Carr's Christmas drinks on Tuesday. The night was young and the town with all its pleasures lay before us, but while we drank beer on the forty-first floor of the Governor Phillip Tower, no Labradors came to sniff us, no cops ordered us to turn out our pockets or strip to our underpants to be searched for drugs.

New South Wales is now the state of the sniffer dog. Off the tops of their heads, Labor advisers can't think of another place in the world where drug dogs and their police handlers roam the community without warrants. At airports and prisons, yes, but not in pubs, clubs, railway stations, grandstands and buses as they do now in New South Wales.

After the Olympics, good homes could have been found for these expensive animals. They might have settled down as loved pets and valued companions. Instead, a new market was found for their talents. The rhetoric is all about catching drug dealers; the reality is all about pulling in users. They do. The stats are a dream. Don't believe anyone who tells you these dogs aren't very good.

Sure, from time to time they detect Oxo cubes and chicken burgers, but they can sniff out tiny quantities of hard drugs. Smelly old cannabis is child's play for a puppy. Dope is also, of course, the drug 40 per cent of Australians use every year.

Air your clothes well after a party. Redfern Legal Centre is warning the public that a jacket worn at a party where dope is smoked can earn you an embarrassing public encounter with a dog and handler.

This is the routine. You're standing on Wynyard Station at peak hour, or the dance floor at DCM in Oxford Street, and the sniffer dog bunts you with its nose or stops and sits beside you. The police handler then says words to this effect: "This is a drug-detecting dog. We have reason to believe you may have drugs in your possession." You are then directed to turn out your pockets, your bag, take off your shirt etc. and be searched. All in public.

A NSW Labor staffer was caught by a sniffer dog at Wynyard a couple of months ago. He had a small amount of marijuana in his pocket and spent some hours in police cells. He works for a government with a policy of keeping users of trivial amounts of dope out of the slammer. Didn't work. Not with the dogs around.

In October, the deputy chief magistrate in the Local Court declared the dogs were breaching Article 17 of the International Covenant on Civil and Political Rights: "No one shall be subjected to arbitrary or unlawful interference with his privacy, family, home or correspondence, nor to unlawful attacks on his honour and reputation. Everyone has the right to the protection of the law against such interference or attacks."

To overturn this pesky decision, Labor and the Coalition combined in Macquarie Street in December to pass the Police Powers (Drug Detection Dogs) Act. Only the Democrats and Greens voted against this bill. There was loads of skylarking in the debate. The Hon. John Jobling (Liberal): "The dogs are highly skilled and highly trained." The Hon. Michael Costa (Minister for Police): "And they are cute." Jobling: "They are much more handsome than the Minister for Police."

Ba-boom.

The bill becomes law on New Year's Day. The attorney-general, Bob Debus, is proud of its civil liberties provisions. Dogs can continue to sniff in licensed nightclubs, bars, parades and festivals but will need a warrant to sniff in restaurants. Coke heads out on the town on Friday nights take note: stick to restaurants.

SEPTEMBER 2006

I was wrong. The dogs and their handlers cost a fortune and turn out to be not much use. Of the people they bail up in the street, three out of four are carrying no drugs at all, the NSW ombudsman reported in 2006. The fourth has, typically, no more than a few shreds of marijuana in a pocket. For every 526 people stopped and searched, only one ends up being punished by a court. "It is clear that drug detection dogs are not an effective tool for detecting persons involved in the supply of prohibited drugs," the ombudsman concluded. The dogs are a farce. But as panic knows no failure, the squads rapidly multiplied across Australia and nosey Labradors became a familiar sight at dance parties and railway stations everywhere.

7.

THE SHAPE OF THE ARGUMENT

I was out of newspapers from 2002 to 2004 presenting *Media Watch* on ABC TV and writing *Dark Victory*, an account of the *Tampa* scandal, with my old friend Marian Wilkinson. These were years in which Australia had a great deal to be worried about. The Bali bombings in 2002 brought terrorism close to home for the first time. We went to war in Iraq in 2003. Fear, not entirely baseless but skilfully exaggerated, was part of the day-to-day politics of the country. Howard would ride these fears to his fourth election victory in 2004. In this atmosphere of threat and contention, Howard's critics came under sustained ideological attack.

29 SEPTEMBER 2004

In the summer of 1997 I flew down to Hobart to interview Brian Harradine. No other interview I have ever done has stuck in my head like this. In those days, Harradine's senate vote could make or break legislation and the only colour in that remarkably bare office on the waterfront was a wall of red Hansards. I remember him sitting in the corner like a grasshopper in grey daks, leading the conversation in odd directions. I should go bushwalking, he told me. Head north and get some perspective on things by walking the Blue Tiers. For a while, he lost me as he rambled through the bush, deflecting my questions about his life, his politics and his faith. Then we got to Hitler.

I'd come to Hobart because I was hacking away at a story – lonely back then – about the resurrection of religion in secular politics. As the nation's leading backroom Catholic warrior, Harradine was shaping the national debate on drugs, sex, film, overseas aid, new technology and the law, shaping it in strange ways according to Christian doctrine. The fact that he was pursuing the Vatican's agenda in the Australian Senate, courtesy of the votes of about 32,000 Tasmanians, struck me as an affront to democracy.

"You remember how Hitler came to power?" Harradine didn't give a fig for the maxim that once you start citing Hitler you've lost your argument. "Hitler came to power by popular vote." I'm ashamed to say when I wrote this interview up for the *Sydney Morning Herald,* I made fun of the senator's shaky grasp of late Weimar politics. Any schoolkid knows Hitler never won a free election but it was unfair of me not to acknowledge Harradine's point: that Hitler was popular. Despite the thugs and violence he could not have done what he did without popular backing. Euthanasia had brought us to this point in the interview. I'd brought along a copy of the Hobart *Mercury* showing 54.3 per cent of Tasmanians wanted euthanasia legalised. That made no difference to Harradine's absolute opposition. He asked: "Should we take account of public opinion polls when we're dealing with fundamental issues such as this?"

What's nagged me ever since is the memory of this strange, unsympathetic man talking life, death and opinion polls. He told me most Australians want the death penalty restored. "Does that make capital punishment right?" But surely we'd all given up on hanging long ago? Later I checked his figures and found he was right. Name a horrible crime – and it doesn't have to be the Bali bombing – and most Australians reckon the guilty should swing. That's a fact, an important fact. But does popular backing make it right? Make it good? Or make any moral difference at all? Harradine hasn't swayed me on condoms, censorship, stem cell research or lesbian motherhood but I've come to see the question he raised in his bleak office in early 1997 as *the* question of the Howard years: do we settle big issues of principle according to opinion polls?

Harradine's challenge takes people like me places we don't want to go. I work to shape opinion. For a long time I believed that winning over the majority – even if way down the track – was what it was all about. But that's naive. It's also an idea Howard has turned brilliantly against his critics. Of all the gambits used to bully public debate in Howard's Australia, the most effective has been this false model of democracy as a perpetual popularity contest. That was *Tampa*. Turning back refugee boats was always going to be popular. Howard wasn't struck by some fresh insight the night he ordered that Norwegian freighter to take – to Indonesia or anywhere – those shipwrecked asylum seekers. Australians had wanted that to happen for a long time. Any politician who could read an opinion poll had known since the first boats arrived in the late 1970s that there's a big constituency hungry to see them turned away.

So why did it take Canberra so long to pursue this sure-fire vote winner? My guess is that good people in politics and the bureaucracy were simply appalled at the prospect of violating Australia's obligations to vulnerable people, to the refugee conventions, to the UN, to world shipping, to the international rules of sea rescue and to our own Migration Act. John Howard's genius was to understand that whatever impact turning the boats away would have on the way the world saw Australia, none of these violated principles would have much traction at home. They could be swept aside by the overwhelming popularity of taking tough action against boat people.

Howard is a master of this brand of raw democracy. One reason Marian Wilkinson and I wrote *Dark Victory* was to try to come to grips with this. The popularity of Howard's strategy was both a starting point for the project and a theme of the book. Even so, we were routinely accused of not acknowledging the support enjoyed by the blockade and the Pacific Solution. Pointing to the many passages in the book where this is analysed didn't get us far. The point being made by our critics was that raw popularity meant there really wasn't much use grappling with the difficult issues of principle raised by the fate of these people. Popularity was enough.

It gets worse. Both sides of politics – Labor and Coalition – claim whatever galvanised Australia in the *Tampa* crisis can't be called racism because it was so pervasive, so popular. Manipulating race for electoral advantage is a hallmark of Howard's government but he insists on the right to cut down native title and turn back boats filled with Muslim refugees "without being accused of prejudice or bigotry, without being knocked off course by … phoney charges of racism". And the press, itself scared of facing the xenophobia of this country, lets Howard get away with it. It's textbook political correctness: the demand that Australia's pervasive racism be shown democratic respect by leaving it unnamed.

Media proprietors read the same opinion polls as politicians. The same focus groups are telling newspapers what they want to read and who they'll vote for. The popularity of what Howard did in the *Tampa* crisis explains, in part, the widespread failure of the media to grasp what was really going on here and cover these events the way they deserved. There were honourable exceptions to this failure – I particularly exempt the *Australian* and the ABC – but to be working inside a newspaper as this shameful episode in the country's history unfolded was to know the power of the media's willed indifference to issues of pure principle when these collide with overwhelming popular support.

These principles were, of course, debated freely on opinion pages in the press, on talkback radio and on television. But the media was too rattled to organise its reporting around the plain violations of due government process going on day after day. The fundamental principles being ignored by Canberra were treated by the media as moot points. Howard and his ministers were continuously offered the benefit of the doubt. Shock was domesticated. Awe went missing. The result was called balance but it was, in fact, poor reporting because the media was missing the story.

This has continued long after the 2001 poll. What is going on here? Blaming it all on media proprietors being too sympathetic to the government is too easy. It's not enough – though true – to argue that Australians don't want to know how the outcome they so welcome has been achieved. The gross failures of reporting since *Tampa* have been driven by the knowledge that Canberra's radical course was hugely popular. The media was not the only institution to fail in the face of this popularity. The courts, the bureaucracy, the Opposition and the media were all rattled.

By the time I moved from ABC Radio National to the *Sydney Morning Herald* in 1996, Labor had met the fate it deserved and Howard's people were taunting their critics with the trademark line: "Don't you know Paul Keating lost the election?" Mocking the democratic credentials of journalists in this way worked particularly well in those early years, tipping them onto the back foot, undercutting their confidence, introducing a note of apology into public debates. And though Keating is a distant memory in 2004, we still hear from time to time this one-size-fits-all rebuke of Howard's critics: "Don't they know Paul Keating lost the election?"

What's the message here? That the people have done more than elect a new government, they've changed the shape of public debate. Those who keep banging on about issues that mattered under the old government – the republic, reconciliation – will be ridiculed as irrelevant, out of touch, members of some self-appointed elite. And if we persist in arguing minority views, we'll be accused of suffering from "moral vanity". Brian Harradine has never been troubled by this accusation. Nor should the press. But this tabloid thuggery has been astonishingly successful in sapping the confidence – and wasting the time – of Howard's critics in the press.

You might imagine those ordering the intelligentsia to submit to the will of the people would remember where they've heard such demands before. What about Eastern Europe before the Wall came down? The same tabloid hacks who – quite rightly – make heroes of Soviet dissenters, vilify Howard's critics for failing to see the prime minister through the eyes of the people. And they're unembarrassed – perhaps unaware – of the grim echoes of their own abuse.

I'd led a quiet life until I went to *Media Watch* in 2002. Then I discovered I was a notorious Lefty. This amused my friends and surprised me. Most of the time, the label was applied as abuse, the counterattack of choice for those we exposed on *Media Watch*. After taking many swings at the *Herald Sun*'s Andrew Bolt over the last couple of years, it was no surprise to read him calling *Media Watch*, "The ABC TV show which Left-winger David Marr uses to attack personal and political foes."

The old tectonic struggle between Left and Right still shapes public debate in this country – less often as a great contest of values, more often as abuse. A twist of history makes this peculiarly Australian. Conservative hard-heads have imported for their own use the wedge tactics of the Republicans, the divisive politics of "the family" and the patriotic rhetoric of George W. Bush's America. But they can't make hay here as they do over there by abusing their opponents as "liberals". Bob Menzies gave that name to his new political party during World War Two and all these years down the track it's just too confusing to tell people to despise liberals and vote Liberal. So in Australia, these warriors of public debate identify their enemy – and the sworn enemy of democracy – as the Left.

Four commentators known for wielding the word are Andrew Bolt, Piers Akerman of the *Telegraph*, Tim Blair of the *Bulletin* and Gerard Henderson of the Sydney Institute. I emailed all four: "I'm trying to pin down what commentators mean by 'Left' these days… how they identify a Lefty in Australia in 2004." I wanted to find what the Left had come to mean, not for the Left itself but for the Left's detractors – a guide to the use of the word as a weapon.

They came to the party. But only on one point did all four agree: the Left they demonise is anti-American. Forget Marx and Engels, the core complaint against the Australian Left today is disloyalty to the United States. That in turn entails for most of them the Left being against the Iraq War, reluctant to tackle Arab extremists, hostile to Israel and pro-UN. On the home front, opposition to private schools is high on the list of Left vices, along with scepticism about Christianity and an indulgent attitude to homosexuals, boat people and the ABC. But thereafter these four lists diverge, often wildly. So here they are as a ready reference for those who may need to know sometime soon what it means to be called a Lefty by Akerman, Blair, Bolt and Henderson.

For that ancient warrior of Murdoch's tabloids, Piers Akerman, the Left are John Howard's opponents: "those who support the admission of undocumented refugees, who are anti-US, pro legalisation of drugs, pro social engineering, opposed to private schools, opposed to parliamentary prayer, support gay marriage, wish to re-regulate the industrial sector, those who fail to see the Iraq conflict as part of the war on terrorism, those opposed to the existence of the state of Israel, those who refuse to support measures aimed at Islamo-fascists."

Those on Tim Blair's Left – "Greens, Dems, the ABC, and the Carmen wing of the ALP" – are chauvinists, republicans and by nature intolerant. His Left "opposes commercial media (except Fairfax), wealth that doesn't grow at the same rate for everybody, lack of media diversity (except at the ABC), media deregulation (except censorship), doing anything that makes Australia a terrorist target (except supporting East Timorese independence), liberation of oppressed peoples by any means other than impossible global consensus, inaccurate commentary (except from John Pilger and Michael Moore), scientific advances in agriculture, and an increasingly pleasant, warmer globe. But what is the Left for? Aside from broad, rarely defined motherhood notions like 'democracy', 'greater accountability' and 'justice', it's hard to tell. A Lefty friend supported the return of South Sydney to the NRL; maybe that's it."

Andrew Bolt's Left is a New Age creature in flight from "the responsibilities and terrors of freedom and into the 'securities' of tribalism". The result is a society breaking up into self-regarding little communities. "So we are divided into First Australians, and given distinct rights on the basis of race. Or we're hived off into a political class called 'women', and given a special bureaucracy to deal with our common claims against the rest. Or we're funded to remain forever Greek, or offered special seats in Parliament because we're Maori. We're given UN recognition if we're of some Aboriginal race and hold out against integrating with more advanced civilisations. We're excused terrorism as Arabs that would never be tolerated among Anglo Saxons. We gloat in our anti-Americanism, and form communities of sexualities." Bolt accuses the Left of inventing its own gods: "Nature gods. Tree spirits. Water sprites. Gaia." He calls these faiths demeaning and incompatible with reason – unlike Christianity. "For that reason, the Left now is not just an enemy of humanism, reason and freedom, but of Christianity, too."

That's a mighty indictment and a very individual view of Christianity. But Bolt is right to raise the issue of faith. It keeps creeping into this argument. What caught my eye in a recent assault on the national broadcaster by Gerard Henderson was his attack on what he called the "leftist orthodoxy" of the ABC. Here was an image of the Left as a bunch of people bound by an old and accepted creed. My immediate thought was: well what is this dogma Henderson's readers are supposed to know all about? What Henderson came up with was both more intelligent and more flexible than a Nicean creed of the Left. This was not abuse but analysis; not a binding set of beliefs but an ideal list of nine points Henderson believes most – but not all – on the Left would share. Here are the points in full.

- A belief in the desirability of wide scale government intervention (funded by taxation) in the domestic economy – in such areas as education, health, welfare and the environment. Along with a corresponding scepticism about private solutions in such areas as education, health, welfare and the environment. In other words, a view that the public sector is good in itself and that the private sector is, at best, a dubious exercise.
- A belief that governments should not interfere in the realms of private morality – covering such areas as abortion, censorship, same-sex relationships etc.
- A scepticism about Western religious beliefs – in particular traditional Christian churches and the emerging fundamentalist Christianity.
- An unwillingness to support the use of military force abroad – along with a disdain for patriotism at home. An ambiguity towards, or outright opposition to, the Australian–American Alliance – along with concern about Israel's role in world affairs.
- An abiding sense of shame and guilt for the past acts of Western

nations in their colonial manifestations – a commitment to reconciliation with native peoples.

- A belief in the sanctity of international solutions to international problems – comprising a commitment to the United Nations, despite its evident inefficiency and virtual impotency.
- Opposition to the globalisation process of economic reform – including a resentment to such international organisations as the World Trade Organization, World Bank, International Monetary Fund. A preference for international aid over the reform of the political systems and domestic economies of third world nations.
- A tendency to be alienated from elected mainstream political leaders (whether conservative or social democrat) and a conviction that the modern democratic system is inhabited by politicians who lie by habit.
- A tradition of moral compromise – leading to a belief that democracies are not much better than dictatorships in the way they operate. In other words, moral equivalence.

Henderson's list gets a bit ragged towards the end. Who beyond a few remnant Stalinists believes these days that democracies and dictatorships are morally much the same? But it's a notion that might spook a few people. On all four lists are ideas capable of sparking fears in the community. But not great fears. The lists don't come near explaining how effectively denunciation of the Left shapes public debate in Australia: rattling the media, sabotaging big public contests of principle this country is so reluctant to face. What is the spectre behind the abuse?

I went back to all four combatants and asked: is it really about money? The Left is never going to seize the assets of the rich, but the Left has plans and they're expensive. They cost a lot of other people's money. Is this where the fear comes in? The idea drew a blank with all four of these anti-Left warriors. But I would put my money on money. No one fears these days that the Left is going to break up the estates and nationalise the means of production. But the contest of Left v. Right remains potent because it's still about public purse v. private purse, wages v. dividends, regulation v. profits, public spending v. tax cuts.

What's worse, the Left challenges the prerogatives of money, and the prerogatives of a government intent on turning Australia into a money-making machine. The problem with "Lefty" journalists – particularly at the ABC – is that they don't give money its due. They keep raising issues like equity, lawfulness, candour, dignity – issues that don't have much to do with money or can stand in the way of money-making. It's bias again. The fear that such people might get their hands on the levers is reason enough to demonise the Left – especially now, in these miraculously prosperous times.

Bullying politicians, rampant populism, nervous journalists, conservative media, subterranean Left v. Right struggles – all shape public argument in Australia today. But one last intangible needs to be thrown into this mix: prosperity. John Howard has been trusted for so long because this country is enjoying the longest uninterrupted run of good fortune any of us can remember. Not for everyone. Not everywhere. But most of us have never been so comfortable. Howard is running the great popularity contest of democracy and nearly all of us are in line for a prize. Measured only by money, these are very good times. And there is a visceral – entirely human – wish to keep it that way. So it is a time to hold back. We don't want the media rocking the boat. We want no distracting rows, no dissent, no great public arguments. We just want to keep going. While it lasts.

8.

SAVING THE NATION 2 OCTOBER 2004

Every twenty-five years or so, the Coalition parties throw decent principles aside in the pursuit of power. Their willingness to do this coarsens the political life of this country. At the backs of our minds we all know that when they feel they must and calculate they can get away with it, the conservative parties break the rules. Australian politics is played out in the shadow of a radical indifference to law and principle that lurks inside the Liberals and their bush brothers the Nationals.

When Bob Menzies tried to ban the Communist Party in 1951, he was defeated first by the High Court and then by the people. Steadiness of principle in that crisis at the height of the Cold War is now the proudest boast of the High Court. But the court did not do so well in the next political convulsion. In 1975 its chief justice Garfield Barwick colluded in the destruction of the Whitlam government, an act that cast a shadow over the court that has yet to be entirely dispelled. The third violation of principle, coming as if by clockwork another twenty-five years later, was the Coalition government's ruthless campaign against refugees. This saw a shameful failure of nerve. A court that is supposed to save us from the fears and enthusiasms of the mob buckled in the face of national panic about boat people.

The name al-Kateb means almost nothing outside gatherings of lawyers. The reason is simple: despite its outcome, the story lasted only a few days in the press. It has become a political issue in this election campaign only on the fringe – which is how we must describe the Democrats these days – and beyond publicly welcoming the power the court handed the Minister for Immigration, the Coalition has been silent about the case of Ahmed Ali al-Kateb.

He was born in Kuwait to Palestinian parents, came by boat to Australia in December 2000 without any papers and was placed in detention. His application for refugee status having failed, he asked to leave but no country could be found to welcome him. Kuwait would not have him back and Israel won't let him enter what's left of Palestine. Everyone – including the Crown – accepts there is no real prospect of finding a country willing to take al-Kateb off our hands "in the reasonably foreseeable future" but the immigration minister Amanda Vanstone wants, nevertheless, the power to hold this stateless failed asylum seeker in detention, if necessary for ever.

For Chief Justice Murray Gleeson, Bill Gummow and Michael Kirby this was an impossible prospect. Kirby expressed it in characteristically bold rhetoric: "Indefinite detention at the will of the Executive, and according to its opinions, actions and judgments, is alien to Australia's constitutional arrangements." Gummow, usually Mr Majority on the court, quoted – not by accident, I suspect – the ultra-conservative Antonin Scalia of the Supreme Court of the United States: "The very core of liberty secured by our Anglo-Saxon system of separated powers has been freedom from indefinite imprisonment at the will of the Executive." And Gleeson, not a man with a taste for sweeping rhetoric, took the ambiguity of the provisions under examination as proof that parliament had not intended to abrogate – via this remote sub-section of the Migration Act – fundamental human rights "of which personal liberty is the most basic".

But that made only three. A minority. The reasons of the majority upholding indefinite detention tell us where liberty stands these days in the highest reaches of the Australian judiciary. It isn't happy news. Michael McHugh, Ken Hayne and Ian Callinan (to my amazement, the court's new recruit Dyson Heydon had nothing at all to say on this great issue) treated al-Kateb's liberty as weightless in the scales of justice. Human rights aren't absolute. They must always be weighed against the legitimate needs of the State. And we have to recognise – however unhappily – that the rights of unwanted aliens aren't going to be given the same respect as the rights of Australian citizens. But what's breathtaking about the *al-Kateb* decision is that the four judges of the majority gave no weight at all to the fact that they were depriving an innocent man of his liberty, perhaps forever.

Detention, said McHugh, was the surest way of preventing unlawful non-citizens from "entering or remaining in the Australian community" and it was quite OK for the minister to order such detention because it's not punitive and "no more an exercise of judicial power than is a law requiring enemy prisoners-of-war to be detained in custody until they are deported from Australia". Again the defence power is dragged into the argument. Like French in the *Tampa* case, McHugh went on and on about war and the authority of a minister in wartime to inter anyone thought to threaten the security of the nation. I only wish Michael McHugh had been around when Rear Admiral Chris Ritchie cautioned naval commanders about to begin the blockade of refugee boats in 2001. "We are talking about people coming to Australia illegally. It is not World War III."

Callinan saw al-Kateb as a cunning litigant to be outfoxed. He wrote contemptuously of the man's "recourse to litigation" and his "litigious endeavours". Callinan feared al-Kateb was pioneering a crafty strategy to earn the hostility of the world in order to compel his release into the Australian community. By making "repetitive unsuccessful applications and litigation founded on unsubstantiated claims, or, if and when it occurs, escape from immigration detention, some aliens may attract so much notoriety that other countries will hesitate or refuse to receive them. In those ways they may personally create the conditions compelling their detention for prolonged periods." And so – if al-Kateb were to establish a precedent – they would then have to be released into the Australian community as de facto citizens. Callinan urged this far-fetched scenario on his brother judges as a "practical consideration".

Callinan is not the comic relief in the case. What Callinan was expressing here is the underlying determination of Australian governments to make the Migration Act impermeable. That legislation be effective is one thing. That it be impermeable is quite another. In *al-Kateb*, Callinan was supporting the long-held argument of governments – Labor and Liberal – that human rights considerations should not be used to break down the wall the Migration Act presents to the world. It was in aid of this extreme ambition that the Federal Court was subjected by Philip Ruddock, the man who is now attorney-general, to an unprecedented campaign of abuse through the 1990s. Callinan, with the mind of a crafty criminal lawyer, saw al-Kateb trying to chip a little hole in the great wall of the law. Better, in his view, that the interloper stay behind the wire.

For how long? The judges of the majority saw no need to fix the time. Hayne thought al-Kateb could sit it out until the problems of the Middle East were – or were not – resolved. He didn't think that would be soon. "His prospects of being removed to what is now the territory in Gaza under the administration of the Palestinian Authority are, and will continue to be, much affected by political events in several countries in the Middle East." So until Israel reverses its hitherto absolute opposition to the return of Palestinian refugees to their homeland, what is to happen to Mr al-Kateb? Indefinite detention in Australia.

But he will have Ken Hayne's personal assurance that he is not being punished. How could this be when His Honour himself observed: "Deprivation of liberty is the harshest form of punishment now exacted for wrongdoing in Australia"? The argument goes like this: it can't be punishment because the man is not being detained "for any actual or assumed wrongdoing". Being innocent is proof his incarceration is not punitive. And we should not be confused by the grim appearance of Immigration Detention Centres. "Because [they] are places of confinement having many, if not all, of the physical features and administrative arrangements commonly found in prisons, it is easy to equate confinement in such a place with punishment. It is necessary, however, to notice some further matters." Those further matters don't include the feelings of Mr al-Kateb as he stares out through the wires perhaps for the rest of his life.

So if he's not being punished, what is being done to him? Segregation. It's an ugly word with an ugly history. It's not remembered very fondly, for instance, by most folks in Mississippi. But that's the word Ken Hayne has picked: segregation, non-punitive segregation. "Only in the most general sense would it be said that *preventing* a non-citizen making landfall in Australia is punitive," the judge observed. "Segregating those who make landfall, without permission to do so, is not readily seen as bearing a substantially different character."

Not readily? Well not by Hayne, Heydon, Callinan and McHugh. So two months ago when the court handed down its decision in *al-Kateb v. Godwin*, Australia became perhaps the only country in the free world – if I can use such an old-fashioned, Cold War term

– where the executive, acting alone, has the power to imprison people perhaps forever.

Call me old-fashioned, but that's a good story. The Minister for Immigration Amanda Vanstone as the government's jailer is a page-one splash. I can see the cruel drawings now: a powerfully built woman with a huge bunch of keys at her waist. But there was none of that. Fear of the wrath of the minister kept al-Kateb from talking to the press. Ditto Abbas Mohammad al-Khafaji, an Iraqi whose parallel case was argued and rejected by the court at the same time. Their stories and their faces were barely known. Eventually al-Kateb gave one television interview one grey day sitting on a low wall at Coogee looking haunted and old. He's not yet thirty.

Reporting of the court's decision was widespread and brief. As a gauge of the state of liberty in Australia today, it was as revealing as the decision itself. The story proved, essentially, to have no traction at all. Tucked away in newspapers across the nation were little stories, most quoting McHugh's perfunctory description of the fate he was imposing on al-Kateb as "tragic". My paper, the *Sydney Morning Herald*, thought the decision worth 226 words on page five. I checked: they were not ambushed by the story. They'd known a decision was on its way for a couple of days. But this was all they thought *al-Kateb v. Godwin* was worth.

The only paper to give the result anything like its due was the *Age* which reported it fair and square on page one as a story about the fundamental liberties of us all. The president of Liberty Victoria Greg Connellan was there expressing grave concern "that the executive arm of government could determine that people who had never been charged with anything could be detained indefinitely". The *Age* did not back its brief news story with the big narrative explanation that stories of this complexity and weight require. But on the Monday there was an editorial calling for a bill of rights.

"Such a bill … would not only protect the rights of asylum seekers in this case, but might also foster a deeper respect for the law and its possibilities." It's the only editorial I've seen anywhere on the case, the only muted thunder.

I expected battles would now rage on the opinion pages. Wrong again. It has to be noted that no commentators came forward to praise the *al-Kateb* decision. The right-wing thugs who are supposed to make our papers lively were silent. That first week there was a lone, combative article by Greg Barns in the *Herald Sun* accusing the courts of failing to protect the innocent. And a few days later the *Age* was the only paper to find room – 195 words on page four – to report the president of the ALP Carmen Lawrence putting herself at odds with her own party by telling demonstrators in Canberra: "This decision should shock all Australians because it shows that in this so-called advanced democracy, we have no effective protections against arbitrary imprisonment by the state."

Week two saw Gerard Henderson of the Sydney Institute deliver a sharp warning to his natural allies on the Right, commending Murray Gleeson's "compelling" dissent. Henderson saw the court's decision as wrong in law, cited the prime minister's praise of the chief justice's "superb legal abilities" and remarked that Gleeson "is widely regarded as the finest jurist of his generation. What's more, he is particularly admired by conservatives for being a legal traditionalist rather than a judicial activist." Henderson drew a connection between *al-Kateb* and one of the most shameful episodes in the Howard government's history. "The Coalition's original error in the children overboard case stemmed from lack of empathy. For different reasons, a majority of the High Court judges have made a similar error." Not a very passionate word, empathy, but not a bad one.

Before the story dropped absolutely dead in the middle of last month, the cadaver twitched a couple of times. In late August,

ABC Radio National's *Law Report* interviewed constitutional law professor George Williams and al-Kateb's splendid counsel Claire O'Connor. It was a few minutes of intelligent radio weeks after the decision. And Richard Ackland of *Justinian* wrote one of his wry Friday columns about this "scary" decision that will see the al-Katebs and al-Khafajis locked up "until hell freezes over, or certainly longer than your average murderer would ever be likely to see out".

Why did the story die? Why has this case not excited fear, anger and public debate? Some high theory lies ahead, but first a practical matter for a practical country. A fortnight after the High Court's decision, Amanda Vanstone gave both Ahmed al-Kateb and Abbas al-Khafaji bridging visas. At that point the story became an abstraction – not about the fate of these two men, but about liberty. There would be no demos to film at the gates of Baxter; no Free al-Kateb campaign to report; no human focus for the kind of long-haul exercise by which the Law Council of Australia finally made this country pay attention to Hicks and Habib in Guantanamo. Of course there are other stateless men in perpetual detention in Australia, but the two who became briefly known to us have been released into the community. Thank God for that. But it means the story – for the press, the community, politicians and lawyers – must now focus on underlying principles. And we're not good at that.

David Malouf has a wonderful theory that it's the English we carried in our baggage that makes America and Australia such different places. In the early seventeenth century, settlers took to America a language of abstractions: "Passionately evangelical and utopian, deeply imbued with the religious fanaticism and radical violence of the time, this was the language of ... dissenters ... who left England to found a new society that would be free, as they saw it, of authoritarian government by Church and Crown." Malouf argues that by the time Australia was colonised, the language had changed. What the First Fleet brought here "was the language of the English and Scottish Enlightenment: sober, unemphatic, good-humoured; a very sociable and moderate language; modern in a way that even we would recognise, and supremely rational and down to earth".

There are some problems with that theory. The Scottish Enlightenment gave us the rhetoric of liberty we still use today. But Malouf is getting to a deeper truth that we all recognise: we don't live in a country or use a language that revels in abstractions. We're not like France and we're not like America. As Liberty Victoria knows to its cost, we don't live in a country where liberty or freedom are the subject of continuing public debate. Liberty is not a part of the political language of John Howard and Mark Latham, but is used – and abused – by George W. Bush and John Kerry all the time. A function of American government – at least according to its own rhetoric – is to provide jobs, defence and Liberty.

George W. Bush declared this the century of liberty in his acceptance speech at the New York Republican convention. "I believe in the transformational power of liberty," he said. "The wisest use of American strength is to advance freedom." A dozen times he promised the delegates freedom at home and abroad and the closing words of his address were a high-flown aria on the theme of liberty. "Like generations before us, we have a calling from beyond the stars to stand for freedom. This is the everlasting dream of America and tonight, in this place, that dream is renewed. Now we go forward grateful for our freedom, faithful to our cause, and confident in the future of the greatest nation on earth."

You never hear Australian politicians saying anything remotely like that. Never ever. Not even John Howard who has done so much to naturalise in Australia the tactics and rhetoric of the Republican Party. At the launch of the Liberal campaign the other day, he mentioned freedom seven times. One of those hits had a vague George W. Bush flavour: Australians want a prime minister, he said, who "will let them get on with their lives and will give them freedom and choice and opportunity". And the other six hits by Howard? Not the freedom of the people but the freedom of small business and independent contractors for whom he promises legislation "to protect them from the deprivation of unions and unfriendly Labor governments who would seek to impose limits and constraints on their freedom to contract".

From the banality of the rhetoric you'd think we were a people who didn't give a damn about protecting our rights and freedoms. But surveys show we do – and show that of all people the most enthusiastic for a bill of rights are Labor politicians. So surely that's a hot topic right now inside the Labor Party? Not a bit of it. Debating Philip Ruddock in Sydney the other day, the shadow attorney-general Nicola Roxon spoke of a bill of rights only as a possibility way down the track. Labor's obligation, she said, was "to lead a debate on this issue … about where we might go sometime in the future". It's a pathetic promise, but my suspicion is that Labor knows where such a debate would take Australia. From a distance the issue looks fine for Labor, but up close the politics would get very messy indeed. Before we can have a frank national discourse on liberty, we're going to have to address the issue of race.

The blockading of the *Tampa* and the outcome of Operation Relex and the Pacific Solution were overwhelmingly popular. The general feeling is that Australia was under attack and Australia was saved. When people are thinking like that – and when judges follow suit – there's not much room for human rights. This is why Australians want that impermeable Migration Act. And if that means refugees are forced out to sea, children put behind the wire and men like al-Kateb and al-Khafaji made to cool their heels in

Baxter, perhaps for the rest of their lives, it's not too high a price to pay – and spare us the details.

We aren't curious to know how Canberra keeps the borders closed. We know enough to know we don't want to know more. In my experience journalists are much keener to pursue refugee issues – and ask the right questions at news conferences – than editors and proprietors are to back and publish their stories. There is more to this than the old political divide between Lefty journalists and conservative proprietors: these stories are not winners. They don't sell papers; they don't boost ratings. And Australians flinch from knowing more because they suspect this, too, would bring them face to face with this country's intractable problems with race.

Despite the High Court's verdict, Ahmed al-Kateb was released from detention by Vanstone because it was prudent not to allow him to become a martyr. And I would like to think that decent men and women in the government had no appetite to exercise the power the High Court had discovered in the Migration Act. Whatever lay behind the decision, the lesson is this: al-Kateb's fragile liberty in Australia was secured by gift not right, by politics not law. The blame for that lies squarely with a rattled High Court.

9

THE HERO OF CRONULLA
13 DECEMBER 2005

By Thursday last week Alan Jones was screaming like a race caller whose horse was coming home: "I'm the person that's led this charge here. Nobody wanted to know about North Cronulla, now it's gathered to this." The riot was still three days away and Sydney's highest-rating breakfast radio host had a heap of anonymous emails to help whip his 2GB listeners along. "Alan, it's not just a few Middle Eastern bastards at the weekend, it's thousands. Cronulla is a very long beach and it's been taken over by this scum. It's not a few causing trouble it's all of them."

Sunday's trouble did not come out of the blue. Jones had been thundering about Lebanese men for months. On one memorable day he threw into the mix "car hoons" racing through the streets of Sydney at night, the appalling rhetoric of preacher Sheik Faiz Mohamad and louts seen on television sniggering during Anzac Day celebrations. "If ever there was a clear example that Lebanese males in their vast numbers not only hate our country but our heritage, this was it," Jones raged. "They've got no connection to us. They simply rape, pillage and plunder a nation that's taken them in. No one who's written to me could believe what they saw. Without exception, you asked what did we do as a nation to have this vermin infect us like this. And what about the sacrifices of our war dead made for this country to make it what it is today and to have these mongrels laugh at them on national television? Tell me we don't have a national security problem in the making."

In early December, a nasty scuffle on Cronulla beach had left two young lifesavers injured. "What kind of grubs?" asked Jones. "This lot were Middle Eastern, we're not allowed to say it, but I am saying it." So began a remarkable week on talkback radio – particularly on 2GB. Radio doesn't get much grimmer than Alan Jones's efforts in those days. He assured his huge audience he understood why that text message went out: "Come to Cronulla this weekend to take revenge. This Sunday every Aussie in the Shire get down to North Cronulla to support the Leb and wog bashing day …" He read it right through on air half a dozen times.

Daily he cautioned his listeners not to take the law into their own hands, but he warmed to listeners who had exactly that on their minds. He commended this listener's plan as a "good answer" to the problems of the beach: "My suggestion is to invite the biker gangs to be present at Cronulla railway station when these Lebanese thugs arrive, the biker gangs have been much maligned but they do a lot of good things – it would be worth the price of admission to watch these cowards scurry back onto the train for the return trip to their lairs … and wouldn't it be brilliant if the whole event was captured on TV cameras and featured on the evening news so that we, their parents, family and friends can see who these bastards are … Australians old and new should not have to put up with this scum."

Last Thursday Charlie rang to suggest all junior footballers in the Shire gather on the beach to support the lifesavers. "Good stuff, good stuff," said Jones. "I tell you who we want to encourage, Charlie, all the Pacific Island people because, you want to know something, they don't take any nonsense. They are proud to be here – all those

Samoans and Fijians. They love being here. And they say, 'Uh huh, uh huh. You step out of line, look out.' And, of course, cowards always run, don't they?"

When John called on Tuesday to bluntly recommend vigilante action – "If the police can't do the job, the next tier is us" – Jones did not dissent. "Yeah. Good on you, John." And when John then offered a maxim his father had picked up during the war – "Shoot one, the rest will run" – the broadcaster roared with laughter. "No, you don't play Queensberry's rules. Good on you, John."

It was horrible stuff, larded with self-congratulation. And pity poor Berta – "not of a Middle-Eastern family" – who tried to argue there were two sides to this story. When she reported hearing "really derogatory remarks" aimed at Middle-Eastern people on Cronulla beach, Jones cut her off: "Let's not get too carried away, Berta. We don't have Anglo-Saxon kids out there raping women in western Sydney."

On Sunday 11 December a crowd rampaged through Cronulla bashing anyone swarthy enough to pass for Lebanese. Thirty-one people were injured and sixteen arrested in running battles with police. Images of the riot were seen around the world. The following night, a mob from the western suburbs counterattacked, leaving one man stabbed and 100 cars damaged on the waterfront.

Yesterday, 2GB broadcasters claimed two-thirds of calls coming into the station supported "what happened" at Cronulla on Sunday. But Alan Jones is not around to deal with the aftermath. He's having a well-earned holiday…

APRIL 2007

The Australian Communications and Media Authority found Jones had broadcast material "likely to encourage violence or brutality and to vilify people of Lebanese and Middle-Eastern backgrounds on the basis of ethnicity". Jones and 2GB rejected the finding absolutely. John Howard sprang to the broadcaster's defence: "I think Alan Jones is an outstanding broadcaster. I don't think he's a person who encourages prejudice in the Australian community, not for one moment, but he is a person who articulates what a lot of people think."

10.

PICK AND STICK DECEMBER 2006

"I think that is so outrageous," brayed Andrew Bolt. We were sitting in the armchairs of the ABC's *Insiders*, cameras rolling, the morning after chunks of Chris Masters's *Jonestown* began appearing in the press. Bolt's voice was steady and angry. "I've read the excerpts that the *Sydney Morning Herald* and the *Age* ran from this book. They all focused on his sexuality and the fact that he was a teacher in charge of boys. And it went, 'Wink, wink, nudge, nudge: teacher, gay, boys.' And I think that is so outrageous. There is nothing to suggest that Alan Jones did anything improper. And if he was not a conservative, but someone of the Left—"

Bolt was making good time. In less than twenty seconds, he had reached the vague, encircling conspiracy of the Left that explains most evils in his world. I groaned, "Oh, dear God," as he thundered on about "rank homophobia". Bolt was the first, but not the last, to bring Kirby into the argument: "If this were Justice Michael Kirby, you would be shocked by this. It's gutless of you not to complain."

The circus that followed *Jonestown* saw star columnists of the Murdoch and Fairfax press performing as a pack. I can't pretend to be entirely objective about this. They savaged Masters but had a go at me, too, for I had helped to choose those extracts. Bolt let his *Herald Sun* readers know I was the crudest kind of "gay-baiter", willing to put aside all my principles to destroy Jones for the crime of being "conservative". Bolt's big finish was addressed to both Masters and me: "So slime him, boys. Slime him again and again and again, until you yourselves are so covered in that stinking stuff that we can't make out a single human feature on your faces."

Piling into the stoush were the *Daily Telegraph*'s Piers Akerman ("A queer crusade to smear a rival"), the *Sydney Morning Herald*'s Miranda Devine ("A journalist's great shame exposed"), the *Australian*'s born-again gay conservative Catholic pundit Christopher Pearson ("Detestable standards") and Paul Sheehan, also of the *Sydney Morning Herald* ("Bullies judged by the book"). Abuse was colourful. Claims were wild. As usual the pack was intent on running fake controversies to mask the real ones. Bolt set the lead on *Insiders*: Masters was to be denounced for making baseless allegations of paedophilia. But where?

Masters spends three chapters of *Jonestown* examining Jones's catastrophic early career as a schoolteacher. Despite bringing sporting glory to a couple of high-end private schools in the 1960s and '70s, Jones left both after humiliating controversies. In the book, former pupils put their names to accounts of inappropriate behaviour. Jones's supporters also have their say. Masters concludes that Jones did himself in at the King's School and Brisbane Grammar through erratic judgment, bad temper, harsh treatment of those he put on the outer, and intense – but not physically sexual – relations with his schoolboy favourites. The headmaster of King's feared lawsuits. Jones went.

Jonestown gets into very murky territory, but makes no allegations of sexual impropriety by Jones as a schoolteacher. Masters wrote, "The story is mostly of emotional manipulation." No evidence of paedophilia is produced and no allegations are made in *Jonestown*. None. Yet the pack detected Bill Heffernan–style claims in the very atmosphere of the book and accused Masters (and me) of advancing the argument that *all* gay men are potential paedophiles. Proof? Not needed. This is the world of Opinion. The pack savaged us for "linking such a high-profile discussion of homosexuality, once again, with that old canard, the predatory homosexual intent on kiddy-fiddling".

Seeing this lot spring so aggressively to the defence of gay men had its funny side. Akerman memorably declared on *Insiders* a few months ago, "You cannot call a relationship between a man and a man, and a woman and a woman, or a man and a dog or his cat or his goat, a marriage." Now, in the aftermath of *Jonestown*, he drew himself to his full height and declared the idea "that sexuality determines an individual's persona is intellectually risible".

Akerman's pronouncement might surprise anyone who has read a biography in the last century but it came as particular news to me. He rarely misses a chance to remind his readers that I am gay. I'm a homosexual commentator, homosexual spokesman, homosexual activist and "the *Sydney Morning Herald*'s expert in matters queenly". I'm "prissy" and "flaccid". I purse my lips. Piers even wants his readers to know that I can be seen at the beach with homosexuals, "disporting with his pals before the North Bondi Surf Club". He may not think homosexuality integral to Jones's persona, but sure seems to think it's integral to mine.

The fake paedophile controversy was at its height in the first week of the book's publication, muffling without smothering real debate over the real issues raised by *Jonestown*. The man in question was absent. Abandoning his 2GB microphone days before the book appeared, he flew to London on urgent business: to see the West End premiere of *Dirty Dancing*. But he was not out of sight. Jones was available to be photographed in London foyers and later at the Melbourne track, looking chipper but saying nothing:

"Mate, I've made a decision not to make any comment on this issue and I'm not about to start now."

He must have wished John Brennan had also stayed mum. No one knows Jones like Brenno: this is the guy who recruited him to radio back in the '80s; failed in the cash-for-comment years to make Jones comply with broadcasting rules; and is now program director of 2GB, the station Jones part owns. Brenno fired off a letter to the *Sydney Morning Herald* comparing his boss to Jesus Christ: "He reminds me of another man some 2000 years ago who had the worst interpretations put upon His kindest actions, yet He went on; who had His words warped, twisted, falsely reported, minimised, yet He went on; was slighted, even laughed to scorn when He gave of His very best, yet He went on. And so will Alan Jones go on …"

Talkback radio hadn't rushed to the barricades for Jones. The world of sport was all but silent. Business was hushed. His old "pick and stick" pal James Packer called him a dear and vilified friend: "My heart goes out to him." Politicians were wary, but the prime minister deplored the violation of Jones's privacy and was among the first to cast him in the role of political victim: "If this had been an issue regarding the sexuality of somebody on the centre-Left, there would have been an absolute uproar." When Jones returned to the microphone on Monday 30 October – still saying nothing at all about the book – Howard offered himself for interview. That nine-minute grilling about school chaplains and interest rates was a telling public endorsement by the prime minister. Jones was not being disowned.

But it is more difficult now. The closet protects everyone. Even if every man and his dog knows someone is gay, they can still pretend otherwise while he stays in the closet. The rights and wrongs of outing Jones was a real controversy inextricably mixed with the sham paedophilia allegations. At stake was not only Jones's fate in a potentially hostile world, but the reputation of all the businessmen, all the politicians who have courted the man to protect and promote their interests, and the pack of newspaper commentators with whom he hunts. *Jonestown* outed them all.

The pack raged at Masters as if they'd never known Jones was gay. But surely these plugged-in commentators knew before *Jonestown*? I put the question to them all. Andrew Bolt declared my question a "red herring". Sheehan wandered past my desk to say he thought the question silly. Devine responded: "Don't know. Don't care." She didn't demur when I said I'd take that to mean she wasn't surprised. Akerman was superbly vague: "Someone had mentioned it tangentially but it had never been a matter of interest, either way." Pearson, who has dealt with his sexuality by taking a late lifelong vow of celibacy, told me that even after reading *Jonestown*, he is still not convinced Jones is gay: "I don't know it at all."

Their bullshit betrays them. That Jones's sexuality has been an open secret for years puts the controversy over his "outing" into its true perspective. At stake was not whether Jones was gay, but whether his sexuality could be publicly discussed. For many – particularly in the gay and lesbian community – it makes no difference that someone's sexuality is widely known by the press, politicians, the public, colleagues, friends and family: his privacy must still be protected unless he's a public hypocrite or his sexuality impacts on public life. But how much privacy did Jones have left to protect? Stacy Farrar, of the *Sydney Star Observer*, wrote, "His homosexuality has been widely known, in the gay community at least, for years … and I personally think that it would be silly and overly squeamish to not at least mention Jones's sexuality in a comprehensive study of his life."

That was Chris Masters's argument, too: "I don't know how you could've written the book and not dealt with it." That's the biographer's defence, but is it enough? Not quite. Obscure civilians should be protected from the necessary violations of privacy involved in biography. But that's not Jones. His political usefulness may be faltering, his ratings are sliding a little, but he remains the most feared man at the microphone in this country. And because he sets himself up as such a ruthless critic of this little world, we all have a right to know where he is coming from and what his values are. After more than twenty years of belting people around the head – at times because he was secretly paid to do so – we have a right to know exactly who Alan Jones is. One of those things is gay.

If the pack hoped to kill off the book, it failed spectacularly. In its first week in the shops, *Jonestown* was the number-one bestseller across the nation. After another fortnight, the $50 hardback had sold a staggering 25,000 copies. Sales were almost as strong in Melbourne, where Jones is not on air, as in the city where he still reigns as the king of breakfast radio. The fear of commercial failure cited by the ABC as its excuse for shamefully dumping *Jonestown* was looking shabbier by the day. The book was a publishing phenomenon.

Silence would have helped Jones more, but this was an opportunity too good for the pack to pass up to have another go at the sinister conspiracy of malice, hypocrisy, naivety and deceit those columnists call the Left. "Might it be," asked Piers Akerman, in the *Telegraph*, right at the start, "that those who proclaim their support of privacy legislation, civil liberties and indescribable acts between consenting adults, are prepared to abandon all principle if they can shred the reputation of those whose success they envy and politics they despise?"

To counter conspiracy theories with facts is probably a category mistake. But here are a few: left-wingers didn't move Jones on from Brisbane Grammar, King's, the Wallabies and the Balmain Tigers.

Something went wrong each time that had nothing to do with party politics and a great deal to do with Jones's character. Nor can left-wingers be blamed for Jones's failures inside the Liberal Party: the failed preselections, a failed election attempt and a curtailed career as a speechwriter for Malcolm Fraser. Nor was the Australian Broadcasting Authority, which tore Jones's reputation apart in the cash-for-comment inquiry, a nest of left-wingers. Perhaps what Akerman, Bolt and the rest of them find most left-wing about *Jonestown* is its way of reminding us that all this happened.

Amnesia has been a great friend to Alan Jones. More than energy and broadcasting skill explain his survival as a big figure in this country. The revelation in 1999 that he sold his opinions for millions should have left him scuppered, washed up, wrecked and finished, there and then. But he survived cash-for-comment, protected by backers and by an audience willing to forget. *Jonestown* was going to be a problem even if it had nothing new to say, for it would sit on bookshelves, fully indexed, within reach, a handy means of recalling all the half-forgotten outrages of his career.

The pack has moved on, hunting the Left elsewhere: under beds, in university corridors, everywhere elites gather to swap their dangerous opinions. And the public, sick of newspapers filled with columnists' endless fake rage, has done the only sensible thing: settled down with a good book called *Jonestown*.

11.

A DAWN SWEEP THROUGH SYDNEY
14 MARCH 2007

Sunil Menon was woken before dawn by a powerful light shining through his window. In the first confused moments he was aware only of the light, "serious knocking" on the front door and a man yelling his name. The door was kicked open and about ten police poured into the house. One identified himself as a member of the NSW counter-terrorism unit. Another was a man Menon often noticed hanging around demonstrations in dark glasses and cargo pants. "I was scared when I saw him." In front of his housemates gathered in the sitting room, Menon was handcuffed and shown a search warrant. "They told me it was to do with G20."

Before the sun came up that morning, between fifty and sixty police from NSW, Victorian and federal squads were out arresting five students in raids around Sydney. The scale of the operation can't be explained by the chaos of Melbourne's G20 demonstrations last year or the relentless campaign for revenge driven by News Limited's *Herald Sun*. The police themselves allude to the real driver behind the raids: the conference of world leaders to be held in Sydney this September. One of the arrested students has been told several times by senior police: "If you guys turn up to APEC we'll smash you."

Tall and black with an unmistakeable face, Menon, 25, works at Sydney University's Fisher Library. A few years ago he was at the centre of a little cause célèbre after being charged with helping an escapee asylum seeker reach New Zealand. Menon's prosecution attracted street demonstrations, pleas from civil liberties bodies and an email from Thomas Keneally. The case collapsed. In August 2005, a Sydney judge ordered the jury to acquit for lack of evidence. On the morning of the Sydney raid in March, Menon was taken to the police centre in Surry Hills and charged with two counts of aggravated burglary and two of unlawful assembly for his part in occupying office foyers in Collins Street at G20.

Dan Jones, a heavy sleeper, was woken in his parents' house in East Balmain by a policewoman tugging his toe. He faced two or three police in his bedroom – who introduced themselves by name and squad as he lay there – and found another dozen in the hallway outside. Among them were counter-terrorist police. Jones, 20, is an arts student at Sydney University with a face known to many sports fans. He was one of the stars – not quite the word – of the SBS reality show *Nerds FC* screened during the 2006 World Cup. The fight against voluntary student unionism drew Jones into campus politics. He was issued with two traffic fines after one of the big anti-VSU rallies in Sydney. He is now the education officer of the university's Students' Representative Council. At the Sydney police centre he was charged with affray, criminal damage and riot at G20.

Daniel Robins was woken at his girlfriend's place at 6 am by frantic housemates in Newtown ringing with the news: "The police are trashing the house and they're looking for you." Later they told him about being herded into the sitting room in their pyjamas while a dozen police searched their rooms. "They videoed my punk t-shirts and all the political stickers on the back of my door," said Robins. "They spread out my documents and videoed them – things like blood tests, union memberships, all these newspaper cuttings. They did the same thing in all the rooms. My housemates were really shaken up." Robins, 23, went to a city police station and turned himself in. A fine-boned restless kid, Robins has been demonstrating for years. He was a schoolboy among tens of thousands of protesters on Melbourne streets during the World Economic Forum at Crown Casino in 2000. He's demonstrated often since and never been in trouble with the police before. At the Sydney police centre he was charged with two counts of affray, two of riotous assembly, two of reckless conduct and one count of intentionally destroying property at G20.

Ten police came for Tim Davis-Frank at his parents' house in the beach suburb of Bronte. "My father answered the door in the dark at 6 am in his dressing gown." As they gathered in the kitchen, Davis-Frank, 22, noticed through the window "guys in dark clothing and gloves sneaking around the back of the house to cut off any possible escape". He knew one of the squad: a Melbourne detective who had interviewed and released him on the evening of the G20 demonstration last November. Davis-Frank's parents explained their son was diabetic and he was allowed to eat a bowl of cereal before being taken to the police centre.

"This arrest is the second time I have experienced the force of Victorian counter-terrorism agents in relation to the G20 protest," wrote Davis-Frank in the *Green Left Weekly*. "On the night of November 18, in Melbourne, I was snatched by about eight unidentifiable men and forced into an unmarked white van as I was walking with friends away from the protest. Without identifying themselves, the men in the van tied my hands behind my back, forced me to lie face down on the floor and proceeded to interrogate me, punching me repeatedly in the face if I didn't answer their questions quickly enough and once for accidentally calling one of them 'mate'." The detective now standing in his parents' kitchen had arranged for his injuries to be photographed and told him he would be charged by summons for his part in the chaotic demonstrations that day. "The next thing I heard about it was four months later when they raided my parents' home."

Davis-Frank studies politics at Sydney University and comes from a political household. He says he was pushed in a pram to an anti-nuclear demo at the age of three months. "If you feel passionately about something, you should make your opinions known to other people," he explained. "Democracy should give space to express your voice. The more people who do, the richer society will be." He was charged with two counts of aggravated burglary – those Melbourne office foyers again – three counts of riotous assembly and one of affray at G20.

At the police centre, the students saw a fifth suspect arrested in the early morning raids: a 17-year-old high school boy from Haberfield. He was leaning on the window of his holding cell: a distraught child on one side of the glass and his ashen-faced mother on the other. At some point in the day he was taken to the Children's Court, bailed and disappears from this narrative. (All he would ever be accused of doing was throwing a bottle at an empty police van.) The four remaining were taken after a few hours to the cells at Liverpool Central Court and strip searched while they waited – most of the day – for the formalities of bail to be completed.

Honora Ryan was at Central Station early in the morning handing out anti-war leaflets to commuters when she heard about the arrests. She joined about thirty people gathered at the court to give the students moral support. A young piano teacher, Ryan was days away from graduating as a Bachelor of Music from Sydney University. She was not at G20, but opposition to the Iraq War had seen her demonstrating when Condoleezza Rice and Vice President Dick Cheney visited Sydney. She has never, she says, been violent at a demonstration. "I've shouted a lot. I go there and march and shout slogans. I'm a pacifist. I believe very strongly we shouldn't be violent – any of us."

As the students emerged from court late in the afternoon, the *Herald Sun* was waiting. Their photograph would appear all over page one of Melbourne's Murdoch tabloid next day under a huge headline: "COP THAT."

Ryan went down the hill to choir practice at Christ Church St Laurence, the Anglo-Catholic redoubt near Central Station. It was dark when rehearsal finished and she emerged to find two big men in suits and dark glasses waiting for her. One held her elbow. They flashed badges. "When I asked to see them again, they wouldn't show me. They wouldn't tell me who they were." But they had a message. "They told me to stop going to rallies. They said they had a file like this on me" – she held her hands a couple of feet apart – "and to watch out or the same thing would happen to me." She took this to mean her house would be raided too. "I was really distressed. Nothing like this has happened to me before."

Australians don't demonstrate much these days. A million marched over bridges for reconciliation in 2000 – at which point the reconciliation movement all but died – and huge crowds turned out against the invasion of Iraq. That proved fruitless, too. Having stopped nothing in Australia in the last decade, it's not surprising that faith in the demo has all but collapsed – except when world leaders gather in exotic cities. The 1999 demonstrations in Seattle against the World Trade Organization began a triple tradition of large turnouts, occasional violence and heavy policing. Politicians are particularly gung ho about keeping the streets orderly. After the World Economic Forum in Melbourne in 2000, Bob Carr denounced the blockade of Crown Casino as "street-fighting fascism". Vietnam certainly knows how to meet the challenge: world leaders gathered in Hanoi for APEC in November last year and there wasn't a demonstrator in sight.

Melbourne hosted the G20 meeting of economic leaders in the same weeks. Roads were barricaded around the Grand Hyatt in Collins Street. Police were bussed in from the suburbs. The press predicted 20,000 demonstrators would converge on Melbourne but the headcount in the end was unimpressive: somewhere between 2000 and 3000. What followed was not an endless melee. Police, politicians and press concur that the following two days were overwhelmingly peaceful. The incidents leading to criminal charges lasted, in total, not much more than one unhappy hour.

Friday 17 November saw a number of brief occupations of office foyers in the CBD, including those of the defence contractor Tenix Solutions and the ADF recruiting centre in Swanston Street. Nothing was taken. Some water damage was reported at the recruiting centre. No arrests were made but three activists – including Menon and Davis-Frank – were afterwards charged with unlawful assembly, criminal damage and aggravated burglary over the occupations. The assistant commissioner of police Gary Jamieson described disruption in the city at this time as "minimal".

Next day saw trouble. Early in the morning, about sixty protesters dressed in white anti-chemical suits burst through the barricades in Russell Street and headed for the Grand Hyatt chanting "our streets, our streets". Their way was blocked by a line of mounted police. The *Age* reported the group called Arterial Block rushed the police lines a second time later in the morning but "dramatically dropped to the ground just a metre before the horses and started laughing. They then headed to join the main demonstration, a line of police horses following. There, they stripped out of their suits and masks and dispersed among the other protesters."

A small march set out from the State Library in Swanston Street. "Initially, the atmosphere was part-protest, part-street theatre," reported the *Sunday Age*. But about eighty to one hundred protesters broke off and slipped through narrow little Alfred Place and found themselves facing a line of water-filled barricades outside the Hyatt. What followed became known as the "Collins Street East riot": the demonstrators emptied the barricades – unbelievably the taps faced outwards – and threw them into the police massed behind. A policewoman, Constable Kim Dixon, was hurt as she steadied the barricades. Her shoulder injuries appear to be the worst inflicted on police at G20. Twenty-one demonstrators – including Davis-Frank and Daniel Robins – were to be charged with riot, affray and reckless conduct for their part in this skirmish.

About 2.20 pm, a group of fifty or so demonstrators set out to march around the hotel but found their way blocked by an empty police Isuzu van – known as the "brawler" van – parked across Flinders Lane. Another melee broke out at this point, lasting six to ten minutes and causing damage worth nearly $10,000. Twenty demonstrators – including Robins and Dan Jones – were to be charged with riot, affray, reckless conduct and criminal damage to the van.

Who did what that day will eventually be decided by the courts. Newspapers also reported "hit-and-run sorties" on police lines; police knocked to the ground; a lone motorcycle cop being rescued by mounted police; Melbourne City Council workers trapped in a truck; a television journalist assaulted; wheelie bins, milk crates, urine-filled balloons and other missiles thrown; and the walls of a bank defaced with graffiti. When the brawling had died down, Peter Costello came out to the barricades to thank the police and condemn the demonstrators as thugs and criminals. "They organised themselves for violence, they prepared themselves for violence, they unleashed violence, they attacked property, they attacked the police, they tried to trash Australia's reputation."

Operation Salver was established within hours of the riot and began rounding up protesters. Police hunkered down to examine 10,000 photographs and 3500 hours of footage with the *Herald Sun* urging them forward. Next day, Drasko Boljevic was grabbed in a shop near RMIT University. "He was thrown into a white van by men who swore at him and failed to identify themselves," reported the *Age*. "He said he was tied up and one of them sat on his head as he was driven around the city. After being taken from the van near Flinders Street station, he was forced to kneel and was told he had been arrested." Detectives handcuffed him and took him to a police station. "I just think it's really bad what's been done to me," Boljevic said. "I just feel traumatised. I thought I was going to die because you don't know who these people are." He claimed he was 100 kilometres away in Malmsbury during the demonstrations the previous day. The chief commissioner of police Christine Nixon later confirmed that a man had been mistakenly arrested.

How much trouble do we allow demonstrators to cause? That democratic question is answered differently in every country. Very little, is the answer here in Australia. Even holding up traffic is verboten these days. As Dick Cheney's plane lumbered towards Sydney in late February, weighed down with armour-plated limousines, Howard, Kevin Rudd and the NSW premier Morris Iemma all insisted anti-war protesters had a democratic right to demonstrate against him – but they could not disrupt traffic. Perhaps it was just a joke. Sydney would endure with good humour four days of traffic chaos necessary to keep Cheney safe – even the Bridge was closed to let him lunch with Howard at Kirribilli House – but on the night of his arrival an attempt by a couple of hundred protesters to march a few blocks down George Street was met with the full force of the law.

Demonstrators are despised by both sides of politics. Kevin Rudd called the old Lefties and young students trying to march along George Street that night "a bunch of violent ferals and they should expect absolutely no sympathy".

Dan Jones was one. "It was a very broad rally. The Hicks issue had brought in a lot of small-l liberals." In Town Hall Square he met old-timers who hadn't been on the streets since anti-Vietnam days. When the crowd voted to march to the US Consulate, he found himself in the front line. He claims that after arguing for the right of the demonstrators to move onto George Street, he was punched three times in the face, had his shirt ripped and was being held on the ground when a group of demonstrators dragged him back into the crowd. "I was basically beaten up."

Daniel Robins was there too. He claims he was dragged behind a police truck, held briefly on the ground, kicked in the groin and grabbed in a move known as the nipple cripple. He says a police-man repeatedly told him: "You've been identified as a wanted person." Wanted for what? The officer wouldn't say. According to Robins, he gave the officer some ID and was then told to clear out. One of the police added: "You're not allowed to be in the CBD today or tomorrow." Robins took the advice.

Early next morning Cheney was speaking at the Shangri-La Hotel in the Rocks. Sixty police standing shoulder to shoulder protected the hotel. A further fifty officers, including mounted police and dog handlers plus a water-cannon, were in reserve. All press reports concur that the gathering of roughly a hundred demonstrators was uneventful until a move was made to arrest two members of the Tranny Cop Dance Troupe doing their usual street theatre routine of mimicking police. In the melee that followed, four arrests were made. The performers were charged with wearing police uniforms when not police officers. Pip Hinman, an organiser of the Stop The War Coalition, said: "It was quite clear to everybody else these young women were simply there as a bit of a gag."

In the shadow of APEC, tempers are short. Police scrutiny is now part of the everyday life of universities. "They are so obvious," says Davis-Frank. "Old men in surf-brand Ts, three-quarter-length pants and running shoes." When rallies of any size are planned on Sydney University campus, security calls in the local Newtown police. When Senator Kerry Nettle addressed a meeting at Sydney University in March about the US Studies Centre to be established on campus, two plain-clothes police joined university security to keep an eye on about forty students. Police deny the man taking close-up photographs of faces was one of theirs. The university, police and students consider such heavy policing absolutely routine.

The dawn raids in Sydney came a fortnight after Cheney's visit. Menon, Jones, Robins and Davis-Frank presented themselves to a Melbourne court the following week. Their bail conditions require them to report to police three times a week and travel to Victoria when required. The bail conditions of the twenty-eight Victorians charged require them to stay out of New South Wales. Going north to demonstrate at APEC will land them straight in jail. Victoria seems to be planning a single monster trial of all the accused G20 protesters late next year.

2008 TO 2010

Melbourne lawyers with long memories of ugly demonstrations say G20 was not the worst the city has seen, not by far. But records were set by the police in tracking down, charging and prosecuting demonstrators. "I've never seen anything like this," said Rob Stary who represented a number of the G20 accused. "It's unprecedented."

Arrests continued for a year. One demonstrator was fetched from Queensland. Another was arrested at Sydney's Kingsford Smith Airport on his way from New Zealand to holiday in Spain. An off-duty policeman at a hardware store arrested a man showing his mates behind the counter his face in a newspaper report of G20. Four children were among those charged. The total number arrested was twenty-eight.

In March 2008 thirteen of the accused appeared in the magistrate's court. These skinny kids didn't live up to their advanced publicity. "Hardcore" was the word politicians, police and press had used about them: thugs, they said, linked to organised crime, inspired and perhaps led by foreign activists. None of this would prove to be true. Most were university students. There was also a librarian, a painter, a performer, a professional abseiler and a New Zealand mother of four – by far the oldest of the bunch – who was thinking of standing for the Maori Party back home.

Only one went to jail. Akin Sari, a Monash student and political refugee from Turkey with a history of psychiatric difficulties, was everywhere at G20: in the occupations, at the Collins Street barricades and smashing the windows of the brawler van. He pleaded guilty to everything the police threw at him and was sentenced to twenty-eight months' imprisonment. Most of the rest of the accused began a long process of negotiation with police that ended in guilty pleas to a few – rather than the original dozens – of the charges they each faced.

Sunil Menon and Tim Davis-Frank were among the very few who argued their case before a jury. At issue was their part in the occupations of various offices including the defence contractor Tenex and the ADF recruiting centre. After a trial lasting two and a half weeks, the jury acquitted them of all the most serious charges but Menon was convicted on one count of unlawful assembly.

The same jury split on a second unlawful assembly count both men faced. Years had passed by this time and with the prosecution determined to push ahead with a second trial, Menon decided to plead guilty and was fined a total of $5000. Davis-Frank went back to court and was acquitted.

That was not the end of it for him. Davis-Frank also had to answer for his role at the barricades in Collins Street. Most of the long list of charges he faced were eventually dropped, leaving him to plead guilty to one count of riot and two of assaulting police. Video evidence showed the police dusting themselves down unharmed and apparently quite amused after a conga line involving Davis-Frank swept them off their feet. Judge David Parsons of the Victorian County Court fined him a total of $3500 in March 2010 but did not record a conviction.

Daniel Robins was also at the barricades. He was accused of helping dismantle them, ram them with a skip and heave the skip into the ranks of the police. Of the Sydney four, Robins was the most severely punished. He would tell the court he had not intended hurting anyone: "I never directed any of those objects to police officers and I never would." He had then gone round the corner and joined the attack on the empty brawler van. He was accused of throwing an empty wheelie bin at an already broken window with what Judge Parsons called "not great force". Most of the charges Robins faced were also dropped. He pleaded guilty to two counts of riot in November 2008 and was fined a total of $10,000.

Also at the van was Dan Jones. All he was ever accused of doing at G20 was throwing a street sign at this van. He pleaded guilty to one count of riot, was fined $1000 and no conviction was recorded. After being targeted by the law again at APEC in Sydney in September that year, he successfully sued the NSW police for false arrest and wrongful imprisonment.

All four men got on with their lives while the machinery of justice ground on in Melbourne. The process was punishing. Menon had remained at his post in the Fisher Library. Jones continued his studies at Sydney University. Robins and Davis-Frank both took master's degrees in teaching from the university. Robins was keen to teach Aboriginal kids and was posted for two years to the outback town of Walgett. Davis-Frank has been teaching in Sydney. All four remain politically engaged.

The charges against the Tranny Cops were dismissed swiftly by Sydney magistrate David Heilpern in July 2007. "Australia has a long history of street theatre as part of demonstrations stretching back to the Sisters of Perpetual Indulgence and the Vietnam Moratorium," he reminded the police. Street theatre, he declared, was a "reasonable excuse" for wearing fake uniforms. "Part of protest has always been challenging figures of authority."

12.

COWBOYS AND INDIANS LATE 2007

Mohamed Haneef was waiting at Brisbane airport to board Singapore Airlines flight 246 when two police entered the departure lounge. "You are under arrest," said Detective Sergeant Adam Simms, "for the offence of supporting a terrorist organisation." The efforts of the last ten frantic hours to get home to Bangalore had come to nothing for Haneef. The doctor was led to a room in the airport, cautioned, questioned for fifty minutes by Simms and Federal Agent 2435 Neil Thompson and then driven to the Brisbane headquarters of the Australian Federal Police (AFP) in Wharf Street. They arrived after midnight.

Haneef was not panicking. He insisted he did not need a lawyer and would stick to that resolve for three days, believing he could straighten this difficulty out: "I would rather answer it myself." He told Simms and Thompson he had been trying to ring British police that afternoon to clear up the matter of an old SIM card he had given his cousin Sabeel Ahmed a year ago. Haneef insisted Ahmed's troubles had nothing to do with him. He said he believed he was being framed. At about 3 am they brought the exhausted Indian doctor a bed and he slept.

"There is a lot of confusion at the beginning of any complex investigation," Commissioner Mick Keelty of the AFP would confess when the case against Mohamed Haneef began to come unstuck.

"Errors in the investigation came to us from the UK." The commissioner's men had stopped Haneef at the airport gate in the belief that the SIM card had turned up at the scene of a terrorist attack in Glasgow forty-eight hours before. The perpetrator of the attack was Sabeel Ahmed's inept brother Kafeel. After failing to set off car bombs outside London's Tiger Tiger nightclub on 29 June, Kafeel drove north in a Jeep Cherokee loaded with gas canisters and drums of fuel to blow up Glasgow airport. It was the first day of the school holidays, and the airport was crowded with families about to fly to sunnier parts of the world when the Jeep rammed the entrance of the main terminal and burst into flames without exploding. Passengers fled but a few brave citizens helped police subdue two figures who leapt from the Jeep – their clothes blazing – punching, kicking and hurling petrol bombs which, again, failed to explode. Kafeel was rushed to hospital with hideous burns. The half-dozen arrests that followed in Britain swiftly made news around the world for many of the still-unnamed suspects were doctors. One was Kafeel's brother Sabeel.

Haneef slept for a few hours before police woke him. Simms and Thompson explained they were off to ask a magistrate for authority to detain him. Again he refused a lawyer. This was to be the first time police used machinery designed to fight terrorism by allowing suspects to be held without charge during lengthy police investigations. Theoretically, Haneef could be held forever but only questioned for a total of twenty-four hours. First up, the magistrate gave them just eight hours. Simms, a Queensland cop seconded to the Joint Counter-Terrorism Team in Brisbane, turned on the tape at 11.01 am. He asked most of the questions. Swift police work meant he wasn't starting cold. The interrogators already had phone and financial records from Australia and Britain. While the prisoner was having breakfast, his Southport flat had been raided, turning up notebooks and diaries. Police had yet to strip Haneef's computer, but they already had evidence of many links – social and financial – between Haneef and his accused cousins. Yet they did not unmask a terrorist that day.

Haneef emerged from the 1616 questions and answers as a nerdy guy with fractured English who has done little in the past decade but study. He denied ever touching a rifle, ever having any training in firearms, explosives or logistics, or ever being part of a terrorist organisation. He denied raising money for political causes and denied knowing anyone who regarded jihad as violent. He denied any foreknowledge of the Glasgow attack and the London car bombs. Asked how he felt when he heard of the terrorist attempts in London, Haneef replied: "Every drop of blood is human, and I feel for every human being."

Whatever else he may have done along the way, Haneef had performed to perfection the classic role of the good Indian son. He told the police: "I am the sole carer for my family." He was eighteen when his father, a teacher in the town of Mudigere, died in 1997. With a little money and a small scholarship, the son entered medical school in Bangalore. His mother, brother and sister moved to town with him and lived very simply in an ugly Muslim quarter of concrete flats. Old neighbours still speak highly of a wholesome and studious boy. His aim after graduation was to become a physician, an ambition that took him to England in March 2004. Money was tight. His interrogators had found the old diary in which Haneef meticulously noted the sums borrowed to stay afloat in his first eighteen months in Liverpool: £180 from one Indian doctor, £290 from another.

His base was a boarding house run by an Indian charity that looks after trainee doctors and dentists newly arrived in Britain. Though mainly Muslim, Mufeed was not a religious organisation,

Haneef explained. But his interrogators were particularly curious about Mufeed's annual summer camp in the Lakes District: was there religious instruction; did you do any self-defence, any white-water rafting, any survival skills? To each, the answer was no. Police would later claim Haneef lived at the Bentley Road boarding house with his cousins Kafeel and Sabeel. He had told them the opposite.

Kafeel, a second cousin on his mother's side, was his only family contact in Britain. Haneef described him as a "short, pretty fat" man of "reserved personality" with a beard. They had not known each other well in India, but Kafeel rang from Belfast to welcome him when he first arrived. Kafeel was studying aeronautical engineering there but was about to move to Cambridge – the town not the university – to begin a PhD in fluid dynamics at Anglia Ruskin University. It was to his cousin in Cambridge that Haneef went for a few days in May after suffering a short, embarrassing setback to his career: he had failed part two of the qualifying exams set by the General Medical Council. "I was a bit low. So I thought I'd just go and visit him. Because there was no-one else my family ..." He stayed three or four days looking around Cambridge, eating and praying with his cousin who gave him £300 to tide him over until he could take the exams again. Kafeel didn't want the money back. "He said: 'Just give it to any of the poor people in India.'"

He passed at his second attempt in November and spent a day celebrating with Kafeel. It was Ramadan. For the next few months he continued working as a volunteer "clinical observer" mainly at Halton Hospital on the edge of Liverpool. Ahead lay a significant hurdle: part one of the Royal College of Physicians exams. These he passed in May 2005. It was a life-changing success. What followed was so Indian, but at every turn, this is a very Indian story.

Haneef returned to Bangalore to bask in his achievement. With a good job lined up at the Royal Liverpool Hospital and the prospect of a fine career as a physician, he found a wife. She was from a family way up the ladder: an IT graduate who lived in a beautiful house in a beautiful suburb of the city. They were modern Muslims. They read and travelled. Haneef's engagement to Firdous Arshiya was announced in July. This alliance did not come cheap: from his brother-in-law-to-be, Dr Siddique Ahmed, Haneef borrowed £3000 to settle his English debts and to pay for the wedding. Here was a source of rich misunderstanding for police who would later find two "S. Ahmeds" in Haneef's financial records: his brother-in-law Siddique and his second cousin Sabeel. It could be so confusing.

Haneef returned alone to Britain to begin work and Sabeel followed a few weeks later. They knew each other well. For many years his younger cousin had been following in his footsteps. They were at Bangalore Medical College together a year or so apart, and now Sabeel was in England preparing to take his General Medical Council exams in Preston. One day that summer brother Kafeel picked Haneef up in a rented car and they drove to Preston together to deliver luggage to Sabeel while listening to a CD of the Koran. After this trip, Kafeel disappeared to India and, it seems, began to drift into extreme Islamic circles.

Once he began earning a decent wage at the hospital, Haneef sent money home to his family. This was done in a way that puzzled Australian investigators but makes perfect sense to Indians: in October 2005, he paid £960 into Kafeel's English bank account on the understanding that his cousin in India would pay the same sum to his family in Bangalore. Haneef told the police: "He made arrangements to pay … in India to my family."

The wedding was in Bangalore in November that year. Both his cousins were guests. "Was it a traditional Islamic wedding?" asked Detective Sergeant Simms, while admitting in the next breath: "I don't know what that means."

Haneef reassured him it was, indeed, traditional: "A lot of people are gathering."

"A lot of colour?"

"Yes."

"And what part did Sabeel play?"

"He just stood there."

The newlyweds returned to Liverpool and moved into a flat in Pembroke Place near Liverpool Hospital. About this time, Haneef bought a mobile phone with a one-year plan from Orange. Relations between the newlyweds and Sabeel were close. Sabeel visited them and ate with them. They spoke on the phone. Theirs was his postal address. They were family. Sabeel was the driver on trips round Britain: to London for a day to see the sights, to a bird sanctuary in Wales and up to the Mufeed summer camp in the Peak District.

"What's that?" asked Simms.

"It's a district in UK."

"Peak?"

"Yes. Peak District is a spot there."

"Sorry, just not aware of that."

The expedition that fascinated Haneef's interrogators was the family trip to the Lakes District and Scotland in the spring of 2006. Haneef rented the car. Sabeel drove. With them were Haneef's wife, her parents and her brother. In Edinburgh they photographed themselves in front of the castle. In Glasgow, they prayed at the mosque, and slept the night in a motorway hotel. Haneef's computer was filling with family snaps.

But for his ambition to be a physician, this young doctor may well have stayed in Britain. He needed to continue his studies in a good teaching hospital. Such jobs were hard to find. "The competition is very fierce there." So he answered an ad in the British Medical

Journal for a post at a hospital on the Queensland Gold Coast, was interviewed on the phone, accepted and prepared for the journey to Australia. The expense of the move was compounded by needing a large sum to pay for his sister's wedding: "I being the only earner and looking after her, for the whole of my time." From his bank he borrowed £2000.

Just before they left, Haneef and his wife took a pile of gear to Sabeel's flat by taxi: a duvet, sheets, crockery, a food processor, a framed picture of Mecca, a winter overcoat and a number of medical and religious texts. Some of this stash was for Sabeel and some to be ferried out to India as friends and family moved back and forth. Haneef also gave his cousin his SIM card. Keeping in contact with their families was obligatory and expensive. In these years they both used Yahoo chat rooms, Skype and mobile phones. Haneef said of Sabeel: "He is talk a lot on the phone, always on the phone." The card had a few weeks and a couple of hundred minutes' credit left to run. But as Haneef explained to his interrogators, the big plus for Sabeel were the discounts offered when the card was renewed for a second year. "They used to … give more minutes at a less cost." The arrangement was that Sabeel would take over payment and transfer the card into his own name. Step two never happened.

Haneef and his wife arrived in Australia in mid-September 2006 with few plans. The taxi driver suggested a motel somewhere near the hospital and after two or three nights at the Motor-Inn, the young couple found a flat nearby in Pohlman Street, Southport. Haneef began work as a senior house officer and enrolled with the Australian College of Physicians to continue his studies. He paid his debts, lived frugally, sent as much money home each month as he could, worshipped at the Gold Coast mosque, and took his wife on brief trips to Sydney and Surfers Paradise. A photograph of

Haneef on that excursion was later leaked by the police to News Limited papers to suggest he may have had plans to blow up one of the apartment blocks in the background.

By November, Firdous Arshiya was pregnant and in March she returned to Bangalore. "We didn't have enough support here," explained Haneef. "We thought it would be better for her to be there with the parents." Her blood pressure was high so their daughter Haniya was delivered by emergency caesarean on 26 June. A few days later, the child contracted jaundice and was brought back to hospital. Haneef was uncharacteristically hazy about the exact date. He said everyone was ringing everyone through this crisis and by Sunday 1 July he felt he should fly home for a visit. But he did nothing until he turned up for work the next day – the day of his arrest.

Simms and Thompson were particularly interested in the narrative of that day: from the moment Haneef received a message that Sabeel was in custody in England because of some "misuse" of the card. Over the next jumbled hours, Haneef was given a week's leave, called his father-in-law for a ticket home, was told by Sabeel's mother on the phone from Bangalore that he must ring a London police officer about the card, tried and failed four times to get through to the officer, then travelled to the airport where Simms and Thompson were waiting.

With breaks for meals and prayers, Haneef's interrogation continued until 5.30 pm. The tone was mostly polite. The prisoner was willing. His answers were detailed. He refused only to give his views on the political situation in Iraq and Afghanistan. "I don't like to comment." Simms and Thompson didn't press the point. They did their chores: quizzing their prisoner about every name in his notebook and everyone he met through Kafeel and Sabeel. They tracked through his studies, his work and his financial transactions. They came back and back to the SIM card.

Before the tape was turned off and the prisoner taken down the road to the Brisbane Watchhouse, Haneef told his interrogators: "I haven't done any of the crimes. Just want to let you know. And I don't want to spoil my name and my profession. That's the main thing. And I've been a professionalist until now and I haven't been involved in any kind of extra activities, what sort of activities which you were discussing earlier. And I just want to live in life as a professionalist in the medical profession. That's what I want."

News of Haneef's detention had broken even while he was being interrogated. The political leadership sang its usual double song: the presumption of innocence and presumption of terrorism. That evening Commissioner Keelty told the ABC his officers believed the Indian doctor was "connected to a terrorist group". It's a word that can mean anything, of course, but in light of what police had learnt from their prisoner that day, "connected" was a bold claim. Even more graphic accusations were being made by police staking out the Gold Coast Hospital. According to later reports, officers were telling the hospital staff their colleague may have been part of a terrorist sleeper cell.

A tabloid portrait of Haneef emerged rapidly: an Islamic radical from his student years; a ruthless terrorist working under the perfect cover of a man dedicated to healing; a prime suspect in an al-Qaeda plot; an absconder from his job fleeing the country to escape detection; and a collaborator in the Glasgow operation with his cousin, the dying Kafeel Ahmed. But from the start, Haneef had vigorous supporters. He was vouched for by family, colleagues and neighbours. Queensland's premier Peter Beattie declared him a "model citizen with impeccable references". As the press began to suggest Haneef's detention was overkill, Keelty stepped in to say there was "a lot more" to the case than mobile phone records. A few days later the commissioner declared: "The links to the UK are becoming more concrete." By this time the press had learnt – and only the police could have leaked the information – that Haneef's international financial transactions were being investigated.

The magistrate's order to detain him, renewed on the evening of his first interrogation, was due to expire late on Thursday 5 July. That afternoon the hard-bitten Brisbane criminal lawyer Peter Russo received a call: "Do you mind coming down to the watchhouse? There's someone who needs a lawyer." The facts are a bit murky at this point, but it seems one of the old cops had finally persuaded Haneef it was time to get help. Russo was not surprised to be rung. "I've been called to the watchhouse on numerous occasions over the years, sometimes just to pacify people who are refusing to give their fingerprints. The guys at the watchhouse know me, and I'm easy to find, I guess." But this wasn't a drunk or a petty crim needing a hand. It was the nation's most famous terror suspect.

Haneef had spent two days and two nights waiting in a double cell with a small five-metre by seven-metre yard attached. He had access to magazines but no daily papers. He had made only one phone call, to the Indian consulate on the morning of his interrogation to warn his family he would not be arriving home. He had been refused permission to speak to his wife. He had not been questioned again. Russo spent less than an hour with his client whose instructions were simple: "I want to go home." The hearing before the magistrate began at 7 pm. Russo was not allowed to hear the police evidence and the magistrate's decision was made in his absence. All the lawyer could do was put on record the fact that his client had been co-operating. Police were given until the evening of Monday the 9th to hold their prisoner.

Extraordinary resources were being thrown at the case. "There is something in the order of 170 AFP officers involved," Keelty told ABC radio's *AM*. "And there would be up to an additional fifty state police officers from Queensland and Western Australia." Keelty and the attorney-general Philip Ruddock urged the public to be patient while an overwhelming mass of evidence was assessed. Keelty spoke of 18,000 files stripped from the doctor's laptop. Ruddock was sombre about the prospects of an early resolution of the investigation: "I am told it is the equivalent of reading 31,000 pages of paper to look at the amount of material that actually has to be analysed that has been retrieved through the exercising of search warrants."

Haneef waited. At Monday's hearing Russo was joined by Brisbane barrister Stephen Keim SC. A week after his arrest, Haneef had still not been told why he was being held. His lawyers were also in the dark. When prosecution lawyers handed magistrate Jim Gordon a dossier of secret information, Keim protested: "That's not natural justice. I've got a right to make submissions. I've got a right to know generally what your case is." He was shown nothing but the magistrate cut the police request for five days down to forty-eight hours. Canberra's lawyers mulled over Keim's demands. He was eventually handed a small dossier. "They gave me thirteen pages of material that two days earlier was so secret and so highly protected, I could not get one letter of it."

At about 3.45 pm on Friday the 13th, Haneef was driven in a police van 200 metres from the watchhouse to Queensland Police headquarters in Roma Street for his final interrogation. Why the police chose to hold the final interrogation at this point isn't clear. The press was restive; lawyers were thundering on opinion pages; the magistrate was growing sceptical; and the manoeuvring of Haneef's legal team had seen the first cracks in the wall of secrecy behind which the prisoner was being held. The dividends of further delay were uncertain: squads of police working on the investigation were turning up nothing of much use. Indeed the case was going backwards.

When Scotland Yard corrected its big mistake is not clear, perhaps as early as 5 July when a chief inspector of the Yard's counterterrorism command arrived in Brisbane. Certainly by the time Haneef's final interrogation began, the AFP knew the old SIM card had had nothing at all to do with terrorism. It was not a bomb component, had played no part in the London and Glasgow attacks and was not found – as the public would continue to believe for a week or more – in the wreckage of Kafeel's Jeep Cherokee. It was with cousin Sabeel in Liverpool.

By this time police should also have been briefed that Sabeel was no terrorist. Suicide bombers traditionally send a message before their deaths. It appears that Kafeel, heading north after failing to set off those car bombs in London, sent his brother a text message with a password that would open an email. According to the *Guardian*:

> Those who have seen the email regard it as Ahmed claiming responsibility for the attempted attacks on London and the one he was about to stage in Glasgow. According to a source, Ahmed says his actions were carried out in the name of Allah. Ahmed writes that his relative would be shocked to read what he is about to tell him about his involvement in terrorism, praises God, and says he wants martyrdom.

Shocked. If this account is correct, Sabeel was clearly not in on Kafeel's plot nor aware of his brother's terrorist ambitions. The *Guardian* also claimed Sabeel was in no position to stop the Glasgow attempt. According to the paper, he did not open the email until an hour and a half after his brother had driven the Jeep into the airport terminal. Sabeel was in custody – but still not charged – for failing to alert police to Kafeel's confession hours after the crime had been committed. So what had this to do with a cousin on the far side of the world?

"Geography was not one of my better subjects at school," Adam Simms admitted in the sixth hour of the interrogation. "Bangalore, where's that in relation to Pakistan?" Detectives on three continents had been gathering whatever evidence they could find about the Gold Coast doctor for ten days, but Detective Simms hadn't opened an atlas. The name Mysore meant nothing to him. He didn't know where Liverpool was from London. The ways of Skype were a mystery: "I'm a bit of a dinosaur when it comes to this sort of thing." His grasp of the ordinary steps in a doctor's career was nil. He had no clue what Muslims do in Ramadan. "Okay," he said when Haneef explained. "Excuse my ignorance, yeah."

Simms emerges as a decent man from the transcripts of these interrogations. He dealt with Haneef politely, hour after hour. But his ignorance of Islam is bewildering. He was, after all, the officer to whom the AFP had delegated the urgent task of discovering whether Australia was holding a man in league with fanatical Islamists who had tried to slaughter large numbers of people in London and Glasgow. Simms knew the term jihad. He was aware of a division between Shia and Sunni. But Islam comes for Simms in only three strengths: moderate, strict and extreme. He showed no expertise in the nuances of fanaticism. Hours were spent that last night asking the prisoner if this or that colleague, friend or cousin was moderate, strict or extreme.

Leafing through Haneef's photographs of family holidays in Britain, Simms asked if religion had been discussed on these travels. "Not normally," Haneef replied. "Just about the faith and the prayers and things we used to say, praying time."

"What sort of discussions were they?" Simms persisted.

"Just the normal things."

"You'll have to tell me because I don't know what you mean by that."

This was not strategy. Simms was stumped every time by Haneef's replies: these people said their prayers; they listened to the Koran in the car; they went to the mosque; they were just normal. He never seemed to know what to ask next.

The final interrogation began at 4.15 pm and continued with breaks roughly every hour until just before dawn on 14 July. Simms took the running but Federal Agent Thompson asked the occasional question after receiving prompts on his laptop. Ramzi Jabbour, manager of domestic counter-terrorism for the AFP, was supervising the interrogation from a nearby room. Sitting with the prisoner was Russo, his knockabout solicitor, with a nasty cough turning into flu.

Though Simms would remind Haneef all through the night that the crucial issue was the SIM card, these hours of interrogation have the feel of a fishing expedition: a team of police hoping to find some more tangible link to terrorism in Haneef's past. So they crisscrossed the narrative of his time in Britain, his travels, his colleagues, his career and the sums of money – mostly small – that flowed in and out of his bank accounts. But always the questioning returned to the SIM card and his cousins Sabeel and Kafeel.

What emerged was a much clearer picture of the intimacy between Haneef and Sabeel. Under questioning, the prisoner revealed a couple of meetings between the cousins not admitted in the first interrogation. None connected him to terrorism. Just before midnight, Simms revealed that in June 2007, Kafeel paid a month's fees on the SIM card. "We believe Kafeel was using the phone also. Does that surprise you?" asked Simms. It did. "Dr Sabeel wanted it for his use. He said he just wanted to make normal calls to India and friends." That line of questioning went no further.

At 3 am, having thrown everything they had at Haneef, the interrogators turned to the suspicious circumstances of his rushed attempts to leave Australia on the night of 2 July. These were crowded hours and police had to judge his account against a timeline of events in Britain and Bangalore:

Tuesday 26 June.
His daughter is born.

Friday 29 June.
London bombs discovered.

Saturday 30 June.
Haneef's daughter admitted to hospital with jaundice.
Kafeel rams the Glasgow terminal.
Sabeel taken into custody.

Sunday 1 July.
Reports of the terrorist outrages and arrests are flashed round the world but the names of Kafeel and Sabeel are not released for another three or four days.

Monday 2 July.
Haneef says he was too busy at work that morning to do more about getting away to Bangalore than make a brief phone call to ask the hospital about family leave. Then, at about 2.30 pm, his colleague and friend Dr Mohammed Asif Ali brought him a message: "You need to call India." Haneef's brother had rung to say Sabeel was in custody; there had been some "misuse" of his old SIM card; and

Sabeel's mother wanted to talk to Haneef. Ali had only been brought into the loop because the brother had been trying and failing to make contact with Haneef all morning.

Haneef went home to his nearby flat and made a number of rapid calls: to his brother Shoaib in Bangalore, then to arrange a week's leave from the hospital, and then to his father-in-law Ashfaq Ahmed to ask for a ticket home. Whether he asked for a one-way ticket isn't clear. Haneef's rather confused explanation was that at this point he had only about $100 in his bank account – as usual all his spare cash had been sent home to support his family – and he would buy a return ticket himself after his next pay.

Simms asked Haneef: "Was the decision to go and take leave made because you found out about this telephone issue?" He replied: "No. Not about that at all." Later he would concede in the interrogation: "This was the second reason probably why I would have gone."

Sabeel's mother now rang and gave Haneef the number of a London police officer who wanted to speak to him about the SIM card. According to Haneef, she didn't explain why there was an issue with the card. Haneef claimed he was still some hours away from learning there was a connection between Sabeel's troubles and the terrorist attempts. Haneef rang the officer's number three times between 3.08 and 3.29 pm but couldn't get through.

Late in the afternoon, he returned to the hospital and put in his leave form. He looked for Ali and found him in the emergency department. The two doctors had known each other since their days together in Liverpool and were neighbours in Southport. Haneef gave him spare keys to his flat and to his new Honda Jazz. When he told his colleague he'd been trying without success to call a policeman in London, Ali lent him an international calling card to try again. This attempt at 4.32 pm didn't work either.

Back at the flat, Haneef had one more favour to ask of his friend: to come and collect for safekeeping his laptop and his wife's jewellery. Giving the computer to Ali was later cited by police as an attempt to conceal evidence. And Simms was sceptical about the jewellery. Haneef explained it was "Some bangles and some necklaces and things." Why not take them home to his wife? "She had enough with her," replied Haneef. "I mean, obviously we were going to come back."

When his e-ticket came through in the early evening, he spoke again to his father-in-law, telling him for the first time about Sabeel and his own name being somehow mixed up in his cousin's phone card troubles. Haneef says Ashfaq reassured him that if he had done nothing wrong there was nothing to worry about. "You're going to come here and we'll have support here for you." Haneef settled down to wait for the airport transfer van due at 8 pm.

The flat was tidy. Journalists who saw the place a day or so later reported a couple of unwashed dishes in the sink but no signs of a rushed departure. As he waited, Haneef exchanged messages in Urdu with his brother Shoaib on a Yahoo chat line. It was at this point, says Haneef, that he learnt for the first time how serious the situation was: "He told me about the thing what was going in the UK. Then he explained to me that Sabeel might have been arrested for this reason. There was the same a terrorist attack." Together they watched the latest report on the attacks on BBC.com, which still did not name Sabeel or Kafeel. How Shoaib knew of the link is not clear, but the transcript indicates the source of the information was their cousins' mother. Whatever the source, the news was clearly travelling from Bangalore to the Gold Coast. Not the other way around. Yet the AFP believed this exchange between the brothers "may be evidence of Haneef's awareness of the conspiracy to plan and prepare the acts of terrorism in London and Glasgow".

Haneef didn't wipe these exchanges. The police would take them from the computer and have them translated. The result was gibberish. Haneef had the original Urdu in front of him, but Federal Agent Thompson brushed aside his protests: "We can go back through it then I'll ask your version." That never happened. Urdu is spoken by a couple of hundred million people, but Australia's frontline counter-terrorism force couldn't find a decent translator. They were undeterred.

The interrogation ended without fanfare at 4.42 am. The police called a break and never came back. Instead they conferred with Jabbour and the team briefed the office of the Commonwealth Director of Public Prosecutions. The police knew they didn't have a case against Haneef, but they had high hopes something would arrive from somewhere. Their optimism was infectious. A decision was taken to charge Haneef. The DPP Damian Bugg QC later tried to spread the blame a little: "This decision was made following advice provided to the AFP by one of my officers that on the basis of the information available at that stage and what was said to be likely to be available and other potential sources of information, the police could have reasonable grounds for believing that Dr Haneef had committed that offence."

About 5 am, the flu-raddled Russo was told his client would be charged with intentionally providing a SIM card "to a terrorist organisation consisting of a group of persons including Sabeel Ahmed and Kafeel Ahmed, being reckless as to whether the organisation was a terrorist organisation".

His lawyers immediately applied for bail. The magistrate, Jacqui Payne, was not impressed with the case against the Indian doctor. She queried the logic of anyone giving a SIM card to terrorists: surely its discovery would immediately implicate them in the crimes? Barristers for the Crown argued the phone was intended to be obliterated in the fire that destroyed the Cherokee Jeep at Glasgow airport. After thinking it over for the weekend, Payne granted Haneef bail that Monday. She noted there was no evidence of a direct link between him and the group blamed for Britain's failed terrorist plot, set bail at $10,000 and, under stringent reporting conditions, ordered his release.

But the freedom she granted was immediately taken away by the minister for immigration. In a move that set off a depth charge in the legal profession, Kevin Andrews cancelled Haneef's work visa on "character" grounds claiming to "reasonably suspect Dr Haneef has had an association with persons involved in criminal conduct, namely terrorism". Andrews was now Haneef's jailor: the doctor was a prisoner of the immigration system. Not complaining was the Opposition leader Kevin Rudd: "These are tough decisions, I understand the complexity of them. I also understand the complexity of the civil liberties argument. But on terrorism we must adopt a hardline posture."

Noël Godin, the great Belgian *entarteur* or pie-thrower, observes that a great deal about a person's character is revealed in the first seconds after they've been hit by a pie. A couple of days after failing to win Haneef's release, Stephen Keim gave the 142-page transcript of his client's first formal interrogation to Hedley Thomas of the *Australian*. Next morning, the prime minister, the attorney-general and the commissioner of police woke to find slabs of the transcript in the paper. They responded with blind rage. "Whoever has been responsible," snarled John Howard, "is not trying to make sure that justice is done." Ruddock put on a grave, grey face and declared "inappropriate, highly unethical" these questions and answers seeing the light of day. Keelty was almost distraught on morning radio: "It's undermined the prosecution."

He was right. For the first time, we read Haneef's protestations of innocence and learnt of his many attempts to reach the British police and his reasons for trying to leave the country in a rush on a one-way ticket. Even at first reading, it was clear the police had no evidence this man had done anything at all. Then two days later, Rafael Epstein broke the news on *AM* that the famous SIM card was not at the scene of the crimes but safely in Sabeel Ahmed's house in Liverpool. The headlines over the next few days told the story: "Terrorism Case Imploding"; "Inept Game of Cowboys and Indians"; "SIM Dim Link Haneef Phone Card Doubt"; "Terror Case Outrage"; "A Case of Plain Old Verballing"; "Haneef Case Turns to Farce." A week later after a brief review by the DPP, the charges were dropped. That weekend, Haneef sold himself to *Sixty Minutes* and finally flew home to Bangalore.

But Haneef's persecution continues. Keelty has announced his officers will continue working on the investigation "until such time as we exhaust all avenues of inquiry about a number of people, including Dr Haneef". The commissioner has also complained officially to the Queensland Bar Association about the "misconduct" of Stephen Keim. Kevin Andrews continues to mutter darkly about Haneef's sins, puts out garbled and misleading material to damn him and expresses his regret that the AFP will not allow him to reveal more. John Howard has signalled it's time to close a few loopholes so the next Haneef doesn't get away: "All of this is a reminder that terrorism is a global threat. You can't pick and choose where you fight terrorism. You can't say I'll fight it over there but I won't fight it here. It's also fair to say that the anti-terrorism laws that this Government has enacted are all, to their very last clause needed … If we need to strengthen them, we will."

The official inquiry into the Haneef mess conducted by a retired New South Wales judge, John Clarke QC, found the AFP had powerful evidence of Haneef's innocence days before they charged him with aiding his terrorist cousin. Scotland Yard had alerted the Australian police to the text of the message Kafeel Ahmed had sent his brother Sabeel:

> This is the "project" that I was working on for some time now … Everything else was a lie! And I hope you can all forgive me for being such a good liar!! It was necessary, Just so that YOU know Alhamdulillah. Everything since last week were executed by me and my team (this is confidential) on behalf of our Amir…

This convinced Scotland Yard the brothers – and hence Mohamed Haneef – were not in league together. But the gung-ho AFP had brushed the message aside as a clever sham to protect the operation. The message was kept from Haneef's lawyers, the magistrates and the DPP. Sabeel would later plead guilty at the Old Bailey to a charge of failing to alert police to his brother's message, but Justice David Calvert-Smith absolved him from any role in the terrorist plot and declared there was "no sign" of Dr Ahmed "being an extremist or party to extremist views".

Clarke concluded the AFP had also known in good time that Haneef's old SIM card did not turn up at the scene of the crime. Not even this gave pause to Commander Ramzi Jabbour, manager of domestic counter-terrorism for the AFP, who was running the Haneef operation. Clarke slammed Jabbour for being "unable to see that the evidence he regarded as highly incriminating in fact amounted to very little" and failing – along with other senior AFP officers – to stand back and reflect on what Haneef was known to have done: "Give a SIM card registered in his name – a card that could have been bought for a small sum of money, even with a false name in the United Kingdom – to his cousin, who had asked for it, about 12 months before the terrorist attack."

Two heroes emerged from Clarke's report: the police officers Adam Simms and Neil Thompson. Clarke revealed they were reluctant to arrest Haneef at the airport and would not charge him eleven days later for they never believed there was sufficient evidence against him. On both occasions they were overruled by Jabbour.

Clarke cleared Haneef absolutely: "I could find no evidence that he was associated with or had foreknowledge of the terrorist events or of the possible involvement of his second cousins Dr Sabeel Ahmed and Mr Kafeel Ahmed in terrorist activities." But this happy verdict delivered in late 2008 and the substantial settlement – perhaps millions of dollars – paid to the doctor in December 2010, lay on the far side of a great political divide. As Australia headed to the polls in November 2007, the Haneef business was another scare campaign gone wrong for the Howard government. Before election day there was time for one last little panic as Vladimir Putin, George W. Bush and Hu Jintao jetted into Sydney for APEC.

13.

SCENES FROM A CITY UNDER SIEGE
SEPTEMBER 2007

Like a parish harmonium in quite good nick, the prime minister can still belt out a tune. He's a bit wheezy and relies too much on the drone, but the tune is loud and clear: we don't want demonstrators making a mess of the streets while the leaders of the world are in town. Kevin Rudd is singing along. So are Morris Iemma and a massed choir of police.

Verse two is just like the first: these things have turned violent in the past, we can't be too careful, better to keep the rabble out of sight and out of mind – or at least out of Sydney's central business district, rebadged the APEC "declared area", running from the Quay to King Street. This is not fenced like some great chook yard. It's just a line drawn on the map. And the strategy is to keep all demonstrators from crossing that line. So while the "heads of economies" are meeting in the Opera House on Saturday morning, the Stop Bush Coalition demo won't be allowed to march up Martin Place.

What possible danger would those demonstrators present at the distance of seven or eight city blocks? Why pick a fight with such a crowd rather than facilitate their peaceful march through the city while keeping an eye out for trouble makers? But the message is: demonstrators like boat people might always be harbouring terrorists.

Yesterday the prime minister refused to say if he had any credible intelligence that the demonstrations planned for APEC might turn violent. "I never talk about intelligence matters," he said after slamming all the demonstrators for being "just interested in making a noisy point" against capitalism and economic growth. As it happens the big complaint of the Stop Bush Coalition is the war: "We will be gathering to protest the ongoing, inhumane slaughter in Iraq and Afghanistan."

But not in Martin Place. There are to be no demonstrations inside the "declared area" and that includes a Friday press conference with Senator Kerry Nettle and twenty-one Greens supporters dressed as lifesavers. What are the police worried about? Concealed weapons?

*

The APEC city is once again hosting the annual gathering of Reporters Without Stories (RWS). Observers of this wealthy international organisation claim its work so far in Sydney compares well with benchmark efforts in Hanoi (2006) and Shanghai (2001). As old and almost as distinguished as APEC itself, RWS is dedicated to the art of making do with next to no news. At multilateral meetings on the margins of APEC yesterday, RWS delegates canvassed a number of initiatives to bulk out the rest of the week's coverage. These include: the supply of acronyms running low; large birds seen circling city buildings in suspicious numbers; children dressed as police turn out to be police.

Some of Canberra's leading pundits are among RWS old hands. Although longing to report the "real" story of John Howard's plunge in the polls, they're sticking to their APEC duties and are grateful for the spirit of co-operation shown this week by senior ministers holding frequent news conferences at which nothing is said. It has been the sort of week where Warren Truss drew record crowds at a doorstop. And the prime minister did what he could for RWS by meeting the press daily in his Sydney office block. The setting is pure Howard: a long brown North Shore dining room with flags and Hansards. As the prime minister talks bilaterals and trilaterals, his hands cut excited shapes in the air. The face is wearing well, but these are the hands of an old man.

Out in the streets, listless citizens get on with their lives while choppers circle overhead. Speculation is growing that those fenced alleys crossing the city are designed for a new APEC sport with its origins in Spain: the running of the presidents. Authorities will neither confirm nor deny.

In Pitt Street yesterday, law and order was breaking down. The *Herald* tried without success to persuade police guarding a major city hotel to book a Mercedes-load of Korean delegates sitting four abreast without seatbelts. A spokesman for the police commissioner declined to comment.

Fresh worries are surfacing about the language used by APEC. A press briefing note describes the ballroom of Government House, where the world's leaders will meet on Sunday, as "an informal, relaxed retreat setting". Where have these people been? It's actually a stiff room in a little palace of great formality, although perhaps if you have President Vladimir Putin's taste for palaces, it may seem a slum.

RWS delegates wandered off after lunch to see if they could make news by getting themselves arrested. Their gloom was lifting. Once George Bush hits town, the real stories might start: half a dozen for the motorcade itself and any number for each traffic jam until he goes. The week is looking up.

*

The scene outside the Supreme Court was chilling: police every-where with nothing to do but flex their muscles. Upstairs inside, Mr Justice Adams had just given the police commissioner exactly what he wanted. In an extempore performance lasting an hour or so, His Honour made downbeat remarks about APEC, President Bush, the war in Iraq – "a subject on which most persons of any sensibility have strong feelings" – and freedom of assembly. But in the end he banned the Stop Bush Coalition from leading a demon-stration up Martin Place on Saturday.

His court was crowded but orderly. The organisers and their friends greeted the bad news in respectful silence. There was no disturbance of any kind. No protests. No shouting. Nothing. Yet waiting outside was a small army of police. Thirty-two officers on foot were gathered in a tight squad by the door. Another ten shel-tered out of the wind – and largely out of sight – in the entrance to the law school. Four more sat on pushbikes on the Phillip Street footpath. "If there is an issue, we can deal with it," explained Inspec-tor Damian Beaufils.

But there was no issue in sight: no sign of trouble, no crowd, no demonstrators, only a couple of activists and a little news confer-ence. That, too, was perfectly orderly. Behind a letterbox on the far side of the road, a tall policewoman was working a strange, hooded camera. I encouraged her to come out from her hiding place and get closer to the action. "This is sensitive," said a beefy constable inter-posing herself between me and the device. But I saw what was being filmed: the journalists. She moved off to continue her important work from the shadows of the arcade of the old Supreme Court.

Meanwhile, around the corner in Macquarie Street waited five police vans, a police truck and an old bus with wire over its win-dows bursting with yet more police. None of it was needed and if police intelligence told them otherwise, we are all in trouble.

This was sheer display, a show of police muscle with a message for Issue Motivated Groups (IMGs), journalists and perhaps the court: look who's in charge in this town this week.

Magistrate David Heilpern found out for himself on Monday. Taking a break in Hyde Park to think through a decision he was about to deliver, Heilpern was stopped, asked for identification and frisked. The policeman agreed not to read the court documents the magistrate was carrying.

The security hoo-ha is nicely focused. A senior barrister who lives in the city was prevented on Tuesday night from getting anywhere near George Bush's motorcade as it sped into town. But when he returned to the overpass near the art gallery yesterday to watch President Hu Jintao of China arrive, there wasn't a policeman in sight. He was shocked: "I could have dropped a brick on his windscreen."

*

Saturday's Stop Bush rally was APEC fear central. The balcony of the Sydney Town Hall, off limits to speakers wanting to address the throng below, became a vantage point for hooded police video cameras. Let's hope they captured every detail of that cheerful crowd and the placards they were carrying: "Marry me Chaser boys"; "Austrians out of Iraq"; "Bush world's worst leader Tony Abbott included".

The scene in the street was so Australian: teachers, Rabbitohs, wharfies, university students, families with strollers and guys from the fire brigade marching in thongs. Boys with fuzzy beards shared the road with ancient aristocrats of the Left who have been at this work since the 1960s. Ditto Peter Harvey executing tricky stand-ups for the Channel Nine cameras as the crowd headed to Hyde Park.

But surrounding the marchers were scenes from another country: John Howard's Australia of fear. Police in Darth Vader gear stood, batons at the ready. Dogs were waiting in reserve. There were machines for pumping gas. The famous black water-cannon crawled behind the demonstrators being funnelled into Hyde Park.

How must Mr Justice Michael Adams of the NSW Supreme Court have felt watching this scene on television? Largely on the basis of police evidence that Martin Place would be too narrow to contain the demonstrators safely, Justice Adams had ordered the march to follow the route the police demanded to a meeting in the park. Now the police were directing thousands of people into an opening at the corner of Park and Elizabeth streets no wider than a city footpath. By a miracle, no demonstrators were injured. No violence flared. But the carnage among the gardenias was terrible.

Watching the crowd file into the park was a plain-clothes man with a squiggly wire in his ear. Whether that meant he was police or ASIO wasn't clear. On the back of his baseball cap was the motto: "Aim to Please. Shoot to Kill." Maybe that's a joke. Certainly the police commissioner, Andrew Scipione, wasn't trying for laughs when he warned the Chaser boys their motorcade in Macquarie Street might have provoked gunfire. "We have snipers deployed around the city," he declared. "They weren't there for show; they mean business."

The police refuse to say what protocols governed the snipers in APEC city. Were there really circumstances in which unarmed citizens might be shot in the streets? They cite "operational reasons" for refusing to say. Let's pray it was just fear-mongering. Sydney was never more John Howard's city than it was last week as he marshalled its fears.

If there is no APEC bounce for Howard in the polls, it may be because there was a feeling in the air that Howard had reached a dead end in the politics of fear. Thank God we all got out alive. But by week's end it seemed we didn't need the kilometres of fences, the water-cannon and the armies of police. They were all a bit of a nuisance. APEC will be remembered for making Sydney feel grubby.

14.

HOME FREE OCTOBER 2007

Smoking a cigarette in the backyard of a Canberra architect's office last Wednesday was a young man with an old face who carries a famous name in the legal history of this country: Ahmed al-Kateb. This week his incredible story reached something like a happy ending when he was issued a card carrying the words, "Permitted to remain in Australia indefinitely."

Nearly seven years after the navy rescued him from a fishing boat washed up on Ashmore Reef, six years after he begged to be deported from the country, and four years after the High Court came to the notorious conclusion that he could be held here for the rest of his life in immigration detention, al-Kateb has his Australian papers. He feels for the first time free to talk, to fill the gaps in his story. "My thinking is confusing," he admits. "Wow, I have a country now. I have somewhere to stay. I have a home. But I remember these things that happened to me. These things will not go just because of the paper."

He is so relieved to have this card in his hands that he is not at all perturbed – as his lawyers are – by the obvious error on its face: "Nationality: Kuwait." The whole point of this saga is that until a week or so ago, al-Kateb was stateless. And what Australia did to this stateless man was done because, when he wanted to put Australia behind him, no other country would take him. Ahmed al-Kateb made legal history as the man who couldn't get away.

He was born in Kuwait, the son of Palestinian refugees from Gaza. His parents had travel documents. He had no status whatever. When life turned sour for Palestinians in Kuwait after the first Gulf War, his family began to scatter. In late 1998 at the age of twenty-two, posing as a pilgrim on his way to Mecca, he slipped into Jordan and lived there illegally for nearly two years. The journey to Australia cost $US4000. "The smugglers suggested why not go to Australia, it's a freedom country, a safe place, have a good life there. And I said yes, all right, and left from Jordan for Indonesia on an Iraqi false passport." For the last leg of the trip he was loaded, with thirty-six others, onto a seven-metre fishing boat.

"Every night we stayed in the ocean it was storms, rain and terrible waves. We stayed about eleven nights. The boat was bad … and the Indonesian sailors lost the way and didn't know where we were going. It was a terrible experience. I stayed about three days sleeping, dizzy and sick and really about to die. We had little bit of food. We had been eating rice, water. The motor was broken." The navy found them stuck on Ashmore Reef a few days before Christmas 2000. Al-Kateb was one of about 200 taken from Ashmore that day and delivered to Curtin, the grim – now mothballed – immigration detention centre in the desert outside Derby in Western Australia.

The system sorted him out swiftly. He was refused refugee status and almost at once began to ask to be sent home. Nothing came of those requests so he ploughed on, appealing first to the Refugee Review Tribunal and then to the Federal Court, "to show I am alive". He lost, and his renewed requests to be sent home yielded nothing.

He fell back into the numbing rhythm of Curtin: sleeping till noon, playing cards, learning to smoke, listening to rumours. "Imagine every day I wake up and I think OK that's my place for ever." This went on for nearly two years. As his spirits sank he became ill. "I am just waiting to die. That's my future. I just wait for death. All sorts of people were trying to kill themselves. I wasn't strong enough to do it." On the advice of an Adelaide lawyer of Palestinian background, Abby Hamdan, he formally applied to be "removed" from the country. Instead, he was taken to Baxter detention centre on the outskirts of Port Augusta in South Australia. There he learnt that Kuwait had refused to have him back and Israel would not allow him to enter Gaza.

Al-Kateb remembers the immigration department asking: "Can you go to Syria or Jordan or Egypt, can you sign a paper for this?" He says he replied: "Anywhere in the world you want to send me, send me. I cannot live in this place … After a while they told me we cannot find anywhere in the Middle East and suggested, what about Asia: Malaysia, Vietnam or Thailand? I told them, wherever you want."

Others were facing the same hopeless diplomatic impasse: in apparently perpetual detention because no country would take them. A queue of these cases was moving through the courts. On 15 April 2003, the full Federal Court ruled that Akram al-Masri, another Palestinian trapped in the detention system, should be released until there was a reasonable prospect that he could be deported. A few nights later, al-Kateb was driven by an immigration officer into Port Augusta and dumped in the town square. "He took our bags and told us to leave the car, turned the car round. And he gone. We did not know anything. We had no money." Hamdan found him after a few hours and brought him to Adelaide. The department presented him with the bill for his detention: $83,000.

By various shifts and complications that have no bearing here, al-Kateb found himself a few months later sitting in the High Court in Canberra. His case had been plucked out of the queue in order that the immigration department might appeal as swiftly as possible against the humane outcome in the *al-Masri* case. The department was determined to assert its right to hold failed asylum seekers forever, if necessary, rather than release them.

Al-Kateb recalls the surprise he felt as he sat in that vast court – surprise that his barrister, Claire O'Connor, stood up to the judges as she did, but most of all surprise that these people were talking about him. "I am tiny. I am just a refugee come to find somewhere to live. I don't want anything more. The High Court! I mean, I was worried. I wasn't sure they think there is a human sitting here. It's his life."

While the judges cogitated – and brawled – for the best part of a year, al-Kateb got on with the little life Australia allowed him on a series of bridging visas. "The first time was for three months. Then it was like three months, two months, two months, three months, one month, two months, four weeks." He was forbidden to work, denied social security and Medicare, and locked out of free education. Lawyers, friends, refugee advocates and Christian charities supported him; TAFE colleges allowed him to study English on the quiet; and he was sustained by contact with Dr Jocelyn Chey, a China expert and former Australian consul-general in Hong Kong. He said: "She is my angel."

They had met in Sydney after corresponding for eighteen months. On the morning in August 2004 that the High Court was to deliver its verdict, Chey suggested he come to her house on the North Shore to hear the result. It was terrible. A majority ruled against the young man. "He was absolutely distraught," recalls Chey. "I have never seen anybody reduced to such a state – unable to move or speak, and dreadfully frightened of being taken back into detention."

That didn't happen. Only one of the dozen men affected by the decision returned – very briefly – to detention. Everyone else remained at liberty, but under the crushing restrictions of their bridging visas. Al-Kateb kept quiet. His name had entered political discourse but his face was unknown. There were no interviews and no press flurry. He moved into Chey's house for eighteen months and did volunteer work, much of the time for Willoughby Council. "I was doing bush regeneration and I was working in the office of civil engineering doing some surveying for the roads and things. Very nice people there. Very helpful people. Very sympathetic."

Late in 2005, after years of campaigning by refugee advocates, the government relaxed the brutal conditions of bridging visas. Al-Kateb was able to get a real job with a Canberra architect – Strine Design, Australian Environmental Designers – using the computer drafting skills he had acquired in Kuwait. He is still with Strine. "Very sympathetic and helpful," he calls his employers. "They understand what I am going through." They say he goes "up and down".

He is clearly not in great shape. "I am always up, down, up, down. When you are up you have a good time. Then something remind you of all this pain, take you down." He works, studies civil engineering at the Canberra Institute of Technology and fills his time pursuing the architects' obsession, petanque. His trophies sit above his desk.

Hamdan kept petitioning immigration ministers – first Amanda Vanstone and then Kevin Andrews – to recognise the impossibility of her client's position and grant him a humanitarian visa. The case has been supported lately by Kevin Rudd and Chey's local member, Joe Hockey. But the intervention that clinched the matter came in late September from the commentator and former Howard staffer Gerard Henderson. With his wife, Anne, he has been quietly and effectively intervening on behalf of detainees for some years. Al-Kateb's case he found "the easiest they'd dealt with". Andrews handled it personally. On 11 October the minister granted the visa.

"May I take this opportunity," he wrote that day to al-Kateb, "to wish you well in the future."

Al-Kateb has no clear idea what that future will be. Surviving, he explains, has meant killing his dreams. Now they must grow all over again. He has found a counsellor, a good doctor and "very nice people" everywhere. But it's still up and down. He holds his papers in his huge hands and admits having them at last has caused him considerable pain. "I paid lots of my life for these papers. I had gone through all this pain here, this worry, all this situation, all this scare – all because this papers." He brushes aside the suggestion that this is the end of a seven-year ordeal. "No. Thirty-one years. I was born a refugee. I go here, I'm a refugee. I go there, I'm a refugee. Now I have a home."

2011

On a day of searing heat in February 2009, Ahmed al-Kateb became an Australian citizen. He finished his TAFE course and moved to Brisbane where he continues to work as a draftsman. He has not recovered entirely from the ordeal of his detention. His friends say he is still up and down.

We live with the legacies of this young man's ordeal. The first is a High Court decision that allows governments to detain indefinitely those who have no right to stay here yet nowhere else to go. On that far-from-short list now are Iranians whose country won't have them back; stateless Biharis who can't return to Bangladesh; the Rohingyas that Burma won't allow to return home; and Tamils who flee Sri Lanka, qualify as refugees but fail ASIO's security checks. They are never told why. "These people are stuck in indefinite detention but it's impossible to find out what the concerns are," says David Manne of the Refugee and Immigration Legal Centre. Those in detention limbo in late 2011 number in the hundreds.

The second legacy of the case gives some reason for hope. In the low-octane campaign for liberty in this country, al-Kateb became a poster boy for the failures of politicians and the common law to protect fundamental human rights. Much quoted were the words of the High Court judge Michael McHugh as he condemned the young man to perpetual detention: "It is an enduring – and many would say a just – criticism of Australia that it is now one of the few countries in the Western world that does not have a Bill of Rights."

15.

TRUST ME APRIL 2008

We have learnt from bitter experience to take great care before bringing to this fragile country anything that might get out of hand. Foxes and cane toads come to mind. So do lantana and gangster rap. Lately, politicians and talk-tough columnists have been mustering their arguments to save Australia from an exotic menace that might ravage our democracy: enforceable rights. That this is the last civilised nation not to guarantee its citizens' rights counts for nothing with them – we don't have foot and mouth disease either. So what's to stop us quarantining Australia against bills and charters of rights?

The NSW attorney-general, John Hatzistergos, has been thundering against them lately in the best traditions of NSW Labor. It's no surprise. Handing out rights citizens can go to court to enforce is something one-party states never willingly allow. "We do not live in a perfect society and never will," Hatzistergos solemnly informed the Sydney Institute last week. "There may well be laws perceived by some to be unjust in our community. It is however wrong to suggest that they can be remedied by enacting charters with wide-ranging values and all will be well."

If only our grim-faced attorney-general had been around in 1791 to tug James Madison's sleeve and stop him making the historic mistake of presenting the US Congress with constitutional amendments guaranteeing free speech and a free press, the freedom to assemble and the freedom to worship, the assurance that life and liberty will only ever be infringed by due process of law – and, alas, the right to bear arms. Two-and-a-bit centuries later in Australia, the courts are all but powerless to prevent these rights being legislated away. And a good thing too, says Hatzistergos: "Transforming social and political questions into legal ones … forces the courts to start making decisions … for which they do not have democratic legitimacy."

That's American talk. Having given the world the great model of entrenched rights centuries ago, America has lately bred the rhetoric to attack the courts as undemocratic for enforcing them. The wisdom of experience? Yes and no. Hatzistergos and his tribe are mouthing the words of those sore losers whose democratic sensibilities are offended by the secular, decent revolution pulled off by the US Supreme Court in the last half century that began in 1954 when *Brown v. Board of Education of Topeka* ended racial segregation of schools.

The court lit a fire under conservative America by banning prayer in those desegregated schools a few years later. But that was nothing to the political volcano that has been spewing lava ever since *Roe v. Wade* in 1973 struck down most laws against abortion as a violation of a woman's constitutional right to privacy. For the clamouring powers of far-right America it just kept getting worse. In 1988 the court gave the nod to pornographic satire in *Hustler Magazine, Inc. v. Falwell*. In 2003 the judges struck down the many state laws across America that still criminalised sodomy and oral sex. Time and again the court has refused to allow public money to be poured into churches.

Democratic? Not according to the losers, though in each of those landmark cases the Supreme Court was siding with mainstream

US opinion. Though the outcomes were achieved not through fresh legislation but an old constitution, the court was with the people. Nevertheless, conservative commentators began attacking the judges as undemocratic judicial activists. The rhetoric was inventive, vicious and exported word for word to Australia. *Mabo* and *Wik* were attacked in language untranslated from the copybooks of fundamentalist America.

Reagan and both Bushes began to stack the bench with judges who could be trusted to reverse the court's fifty-year tradition of tolerance and liberty. That's happening – unpredictably but not slowly. And as it does the brickbats are turning to bouquets. In June the reconstituted court will decide the ambit of Madison's right to bear arms. If, as is highly likely, the justices decide that Washington, DC, cannot ban handguns as it has for the last thirty years, those who once campaigned against judicial activism will break out the champagne. Their big wish is still that someday soon the court will reverse *Roe v. Wade*. More than anything, the US campaign against constitutional rights we've mimicked on this side of the world is driven by the hope that once again abortion will be a crime.

Was all this history going through John Hatzistergos's mind last week? Probably not. He was borrowing the rhetoric to make his own point: that in New South Wales Labor politicians don't like to be hobbled. He should be listened to politely, of course, but taken about as seriously as a burglar advising citizens not to invest in bars and alarms.

16.

NAKED AS THE DAY MAY 2008

Richard Jinman placed the photograph of a naked child on the table and asked the *Sydney Morning Herald*'s morning conference: "What do you think of this?" A rangy Brit who edits the paper's arts pages, Jinman had been troubled by the invitation to Bill Henson's new show from the moment it arrived. He'd quizzed his colleagues about the picture: did it worry them? He noticed he kept the invitation face down on his desk. With the exhibition due to open next day at the Roslyn Oxley9 Gallery, Jinman was pitching to the editor a story about Henson for the following day's paper. He was agitated, raising the issue even before the editors settled down in their chairs. "I think it's a bit off."

Jinman's worries would set off a bonfire that had been standing unlit in the national paddock for years. Everyone loves a bonfire. We're mesmerised by the flames. This one would rage for months leaving a great circle of white ash and the nagging question: what on earth was it all about? One thing we knew all along: bonfires can be hard to get going. It took a few attempts. The first matches didn't catch. But then someone came along with a bucket of kero and the Henson blaze went up with a satisfying roar.

Jinman's worries didn't reserve a place for the Henson story in the news pages planned for the next day. Some of those around the table were also appalled by the sight of the naked child on the invitation. Others thought the Henson story old hat: hadn't he been doing this sort of thing for years? The story of the famous photographer's new exhibition was assigned to the arts section. The news next day would concentrate on rising petrol prices, the big rugby league clash between the Blues and the Maroons, the triumphant return of Cate Blanchett from the *Indiana Jones* premiere in Cannes and the sentencing of Milton Orkopoulos on thirty drug, child sex and child pornography charges.

The Orkopoulos case was dry kindling at the heart of the fire. His crimes confirmed the nightmares of those who believe paedophiles are a protected species operating at the highest levels of society. As minister for Aboriginal affairs in the NSW government, Orkopoulos groomed fifteen-year-old boys by plying them with drugs and excursions to parliament – often simultaneously. Early warnings went unheeded. The whistleblower who brought the minister undone was sacked by parliament. The sentencing of Orkopoulos was not going to be the end of the matter for the Labor government of Morris Iemma. The opposition was determined to prove the premier was soft on paedophilia. In the following day's paper a chunk of page one and at least one inside page was set aside to wrap up the Orkopoulos saga.

Conference wasn't done with the Henson invitation. "Miranda might be interested," said the acting opinion editor Daniel Lewis. "Her column tomorrow is on the sexualisation of young girls." He might have added: "Again." Defending the innocence of childhood had become Miranda Devine's trademark and she had, in the previous year alone, devoted six slashing columns to the issue. Though hers was only one of many voices that persuaded the Senate to hold a rather perfunctory inquiry into the subject – an inquiry in its last stages at this point – no one wrote about the perils of growing up too soon with anything like Devine's verve. Until Lewis brought her the Henson invitation after conference, she had known nothing about the exhibition. "I had my news hook," she says. "And it was pure coincidence."

Over breakfast the next morning politicians, police officers, political staffers, journalists and radio producers who would be in hot pursuit of Henson later in the day read the harrowing rhetoric in Devine's column but, for the moment, did nothing. Her words alone were not enough to light the fire:

Opening tonight at the elegant Roslyn Oxley9 Gallery in the heart of Paddington is an exhibition of photographs by Bill Henson, featuring naked 12- and 13-year-olds. The invitation to the exhibition features a large photo of a girl, the light shining on her hair, eyes downcast, dark shadows on her sombre, beautiful face, and the budding breasts of puberty on full display, her hand casually covering her crotch.

Such images presenting children in sexual contexts are so commonplace these days they seem almost to have lost the capacity to shock. The effort over many decades by various groups – artists, perverts, academics, libertarians, the media and advertising industries, respectable corporations and the porn industry – to smash taboos of previous generations and define down community standards, has successfully eroded the special protection once afforded childhood.

It is now impossible to shield children from a culture dripping with sexual imagery, in which Saturday morning cartoons are interspersed with soft-porn music videos, pole-dancing kits with sexy garters are marketed to little girls …

*

The Henson invitation has few friends. I have yet to meet anyone who says they opened the envelope with wholehearted pleasure. Even those who admired Henson's naked junkies in the 1980s, and didn't flinch from his gawky adolescents in the 1990s partying by night in piles of wrecked cars, were unnerved by the beautiful image of that twelve-year-old child. "Here's trouble," many said to themselves.

Hanging on a gallery wall or tucked inside a catalogue, that image would not have provoked the same response. But the invitation was being used to sell the show. Its deliberately commercial purpose was unsettling. And Devine was right to identify, in her roll call of horrors, a broken taboo. Without breasts or with full breasts this image would also have caused less fuss. Perhaps it would have passed unremarked. But these are budding breasts, rarely seen and almost never celebrated. In our culture, budding breasts are extraordinarily private. These things aren't sacrosanct but Henson had broken a powerful little taboo.

He chose *Untitled (#30)* for the invitation because he thought it was the most alive in the exhibition. He was fiercely proud of the picture taken after working for many months with the young model. "I can speak about how fantastic images are, without it being at all egotistical on my part," Henson claims. "It's as though the pictures make themselves. Obviously they don't, but it feels like that. You have this strange feeling that it's so good that it almost has nothing to do with you. You are along for the ride." He says he heard no warning bells. This was the picture he wanted and he chose it with "no thought at all for what if, and who and other things".

Roslyn Oxley, an elfin woman with a great mane of hair and a vague smile, had qualms from the start. Over nearly thirty years, the gallery she runs in Paddington with her husband, Tony, has gathered under its wing most of the leading contemporary artists in Australia – the big names, the bankable ones, those who represent their country abroad. In that company, Bill Henson was blue-chip. Usually Henson gives her two or three choices for the invitation. Not this time. "Ros," he said, "it has got to be this." She kept her worries to herself. "As far as he was concerned, that was the image. So … fine."

Roughly half the forty-one huge – 127 by 180 centimetres – prints he had brought up from Melbourne were sombre studies of imperial Rome, sarcophagi, dark forests, twilit cloudscapes and huge heads in close-up. The rest were nudes: one of an unknown girl lying on her back in the dark, two chaste portraits of a young boy, and fourteen pictures of the girl on the invitation. She is alone, pensive, withdrawn and entirely naked in them all. Her nipples are visible in nine and her crotch can be seen faintly in one – but not in *Untitled (#30)*, where her pubis is lost demurely in deep shadow. Though troubled by that image on the invitation, Oxley's verdict on the show was: "One of Bill's most restrained."

The morning of his opening saw Henson back in the gallery on Soudan Lane. Beyond fiddling with the lights, there wasn't much left to do. About midday the new pictures went up on the gallery website. An ABC crew was quietly filming the exhibition for the inevitable new documentary on the photographer. There wasn't much media hype about the show. This was going to be a low-key opening, something for the connoisseurs. His face was here and there in the papers: the image of the Melbourne artist in his prime, balding and bearded, all in black with deep black eyes.

At Richard Jinman's urging, the *Sydney Morning Herald*'s Josephine Tovey had asked Henson why he worked with models so young. It's a question he'd answered many times over many years. "It's the most effective vehicle for expressing ideas about humanity and vulnerability and our sense of ourselves living inside our bodies; the breathtaking moment to moment existence as you're walking down a street and feel a cool change come through, feel the weather on our bodies and the way we feel about being in the world. All of this is focused more effectively through this age group, so it's the age group I work with." Did he sense a media frenzy boiling up over the sexualisation of children? He did not: "There is always something being boiled up. George Steiner once said that the media's only job is to create and maintain a state of emergency. About what, doesn't matter."

*

About 1.30 pm Darren of Engadine emailed one of Sydney's most aggressive broadcasters, Chris Smith of radio station 2GB: "Chris I saw an article by Miranda Devine in today's *Herald* where she mentions that the Roslyn Art Gallery in Paddington has a display of photographs of naked twelve- and thirteen-year-old girls. I'm looking at their website. They are displaying the images there as well. Surely this cannot be legal?"

The 2GB day, which begins with the indestructible Alan Jones hectoring his listeners from dawn, reaches Smith at 1 pm. He is a knockabout tabloid radio and television reporter with a sideline in writing thrillers. Stunts are a big part of his schtick: celebrity camel-racing and having himself tattooed on his forty-fifth birthday. He was already on air when Darren's email arrived, and within minutes his producer Phil Sylvester was on the case.

"I was getting fodder for a radio talkback show," says Sylvester. "It's one of the great topics: what is art and what is porn? And here it was again." The tabloid possibilities were infinitely rich. Stories about deceit in the art world have a strange power to convulse the Australian media. It goes way back. Ern Malley, the fake poet, is part of folklore; the martyrdom of the painter Bill Dobell, accused of passing off caricatures as portraits, is not forgotten; Helen Darville's fake Ukrainian ancestry is a live scandal more than a dozen years after the publication of her Holocaust novel, *The Hand That Signed the Paper*. Now 2GB was presented with a chance not only to grandstand about children but portray this celebrated photographer as another artist fake: the photographer as pornographer. The Henson story had the makings of a great afternoon's radio – kids, cops, artists, nudity, socialites and politicians. But even the best beat-ups work only if there is some issue in the mix that really matters. There was here: children and their protection.

Smith got on with other things at the microphone while Sylvester tried to find someone who could come on air at once and explain the difference between art and porn. That his search would prove fruitless says a good deal about the complexities of the row that was about to break. The Classification Board wouldn't help and flick-passed him to the attorney-general's department in Canberra. They couldn't help. But by this time Smith was raring to go. A few minutes before the 2 pm news, he told his listeners about Darren of Engadine: "I've got a copy of exactly what Darren is referring to and what Miranda Devine wrote about today. I don't think I've seen anything more disgusting. How the people at the Roslyn Art Gallery in Paddington think this somehow comes under the category of art defies logic. It is disgraceful. It is disgusting. It is pornographic. It is woeful." There followed the sound of paper being crunched and flung in a bin.

Sylvester kept at it. He turned next to Tony Ritchie, former head of news at Channel Nine and now media adviser to the NSW commissioner of police, Andrew Scipione. Could Ritchie find someone in the force to come on the show and talk about art and porn? By another of the blind accidents that make sense of this story, Deputy

Police Commissioner Nick Kaldas was sitting with Ritchie as he opened Sylvester's email and clicked on the link to the gallery's website. "That better go to the Child Protection and Sex Crime Squad," said the deputy commissioner. The whole transaction took only minutes. Ritchie was sending the link through to the squad about the time Smith came back on air to hammer the story again.

"Here's a suggestion for you," Smith began. "Either read Miranda Devine's column in the *Herald*; try and Google this and have a look on the website – though I wouldn't advise it because you might puke – or even better, phone the Roslyn Art Gallery in Paddington and give them what for. If they think that kids in a state of undress is somehow art, it's got me beat. I know I've said that before because I don't have a great appreciation for anything artistic, because I'm a little bit of an artistic moron, but in this case it is just off. It's sickening. So give them a call and tell them what for, especially if you know a little bit about what they're showing, and I'm not going to put it on the website or anything like that because it's just off." The phones began to ring at the gallery a few minutes later.

Affable Barry O'Farrell, leader of the Opposition in NSW, was the first politician to clamber onto the story. His press secretary Brad Burden was monitoring 2GB. After checking the Oxleys' website, he contacted Simon Benson, the state political editor of that remarkable Murdoch tabloid the Sydney *Daily Telegraph*. O'Farrell's man urged Benson to overlook his paper's reluctance to follow up a column in the rival *Sydney Morning Herald* and pursue the Henson story. The strategy positioned O'Farrell in the shadow of the Orkopoulos case to take a stance on child protection in the pages of the biggest-selling paper in the city. "After viewing the gallery's website and viewing those images displayed," says O'Farrell, "I gave Brad some lines to use." These were:

Sexualisation of children under the guise of art is totally unacceptable. Art will always push society's boundaries but protecting our children must be the priority. It wasn't OK for a fourteen-year-old model, fully dressed, to be on the catwalks for Australian Fashion Week. It is definitely not OK for naked children to have their privacy and their childhood stolen in the name of art.

Of all the politicians who would denounce Henson over the next twenty-four hours, O'Farrell was the most familiar with his work. He had been among the 115,000 Australians who saw the huge retrospective *Bill Henson: Three Decades of Photography* staged by the Art Gallery of New South Wales and the National Gallery of Victoria in 2005. He made no protest at the time and now says he can't even remember the walls of photographs of naked adolescents, photographs far more confronting than anything waiting to be seen that night at the Roslyn Oxley9 Gallery. "My memory of it was more about buildings and more mainstream images."

The *Telegraph* assigned Clare Masters – one of the Masters family of writers and journalists – to the story and about 3 pm she rang Morris Iemma's office for comment. The premier's staff promised to get back to her. There was a problem: Iemma was in northern China inspecting a railway carriage plant, and would be out of range for a couple of hours. They put some questions to the office of the police minister David Campbell: what's the story; is there an issue here; what are the rules? After passing swiftly through several hands, those queries landed on the desk of Assistant Commissioner Catherine Burn, commander of the Central Metropolitan Region. Knowing nothing of the gathering Henson storm until this point, she contacted Superintendent Allan Sicard of Rose Bay whose patch covers the Oxleys' gallery in Soudan Lane. Sicard had already had calls about the exhibition. Burn placed him in charge of the operation.

This would not have been happening – certainly not at this breakneck speed – without the internet. Links to the gallery's website were flying around town. People could *see* what Devine was writing about and Smith was fulminating against. Their outrage found its echo inside the force. Police were disgusted by what they saw on the net. Emotions were running high. They didn't know and didn't particularly care who this photographer was – he had no history in their eyes – but his work looked like porn to them. Police at Rose Bay, Kings Cross and The Rocks were taking furious calls from the public complaining about Henson's work. None of the callers had been to the gallery but the offending work was only a few keystrokes away online. As 2GB pursued the story, the public response was swift and raw. Not much more than an hour after Henson's exhibition was first mentioned on air, police were preparing to act. A visit to the lane by Sicard's constables was inevitable. "Everyone," says a police source, "knew it was not going to be a pretty scene."

*

By mid-afternoon, Chris Smith was giving the story the gun: "Geoff from Gymea has sent me an email: 'I have looked at it. It is simply wrong.' Lorraine from Kings Langley: 'I've Googled. What the heck were those children's parents thinking?' Phil from Lidsdale: 'Can you find out if this so-called art gallery receives any government or corporate funding? Disgraceful. Filth. Where are the parents? Maybe DoCS [the Department of Community Services] can look into it.' Cathy: 'Bloody hell. Who's this Bill Henson that he can take these pornographic photos of girls? Surely it's a crime?'" Smith's first mention of the police a little before 3 pm instantly raised the temperature. "I understand a squad is interested in the exhibition," he said. "We will check in with the police and hopefully they will do something about it."

A little press tornado was blowing behind the scenes. Radio producers were talking to television producers. Newsrooms were monitoring 2GB. Journalists were already gathering in the lane and more were on their way the moment the police were mentioned. Now the abusive callers to the gallery were joined by journalists asking the Oxleys for interviews. All were refused. As she always does on the afternoon of an opening, Roslyn Oxley slipped out at 3 pm to have her hair washed – and found herself facing a television news crew. "I nearly died." With Channel Seven reporter Robert Ovadia in pursuit, she made for her car, at first shielding her face from the cameras. Would she let Henson put her own daughter "on public display" asked the reporter? "She's been in some of his shots," Oxley replied and drove away.

Morris Iemma, having praised the capacity of the Changchun rail plant to deliver "the largest single rolling stock order in the shortest delivery timeframe ever ordered by an Australian railway", sped back to Beijing. Once he was in range, his Sydney staff sent a few Henson images to his BlackBerry. The premier said he would take a look and get back to them. They expected a hostile response – Iemma had bought into a press flurry the month before about the use of young catwalk models in Australian Fashion Week. "We need to let children grow up without unreasonable pressure being placed on them and they should never be portrayed in a sexual way," he said at the time. "As a father, there is no way in the world I'd want my daughter to be in that position. The interests of the child must always come first and that will never be compromised."

*

Soudan Lane ends at a cliff face. Even empty, it feels claustrophobic. When Roslyn Oxley returned at about 4 pm with her hair washed the lane was crowded with press. She slipped inside to find the staff dazed and at times in tears as they answered often wildly insulting calls: "You're all pornographers"; "We know where you are"; "We're going to burn the gallery down." At least they now knew who had alerted these abusive callers: one of Henson's fans had just rung to wish the gallery luck for the opening and identify the culprit – 2GB.

When Smith handed the microphone to his colleague Philip Clark at 4 pm, the station's message didn't change. "I was appalled when I saw these photographs, I really was," trumpeted Clark. "The opening is tonight. The photographs are by Bill Henson who's a very famous photographer. His photographs sell for tens of thousands of dollars. In reviews by curators etc. Bill Henson's work is described as 'A triumph of taste. While the subjects are in that in-between age of adolescence, caught between childhood and adulthood, faces oscillate between the familiar and the anonymous ...' goes the waffle associated with Bill Henson's work. Look, people go to jail for possession of images such as these; 1.27 metres by 1.8 metres is the size of these images and they are images of twelve- and thirteen-year-old girls naked. Don't tell me they're not pornographic because they are. As I say, if they were found on someone's computer in the workplace, you would call the police."

About 4.30 pm, with the tide of abuse still rising, the gallery stripped the images from its website after less than five hours. Though the Oxleys had no way of knowing this, removing them was a strategic blunder. The two organisations that decide what Australians can read, see and hear had both looked at the Roslyn Oxley9 website by this time and decided there was nothing up there to worry about.

The Classification Board, little known outside the worlds of film, porn and civil liberties, is the national guardian of community standards that classifies and sometimes bans films, DVDs, books and magazines according to guidelines set down by all the attorneys-general of the Commonwealth, states and territories. The board had been taking calls from the press all afternoon at its loft offices in Sydney's Surry Hills as 2GB cranked up its campaign. Three senior classifiers had downloaded the Henson images. These professionals, with long experience of administering the guidelines, concluded at a glance that there was nothing in 2GB's claim that the Hensons were porn. Not remotely. They realised that the board could well be the circuit-breaker if the hubbub of the afternoon developed into a major furore. But, for the time being, the best it could do was watch and wait.

But the Australian Communications and Media Authority was ready to act. As well as keeping an eye on broadcasting standards, ACMA has the near hopeless task of cleaning up the net by issuing "take down" orders to local websites and alerting its overseas counterparts to the presence of illegal material on foreign websites. ACMA officers had also taken a look at the Hensons earlier in the afternoon and were not worried by them either. This was not illegal material. They were keen to intervene but needed a formal complaint to set the machinery in action. All afternoon, angry members of the public ringing ACMA were asked to put their objections to the Hensons in writing. The police were the first to do the paperwork. Their complaint arrived about 4.15 pm and an investigation team was called together a few minutes later. But by the time they logged on to the Roslyn Oxley9 website at about 4.45 pm, the images had gone. ACMA, too, was going to have to wait for a chance to bring some professional clarity to the uproar.

Henson was finding the atmosphere in the gallery becoming stranger by the minute. "A few clients of Ros's had been through, people were coming in and putting stickers on things. The National Gallery of Victoria had reserved two; the NSW Art Gallery had reserved two, so that was just ticking along a bit." The abusive phone calls continued unabated as the staff went about the usual chores before an opening. "People were still answering phones, cleaning up, bringing drinks." He stepped onto the balcony and was shocked to see how the crowd of journalists and cameras had grown. Almost the only television footage of Henson shown in the following weeks were these few seconds of him looking absurdly like an artist – bearded and aloof, his eyes scrunched against the light – before ducking swiftly back inside. "At a certain point I said, 'Do you think we should call the police?' After I made that suggestion – it was mine, I think – within five minutes, ten minutes, these two guys walked upstairs."

The officers from Rose Bay were low-key. At first they seemed only concerned about crowd control. Oxley says: "We were relieved." But after making a few calls, the two were joined by their commanding officer Superintendent Sicard. "We do have a bit of a problem," he told the Oxleys. "We need to wander off and look at the gallery."

Channel Ten's 5 pm news crossed live to its reporter in the lane. The story jumped to television. Even more press now headed for the gallery. At roughly the same time, on the other side of town, Iemma's staff received their instructions from the premier in China: they were to draft a statement strongly disapproving of the pictures and the girl's parents for putting a child in such a situation. The finished words were given to Clare Masters for publication next morning in the Telegraph but at least the gist of the premier's views was also sent through to the police. Though he could not direct them, Iemma could let them know what was on his mind.

Sicard and his men finished their tour of the exhibition. "I'm really concerned about potential damage to the work," said the superintendent. Henson was too – the prints weren't behind glass. One nick with a Stanley knife would see them ruined –but he was more immediately worried about the gallery staff if things should turn nasty at the opening. By this point, Sicard's qualms about the pictures themselves were also on the table. About 5.15 pm, he asked the gallery to suspend the exhibition "to allow inquiries of legality of photos". The Oxleys took their lead from Henson. He didn't put up a fight. "I said, 'Right that's it, let's shut it.'" A few minutes later a notice was put on the roller door downstairs:

Tonight's opening has been cancelled. Apologies for any inconvenience.

*

The jocks at 2GB had done well. In a little over three hours – inspired by Devine, powered by the internet and backed by the police – they had shut the exhibition down. Debates familiar in the art world for more than thirty years about Bill Henson's use of kids had jumped the tracks in a single afternoon. Not that debate is the word to describe what 2GB had staged that afternoon. The Oxleys and Henson were refusing to go on air, but 2GB found no other voices to defend the photographer or the gallery against the rolling thunder of its own accusations that this work was, beyond any doubt whatsoever, child pornography. "And wankers," said Phil Clark, "walk around with glasses of champagne and call it art."

Gallery staff hit the phones to try to warn about sixty guests not to come to Soudan Lane but go straight to dinner at Carthona, the Oxleys' house on the harbour. By this time a fourth policeman had appeared. "They asked Bill about the girl and how old the girl was, and that sort of thing," recalls Tony Oxley. Henson chatted amiably with the officers, giving them his address and telephone numbers, the names and ages of the models, and the names and addresses of their parents. Everything was calm and co-operative until police asked to photograph the exhibition. Roslyn Oxley baulked: "It was my instinct not to let them. To hell with them, that was my attitude."

One of Sicard's men, Detective Senior Constable Martin Kiernan, was despatched to the Waverley court to ask for a "crime scene" warrant for photographing the exhibition. By this time the Oxleys were impatient to be home where their guests would already be arriving. The magistrate Jason Day rejected the police application some time after 7 pm. Henson recalls the police still in the gallery having one last go when the news came through. "The two young guys just came over, did their casual thing, and said, 'We want to get out of here. Would you mind if we just take the photographs ourselves?'" A lawyer friend had joined Henson. "He said, 'No, sorry,' and they just went, 'Fair enough,' and walked down the stairs and left."

At about 8 pm the Oxleys led the way up the fire escape to waiting cars, leaving the lights blazing behind them, tubs of ice melting, the phones still ringing, the website crashing and baffled Henson fans beating their way up Soudan Lane against the tide of dispersing journalists only to find, instead of the familiar open foyer with the name of the artist spotlit on its bare white walls, a roller door locked to the ground.

*

Carthona sits on the tip of Darling Point. Fig trees tower over the garden. The water laps its walls. At first glance, such a romantic old place seems an odd base for a couple who have spent thirty years pursuing their simple faith in contemporary art. But the Oxleys' is also a marriage of Sydney fortunes: Bushells tea and Waltons stores. Knots of anxious guests surrounded lawyers on the lawn. Sydney QCs were delivering Opinions gratis. Melbourne folk were on their phones to QCs back home. Among the waiting guests was Henson's young model. She seemed calm if a little cross to have missed her chance to star at the opening.

Emerging from the Oxleys' Mercedes when it came down the drive, Henson seemed extraordinarily calm; Tony appeared shaky; and Roslyn dazed. "She gave me the impression that she was some-one from another world," recalls Jana Wendt, who was meeting her for the first time. "Someone who had suddenly been dropped onto a planet that was crazy and she didn't understand how this particu-lar planet worked." The waiting guests were a few steps ahead of their hosts for, confused as they were, they had at least seen the evening news. The Oxleys and Henson, caught in the eye of the storm, had seen nothing. They had no idea the reporting was so savage. Roslyn Oxley was soon locked in a brawl with her brother John Walton. "My brother was so aggressive. He kept on grabbing me saying, 'Roslyn, you have got to get someone to help you. You have got to get someone to help orchestrate this whole thing.' He was so full on. 'You've got to sit down right now and get someone on the phone and if you don't, I will.'"

At a council of war in the kitchen, Walton persuaded his sister to engage the spin-doctor Sue Cato. This rather jagged woman enjoys an unusual level of trust in the "issues management" game, as she labours invisibly to make her clients' troubles disappear. Apart from being one of the city's canniest public relations opera-tors, Cato is nuts about contemporary art. She had reserved one Henson from the new show and was considering buying another. She'd cancelled her plans to attend the opening – her office was, in the ordinary course of things, monitoring the media all afternoon as the storm broke – and was having a quiet night at home when the phone rang at 9.30 pm.

Cato spent the next hour and a half talking to the team in the kitchen. "I knew that in the wider world of tabloid media and politics Bill was not going to find ready allies, and that this was going to be sensationalised immediately." She feared he was about to become a major football. "So I wanted to sit back, take a deep breath, work out exactly what the lie of the land was before we moved." Her instinct was to put a lid on the whole thing with the child sheltered absolutely from the press and everyone else shutting up. It was agreed the team would meet early next day in her office.

*

The *Daily Telegraph* that morning produced a tabloid front page of genius: a huge picture of a couple of heavy-set coppers heading up the stairs of the gallery beside a massive headline:

CHILD
PORN
"ART"
RAID

The strap across the top read: "Victory for decency as police close gallery." Commentators bluntly declared Henson a child pornographer. Morris Iemma was venting. No one reading the paper that morning could doubt that the premier of New South Wales was a far from happy man: "The cornerstone of any civilised society is the protection of its kids and there can be no justification for some of these images. I'm all for free speech, but never at the expense of a child's safety and innocence."

A little before 7 am, the prime minister Kevin Rudd arrived at the Channel Nine studios for one of his regular appearances on *Today*. He could not have come to the Henson issue unprepared. Any prime minister appearing on morning television would be briefed to expect questions about a *Telegraph* page-one splash. The host Karl Stefanovic quizzed him for a few minutes about petrol prices before getting down to business. "I want to show you some photos," he said. "These are images from Bill Henson. Now, one critic says that he is an artist of ferocious integrity who depicts androgynous girls and boys adrift in the nocturnal turmoil of adolescence. What we say is, that is crossing the line."

As he spoke, Rudd and the viewers were shown five images of the girl taken from a slideshow that had gone up on News Limited websites the previous night. Thick black bars covered the girl's nipples and her already heavily shadowed genitals. Across the bottom of the screen was the title: "Outrage over child-porn art." After flashing through all five images in less than twenty seconds, Stefanovic asked the prime minister: "What do you say?"

Rudd looked slightly dazed. "That's the first time I've seen them. I think they're revolting."

"As a dad how do they make you feel, those photos?"

"I've just said, it's the first time I've seen them, I find them absolutely revolting." With his voice rising and his hands chopping the air, Rudd continued: "Kids deserve to have the innocence of their childhood protected. I have a very deep view of this. For God's sake, let's just allow kids to be kids. Whatever the artistic view of the merits of that sort of stuff – frankly, I don't think there are any – just allow kids to be kids, you know. You know."

Sue Cato was watching. She had been up early scanning the papers, monitoring the news and listening to early talkback. The *Telegraph* was hyperventilating and 2GB was celebrating the shutdown with whoops of triumph but reports of the Henson mess were tucked inside the broadsheets. It was not yet a huge national story, not until Rudd came on television. As Cato watched the prime minister on *Today* she said to herself: "This is incendiary."

JUNE 2008

Bill Henson disappeared to Melbourne and remained silent inside his warehouse studio as a tumult of outrage swept the country. His detractors didn't hesitate to call him a child pornographer. By this time the NSW police had seized dozens of Henson's prints from the Oxleys' gallery. Some dated back to the early 1980s. They also carried off to the cellars of the Sydney police centre a stack of invitations. In the days that followed, Henson's pictures were impounded at the National Gallery in Canberra and stripped from the walls of regional galleries in New South Wales. Steve Bush, the nervous proprietor of a lavish new art magazine, pulped 25,000 copies of his next edition celebrating the Sydney exhibition. He said: "It felt like a witch-hunt."

Labor was silenced by Rudd's stand. The Coalition joined the attacks on Henson. The only politician in the nation to show, briefly, courage in the face of this panic was Malcolm Turnbull: "Before we have policemen tramping through art galleries, tramping through libraries, going into newspaper offices, we have got to think freedom is what makes this country great and that is what enables us to be the type of nation that we are. So, Mr Henson has to obey the law, we all have to obey the law, and if he is charged with an offence then the courts will deal with it and they should do that. But just remember, freedom is what makes Australia great."

But the law had no quarrel with Henson. Within a fortnight, the Classification Board declared the "image of breast nudity" on the invitation "creates a viewing impact that is mild and justified by context … and is not sexualised to any degree". This was not porn, only PG: "Not recommended for viewing by persons under 15 without guidance from parents or guardians." The board placed no restrictions whatever on its exhibition. The police were advised by the NSW Director of Public Prosecutions that Henson had no case to answer. A team from the Oxleys' gallery retrieved the pictures and the exhibition reopened: entry by invitation only. Henson came out of hiding.

I underestimated Chris Smith. Not until after my book about the Henson case was in the shops in October 2008 was I alerted to the strange shape of Smith's career and saw how his crusades on 2GB might be driven by peculiar demons. Back in the 1990s Smith was caught forging a signature in order to spring a prisoner he wanted to interview for Channel Nine's *A Current Affair*. *Media Watch* nabbed him and the courts gave him a two-year suspended sentence. Nine took him back but he was soon in trouble again. Drunk at a farewell party in the station's boardroom in October 1998 he gave a couple of women the good news that he had a very big penis and opened his pants. He was sacked. After a stint in China he returned to join 2GB where his particular line in moral indignation earned him a huge audience. Though he had put forgery behind him by the time he drove the Henson panic of 2008, he remained a prey to other dark impulses. "I've had some terrible problems handling alcohol," he confessed after the station suspended him for groping four women at the station's Christmas party in 2009. "If you're bipolar and you have an alcohol problem then you're a runaway train." He was back on air after six weeks.

17.

THE WASH-UP DECEMBER 2008

I was putting on a bit of dog for the fresh envoy of a Great European Nation. This was deep in the Howard era, and we were drinking coffee in one of the sitting rooms the *Sydney Morning Herald* used to have for receiving notables. The new ambassador, a man of pugnacious energy approaching his last post, wanted some tips about Australia. "What you have to understand," I said solemnly, "is that we're new, rich and free but have a petit-bourgeois government." He snorted. "All governments are petit-bourgeois."

Watching the smouldering ruins of the Henson bonfire in the past few months, I've had reason to recall the old ambassador's wisdom. The transition from Howard to Rudd has seen not much change from the social caution of the old era. The liberals inside Labor are almost as embattled as they were inside the Coalition. That Rudd is, as we were warned, very, very conservative involves more than maintaining the American alliance. It also means continuing to promise fearful Australians protection from the excesses of art, film, television and now, above all, the internet.

As the year drags to a close, Communications Minister Stephen Conroy is fine-tuning a regime of internet censorship unique in the democratic world. Under direction from Rudd, the Australia Council is drafting protocols that will tie in bureaucratic knots any artist dealing with children and present extraordinary obstacles to their work being put on the net. And the nation's attorneys-general are roaming the outskirts of censorship law to try to crack down on images of naked children. Kevin Rudd's Australia is in a rage over art and kids.

The prime minister chose Frank Lowy's Westfield shopping centre in Parramatta, the old city embedded in the Sydney suburbs, as the spot to address the latest eruption of community rage about Henson. The *Telegraph* had just picked up on my report that the principal of St Kilda Primary in Melbourne had allowed the photographer to cast his eyes over the schoolyard. He did not approach the children but asked a couple of sets of parents if they would allow their kids to pose for him. He'd been doing that for years. Janet Hawley in a big profile of the photographer in the *Good Weekend* in 2004 wrote:

> He has just spent a week in a girls' private school, under the auspices of its art department, searching the faces of 2300 girls. He saw only two that were "perfect" for his new series, but their parents declined permission.

Her report had gone unremarked. But the times had changed. In Parramatta the day after my story appeared, Rudd had the words ready: "If the report is accurate, I'm disgusted by it. I think parents would be revolted and horrified if this were true."

This was the third wave of panic. The Sydney exhibition provoked the first. Henson was cleared. The July issue of *Art Monthly* dedicated to the controversy and illustrated with familiar, art-world photographs of naked children provoked the second. The magazine was cleared by the Classification Board. News of the visit to St Kilda provoked the third and perhaps mightiest wave. A month later the principal was cleared by an independent inquiry: Henson's visit was declared kosher. The children were considered safe. But that seemed to change nothing. The defining mark of this controversy is that all the official acquittals have counted for little or nothing at all.

Nothing prepared me for the rage I provoked by reporting the Henson story. I had a good run on radio and television in those mad days but it was a lonely business. After lobbing a few grenades, the politicians went silent. Gutless wonders. Malcolm Turnbull, the political hero of my book, turned tail once he became leader of the Opposition and was no longer saying brave things about art and freedom and the law. Peter Garrett concentrated exclusively on saving coral reefs. Though the Henson row is probably the biggest art controversy in half a century, the nation's arts minister had nothing to say. No politicians were game to stand up to the guardians of childhood and say the obvious: this was getting way out of hand.

Rudd was largely the reason. He denounced Henson without discussion. His door was closed to differing opinions. The only other prime minister of the past few decades who tangled himself in the arts was Paul Keating. His message to Australia was to lift its game. Though something of a connoisseur in his private life, Rudd has other instincts and another agenda. The cultural power of his office is to be exercised to reassure the fearful. Rudd has been splendid on the Apology and good on gays, but he is going back into the censorship business in ways not even Howard's government contemplated.

Terror of the internet seems to be at the heart of it. The Australia Council's new protocols are being imposed as a condition of subsidy on all artists who paint, photograph or sculpt children, and on the publication or exhibition of every artwork made in this country in the past twenty-five years that includes children clothed or naked. Artists working with children in future will be reminded to obey the law and parents will be asked to supervise the process more closely. Fair enough. But publication of the work – particularly on the internet – will become virtually impossible without complex permissions being sought and gained.

Art is being boxed in. Pictures that newspapers wouldn't hesitate to print or put on their websites will be locked away forever because the artist or gallery or website can't get the permission of every parent of every child appearing in the image. Ask officers of the council what protection such rules offer real children from real harm, and their rather forlorn reply is that publication on the internet is by definition exploitation. They don't sound convinced. No wonder. This is being imposed on them by a government toying with the impossible dream of cleaning up the internet.

By Christmas, Stephen Conroy hopes to be road-testing Labor's policy of compulsory internet filtering. He has $44 million for the task. Among the young and the web savvy, Conroy has become a despised figure as the scale of Labor's ambitions emerges. China and Iran have their own schemes and their own reasons for censoring the net. But Labor would make Australia the only democracy on earth delivering a mandatory "clean feed" to every home in the nation.

We're told it's all about protecting kids. We always are. But Conroy is on about much more than that. Quizzed by the young, new Western Australian Greens senator and graphic designer Scott Ludlam, the minister snapped: "Illegal material is illegal material. Child pornography is child pornography. I trust you are not suggesting that people should have access to child pornography." By the end of their testy exchange at a Senate estimates hearing in October, Conroy had admitted his net police will also be cleansing the feed of material on euthanasia and anorexia. Indeed, everything banned under the grab bag "Refused Classification" provisions of the national censorship regime is to be filtered out. Compulsorily.

Independent senators, whose support is crucial for the passage of all contested legislation, are writing their own wish lists. Family First's Steve Fielding wants mandatory filtering of all hardcore porn and all fetish material. Anti-gambling campaigner Nick Xenophon wants the blocking of all online casinos. "The black list," Ludlam remarked, "can become very grey."

Labor's plan faces big technical challenges. Can software be written that will distinguish between porn and public health? How much over-censoring or under-censoring will be allowed? How will the filters affect the speed of the internet? What slowing of the whole system will be tolerated in the pursuit of a clean feed? What will be done to try to thwart the young and the tech savvy who are already working out high-tech strategies to avoid the coming regime, strategies pioneered to beat internet-blocking in Burma and China?

Disbelief is the default response of Labor's liberals and those who remain so grateful that Howard has gone that they're not going to look too closely at the continuities between then and now. There are those who wonder if the Australia Council and Conroy aren't really setting out to show that these filters and protocols simply won't work: the sillier the better and they will all go away. But they don't understand the deep politics of censorship that survives untouched by time: being effective is never what counts. Governments only have to make gestures, show they are taking action – no matter how ridiculous.

2010 TO 2011

Henson was winded. "I think you lose a bit of time and energy because of the logistics of all that nonsense," he told art students in Sydney. Yet he believes he has come through unscathed: "I don't feel as though I'm working any differently to the way I worked before." Time will tell. He was slow to show again. When he did in May 2010 at the Oxleys' gallery, the work was dark and chaste. The tabloids left him alone. A year later the Melbourne Establishment turned out in force for his first show down south since the hullaballoo. Mostly nudes. Premier Ted Baillieu came to Henson's defence when the *Herald Sun* tried to light the old bonfire. "Class groups view provocative teens at photographer's latest show," ran the page-three headline. "Too nude for schools." But no one was complaining. The premier of Victoria reminded the paper: "Bill Henson is an internationally renowned artist."

But in the subterranean world of morals politics, the Henson case continues to fuel demands that making and showing pictures of naked children should always be a crime. The crusaders are mounting a double attack. Their first target is the Classification Board and the classification guidelines – this because Henson's pictures in 2008 were given the mild PG rating instead of being banned as porn. Their second target is the concept of "artistic merit" – this because of a mistaken but unshakeable belief that Henson would be a convicted criminal today but for the law allowing him to claim he did what he did as an artist. These attacks are determined, persistent and far from played out.

Conroy has only put on hold his plans to clean up the net while the Australian Law Reform Commission examines what should or should not be "Refused Classification" – banned – in art galleries, at the movies and from the internet feed reaching every Australian household. Though the fresh inquiry is music to the ears of Henson's detractors, its real purpose is to deal with the growing opposition to Conroy's filtering ambitions. The minister wants to show he has the public behind him. So he has asked the commission to see if the material now refused classification "correctly reflects current community standards". Conroy says once that exercise is finished in early 2012 "we will be moving to implement our policy".

18.

ONE HOT NIGHT FORTY YEARS AGO
JUNE 2009

When Judy Garland died in London in June 1969 after slurping too much Secanol, her body was brought back to New York where 20,000 distraught fans filed through the Frank E. Campbell Funeral Home on Eighty-First Street to catch a last glimpse of the fallen diva. It's a fair guess many of those mourners were gay but despite all that's been said since, their grief did not make history.

In the same city on the same hot weekend Garland was buried, a gay riot broke out after police raided a dive in Greenwich Village called the Stonewall Inn. There's no evidence the two events were linked in any way, yet by now it's hard to think of Stonewall without crediting Garland's emotional fans with striking this early blow for sanity in a world still deeply troubled by gays.

Stonewall has become smothered in legends and honoured by the powerful. That corner of Greenwich Village was declared a National Historic Landmark a decade ago and President Obama has lately enraged militant Christians by declaring June 2009 the month of Lesbian, Gay, Bisexual and Transgender Pride to honour those patrons of Stonewall for resisting police harassment: "Out of this resistance, the lesbian, gay, bisexual, and transgender rights movement in America was born."

Not really. Stonewall wasn't the first time such violence erupted nor the first time political headway was made in the uproar that followed. The club's patrons were not the frontline troops. Nor was gay liberation born solely out of such violence: Stonewall would not have led where it did if the rights movement had not already been well under way in America and even here in timid Australia.

Don't get me wrong. Stonewall's fortieth birthday is worth the celebrations round the world this weekend. But the legends are getting in the way of the lessons Stonewall has to teach about winning sensible and popular reform when police and politicians are hellbent on standing in its way. Stonewall is about the power of mockery and fun and celebration; about shabby violence and brilliant political invention; about the riff-raff and the reputable working hand in hand; about the need for supporters of sensible but difficult causes – gay rights, euthanasia, drug reform – to show their faces in daylight. It's about the power of coming out.

The Stonewall Inn on Christopher Street was a trashy firetrap run by the mafia. The walls were painted black, the drinks were watered and the toilets overflowed. Men were allowed to dance with men, women with women. This was no safe haven. From the moment Stonewall opened in March 1967, it made a fortune for the mob from blackmail as much as liquor. None of it was ploughed back into the business.

The police crusade against homosexuals was more determined than ever in the 1960s but the courts were proving troublesome to the forces of purity. Test cases brought by advocates of gay law reform had shown it was not against the law in New York to serve liquor to homosexuals, nor to let them dance together. But it remained a crime for men to wear women's clothing and vice versa. The nineteenth-century labour law in question required citizens of New York to wear no less than three articles of clothing appropriate to their sex. When police raided Stonewall early on the morning of

28 June 1969 – the second raid in four days – they were looking for women in overalls and men in frocks.

About 200 customers were packed into the inn's two bars when the music stopped and the lights came on at 1.20 am. Tempers were frayed. Drag queens refused to go to the toilets to be "checked out" by the morals squad. Men dressed as men released into Christopher Street hung around under a full moon jeering at the police as they led their prisoners to the paddy wagon. They were joined by street kids, the scruffiest end of the gay world who would be the shock troops of the confrontation.

The atmosphere was street party until one of the drag queens swung at a cop with her handbag and was clubbed in return. Then a handcuffed lesbian was dragged from the bar kicking, cursing and screaming. She fought all the way to a waiting squad car from which she escaped twice before being driven away. It was this unknown woman who taunted the crowd by calling out: "Why don't you guys do something?"

Loose change was already showering down on police. Now pennies were followed by bottles, bricks and cobblestones. Vastly outnumbered by the swelling crowd, the police retreated into the club and barricaded the doors. The crowd erupted. Celebratory accounts of Stonewall usually skate over the details of the next hour or so. About 400 people took part in the melee. Most of them were street kids. Everything was being hurled at the bar. All its windows were smashed. Attempts were made to set it alight. An uprooted parking meter was used to batter open the bar's heavy doors. Crude Molotov cocktails were thrown inside and extinguished by the police.

Then the cavalry arrived: two fire engines, a paddy wagon, several patrol cars and two buses filled with members of the heavily armoured Tactical Patrol Force. As the TPF advanced in line abreast, street kids met them with an impromptu high-kicks chorus line.

In *Stonewall: The riot that sparked the gay revolution*, David Carter wrote of witnesses "amazed at the courage of the street kids who dared to mock the TPF to their faces". The brawling ended sometime after 3 am. The next night a crowd of several thousand gathered outside the reopened bar and blockaded the street. This was, for the time, barely imaginable: a public gathering of men and women identifying themselves as homosexual. They were there because they wanted to be there and they were angry. It took 300 police two hours to clear the streets.

That's Stonewall: sixteen rioters arrested and four police hurt over two nights with the trashed club reopened at once by a determined mafia management. Press accounts of the fighting were brief and mocking. It was too soon while the streets were still being swept to cast these events in a romantic light. The respectable forces of gay law reform considered the riots a setback to their agenda.

Stonewall was not big news in the outside world but the story quickly reached Australia. The *Sydney Morning Herald* would take a stance of haughty disapproval of the gay movement for the next decade or more but it carried a sympathetic account of the upheaval in Greenwich Village by a very individual Australian journalist based in New York who already saw Stonewall as it was going to be seen. "Homosexuals, understandably, are anxious to avoid trouble," Lillian Roxon wrote. "Last week the police moved in on a place called the Stonewall, expecting the usual lack of resistance. But revolution is in the air, and what has been confined until now to the ghettos and the universities suddenly happened on nice, quiet, tree-shaded Christopher Street. Instead of the skulking shamefaced deviates they were prepared to encounter at the Stonewall, the police ran slap bang into a mob of terribly angry men."

Though the American press that weekend had been merciless about men in frocks and assaults with beaded bags, Roxon noted:

"Those lithe figures in the sequined sheaths and the feather boas also happened to be in very fine physical nick. 'If the queens of America ever get together,' said one redhead, aiming 'her' stiletto with vicious precision, 'it's the end, baby. We've had enough.'"

Brawls with cops outside gay bars had been going on for years in America. The anger and the violence at Stonewall were not unique. Stonewall was turned into myth by a group of astute gay politicians who took the daring decision to commemorate the first anniversary of this scruffy riot with a parade of gay men and women through New York city in broad daylight. Stonewall became a marker of profound change because that 1970 march stretched fifteen blocks.

Stonewall was not a rallying cry in Australia. Indeed, the magazine *Camp Ink* warned campaigners in 1970 not to follow the example set in New York. Rebellion was not the Australian way. The fledgling gay reform movement out here was still taking its cue from England where civil liberties campaigners working through parliament had seen sex between men in private decriminalised in 1967. That was another beacon to the world. South Australia followed suit in 1972. Everywhere else in Australia sex between men would remain a crime for years.

But Stonewall was working its rebellious magic. "Australian queens began to turn from British to American gay life as the beacon on the hill," says historian of the gay movement Garry Wotherspoon. "Prior to Stonewall all the queens would go to London. From the '70s on, they went to Los Angeles, San Francisco and New York. It was a real turning point. Let me tell you, London in 1970 was boring as shit compared to LA in '73."

Though branded a Stonewall celebration, the famous 1978 march in Sydney was actually held at the request of Harvey Milk's people in San Francisco seeking international support to prevent gay teachers – and all teachers sympathetic to the gay movement – being expelled from the Californian education system. Though the link with Stonewall was tenuous going into the event, it was profound by the time the night was over.

In the early morning of 25 June, police ambushed the marchers in Kings Cross, beat many and arrested fifty-three. Days later, a big gay demonstration wound its way through Sydney in broad daylight. Just as in New York in 1969, a mighty impetus to change was given by police going too far in pursuit of an old morals agenda at a time when public opinion had undergone a radical shift. Police violence jolted the reform movement back to life.

Change still took time. Indeed, not everything has been achieved. But the lessons of Stonewall are there to be applied to other reforms police and politicians continue to thwart. Change takes respectable lobbying to prepare the ground, outrageous behaviour in the streets to confront authority and mass coming out to show the days of shame on this one are past. We could start with the hardest, the issue still policed as gay sex once was with tough laws and hefty prison sentences that achieve little while destroying lives along the way: drugs.

2010 AND 2011

Perhaps I'm a bit of a Pollyanna when it comes to society calming down about poofs. Nasty skirmishes continue on the frontier between gay and straight. In May 2010 Channel Seven destroyed the career of the NSW minister for transport David Campbell by filming the huge-girthed politician leaving a gay steam bath in Sydney. The station tried to justify the outing with a cockamamie complaint about misuse of a ministerial car. The Australian Communications and Media Authority defended the broadcast because the public was owed a "deeper explanation" for Campbell's sudden resignation hours before the story went to air. ACMA's message seems to be: when grossly violating the privacy of a public figure, avoid half measures. Destruction or nothing.

From the other side of the world, Miranda Devine could see what lay behind the riots that tore a number of British cities apart in the summer of 2011:

> As a Catholic, I believe the push for same-sex marriage is not about enhancing the lives of gay couples. In countries where it has been legalised, there has been no rush to the altar. The issue is largely symbolic. It is simply a political tool to undermine the last bastion of bourgeois morality, the traditional nuclear family. You only had to see the burning streets of London last week to see the manifestation of a fatherless society.

The last surviving anti-gay warriors have had a fresh lease of life since gay men and women began agitating for the right to marry their partners. In August 2011, the National Marriage Coalition held a hate fest in the Great Hall of Parliament where preachers and politicians denounced lesbians and homosexuals as selfish, destructive, ridiculous, anti-children, despotic, foes of liberty, evil, hateful, useful to Satan, liars, vicious, narcissistic, empty, insatiable, oppressors of the church, insidious, bullies, power-mongers and promoters of massive evil. Independent MP Bob Katter donated his hat to the cause and begged for "gay" to be given back to decent folk: "Nobody has the right to take that word off us." But the most colourful attacks came from Mrs Rebecca Hagelin, the keynote Christian flown in from America:

> It won't stop at homosexual marriage. Once the historical and legal definition that has withstood through the ages is changed,

anything can be called marriage. Look for polygamy, and marriage between adults and children to be legalized. There is no greater dream for a paedophile than to be able to legally claim a child as his lover. If the enemy is successful in destroying marriage, then every other institution and freedom we hold dear will also eventually be destroyed.

19.

TIME ON THE ISLAND SEPTEMBER 2009

In a tin shed on Phosphate Hill, a brisk woman from the Department of Immigration and Citizenship sits facing a slight kid of seventeen. Though Ali Jaffari knows something of what is coming, he is battling nerves. His face is grey. One leg is trembling. His father, Sharif, sits quietly beside him, his head bowed. An air conditioner thunders in the background. Both men keep an eye on the envelopes the DIAC officer has on the table: brown envelopes that hold the answer to the rest of their lives.

The Jaffaris are Hazaras from Afghanistan, a people long persecuted as Shia Muslims in a country overwhelmingly Sunni. Sharif was still a boy when he fled the country to grow up in the large Hazara community in Iran. At some point, he moved to Pakistan and raised a family in Quetta. But as inter-faith violence intensified in Pakistan over the last year, the city became dangerous. Sharif talks of more than sixty Hazaras murdered in the city. The Jaffaris narrowly escaped death. "Two persons came by motorcycle. They stopped. They fired on us and they escaped." It was time to leave. "There were rumours Australia accepted refugees and it's a safe and secure country. So therefore we decided to come to Australia. That was our plan."

Their arrival on Christmas Island in early May, along with another 185 refugees collected by HMAS *Tobruk*, provoked fresh denunciations by the Opposition of Labor's "soft" response to boat people. "There cannot be any serious argument about it now," said Malcolm Turnbull. "It has failed to stop the dreadful business of people smuggling." Hate was back in the air. The press noted the biggest spike in "unauthorised boat arrivals" since the heyday of the Pacific Solution in 2001. The island was said to be reaching bursting point. As always, Christmas Islanders gathered to watch the refugees brought ashore. It's a spectacle that predates the *Tampa* affair by a decade. But things have changed: the islanders were no longer held back by police barricades, and there were no guards in riot gear on the barges.

Flying Fish Cove lies under cliffs covered by dark forests. Jurassic birds wheel overhead. The dusty hulk of the phosphate loader waits for ships. Along the shore are barracks, warehouses and a little mosque. This was not where the Jaffaris expected to find themselves. That all boat people heading for Australia are now held on Christmas Island came as a complete surprise. "No one told us." They hadn't heard of attempts by Labor and Coalition governments over nearly two decades to deter people like them from coming here by boat. The messages had fallen on deaf ears. The Jaffaris paid a smuggler to bring them to this country because, where they come from, Australia has a vague reputation for decency.

As Ali was only seventeen, father and son were not taken to the high-security immigration detention centre at North West Point but to the old Construction Camp on Phosphate Hill above the town. The immigration minister, Chris Evans, says Labor converted the facilities here to give children and families a "community environment". It's a grim fib. A high fence was torn down, but what's left is a cluster of tin boxes and concrete walkways surrounded by gravel. Workers building roads in the bush sleep in dongas like these and are well paid for their discomfort. But on Phosphate Hill families sit behind closed doors day after day with air conditioners working away. There is little privacy. Heavy rain turns the camp into a mosquito-ridden swamp. Although the guards have gone from the gates, no one is free to leave without an escort. "It's not a community," said an islander who knows the place intimately. "It's a shithole."

Under John Howard, boat people were held in detention for years as a harsh warning to those who might follow in their wake. Labor has dramatically sped things up. The Jaffaris have waited only two months and twelve days for this encounter in the rec room with the woman from DIAC.

Her news is all good and delivered swiftly: "The paperwork has gone very quickly and I'm pleased to let you know that the minister has granted you a protection visa." Ali sags a little and thanks her quietly. The father nods. In real life, victories aren't marked by shouts and high fives, but relief that mimics exhaustion. She slips documents from the envelopes for them to sign. Ali asks that word be sent to a friend he made on the boat who is being held at North West Point. Ali wants to say goodbye. "I only know his name as Said." Promises are made. (And kept.) There follows a last, bizarre interrogation. It's so pointless it's almost insulting, yet it's proof the Jaffaris have now achieved the privileged status of ordinary travellers.

"Are you," asks the woman from DIAC, "carrying goods that may be prohibited or subject to restriction such as medicines, steroids, firearms, weapons of any kind?" Ali and his father confer. "No, we don't have any." Nor do they have $10,000 or its equivalent in foreign currency. Nor any dried, fresh, preserved, cooked or uncooked food. The translator labours away and the woman from DIAC crosses each box in their entry cards. Tomorrow they will be driven to one of the most fickle airports in the world, where a plane will be waiting to take them 2600 kilometres to Perth. The scene is not quite finished. The air conditioner is turned off and in the silence that fills the shed, Ali thanks those who have looked after them on the island. "We can't consider them as human beings," he says, "but better than human beings, like angels. We are very pleased being treated well and feeling safe and secure here. It can't be described by words."

*

Christmas Island is not a sunny atoll but a gloomy mountain sticking out of the Indian Ocean. It appears from the air black, cloud-smothered, defended by cliffs and ringed by surf. It's tiny and a long way away. The sea is everywhere. It sets the moods of the place, brings the cloud and nights of thundering rain. It's a tough stretch of ocean ending in the poor harbour of Flying Fish Cove. A navy boat has been hovering off the coast for days waiting to intercept little boats making their way down from Indonesia. It's an island for waiting: waiting for something to come along, waiting for the supply ship, waiting for friends to visit, waiting for the weather to clear, waiting to get away.

Seven hundred detainees, housed in town, up in the Construction Camp and out in the forest detention centre, are waiting for news of hearings and applications and visas. Driving around trying to make sense of this baffling place on my first afternoon, I find the oval on Phosphate Hill just as it is getting dark. Gnarled frangipanis guard the gates. Lichen grows on the goal posts. Eighteen young men are playing soccer, the jungle behind them a hazy shadow in the mist. They are waiting, killing time in their own way. Clouds sweep across the field and the men disappear, disembodied, lost except for their shouting.

This rock was given to Australia in the great dispersal of the Empire fifty years ago. Jakarta is the nearest big city. Buddhism is the main religion. Most of the island is locked away in a national park. The tiny population is 60 per cent Chinese, 25 per cent Malay and the rest European. They live in little suburbs scattered over the cliffs above Flying Fish Cove: below Drumsite come Poon Saan ("half way") and Silver City, with the offices and big houses of the Settlement running along the waterline. All told, the permanent population is less than 1500. Christmas Island is so tiny it's not so much a territory as a parish of Australia.

What to do with the place has intrigued Canberra for decades. One inquiry is barely finished before the next begins. Reports pile up while life goes on. Big visions disappear in the tropic heat. A casino used by Tommy Suharto and his mates to wash their loot collapsed a decade ago. The satellite launching pad never got anywhere. Phosphate mining has kept the place in work since the 1890s but perhaps for not much longer. For years the mine has been threatening to close down in four or five years' time. It wants another 256 hectares of forest to strip and mine. Peter Garrett's decision will shape the economic fate of the island. Meanwhile, the place has been handed another future: as a prison for refugees.

At the Australian National University in July 2008, Chris Evans laid out Labor's new regime for handling boat people. Much of the tough Howard architecture would remain: excision, military interception and mandatory detention. But now detention would be brief: only as long as it took to carry out health, identity and security checks. After that, asylum seekers would be released into the community while waiting to see if Australia would take them as refugees. The process would take months instead of years. But it was to happen a very long way away: "Those unauthorised arrivals," said Evans, "will be processed on Christmas Island."

Why, all the way out here, is one of the puzzles of our time. Everywhere on Christmas Island you hear of changes for the better since Labor came to office. That a great shift has happened is undeniable. Despite a core of boat people haters among DIAC employees, relations between detainers and detained have been transformed. Fine professional services are on hand. Processing so far away from Australia has many risks – particularly for children and damaged souls disembarking from the boats – but Canberra appears willing to throw money and expertise at minimising those problems. Money is no object. The result is a logistical miracle. But to be doing this out here is utterly bizarre. We're still caught in the toils of border protection politics.

Who is the audience for this operation? Evans concedes everything done here could be done on the mainland – "It was in the past" – and done infinitely cheaper. And he makes no big claims that processing on the island deters the people smugglers: "I think it offers a message about excision and a strong commitment to ensuring people who seek to come to Australia arrive lawfully." But isn't that a message for home consumption: that these people are being held, checked and sorted a long way away from Australia; that only the chosen will be allowed to reach the mainland; that the boats are under control? "That's not part of our rationale," replies the minister. "But I think there probably is something in that." It's political theatre.

Evans treads gently. Rudd laid down Labor's policy on boat people early in his time as leader of the Opposition. Nauru would be closed, but all processing of boat people would continue way offshore. "If people are on the high seas and then indicate that they are going to seek asylum in Australia … then they should be taken to Christmas Island for processing," said Rudd. "That's our policy." Howard had held some boat people on the island, but Rudd would use the island as a prison for them all. Evans's number-one reason for the enormous effort that's since been put into this operation is unambiguous: "It was an election commitment."

*

The weather on the island is brutal. It wipes inscriptions from graves. Television sets last a couple of years. Duco warps and shreds like skin with strange diseases. Buildings rot. All that's left of the old CI Club, one of the great institutions of the island, is falling apart in the trees behind Flying Fish Cove. Here in March 2002, the minister for territories Wilson Tuckey called a meeting that's seen as a turning point by the islanders. He told them: "You're going to get a new detention centre and I'm not here to argue."

Canberra had a problem. Stopping the *Tampa* six months earlier and warehousing boat people in the Pacific Solution helped win Howard a mighty election victory, but the camps on Nauru and Manus Island were reaching capacity. If, as Howard had promised the Australian people, no boatperson was ever to set foot on the mainland, another big holding camp was needed offshore. Tuckey announced a plan to spend $220 million building a 1200-bed camp very rapidly on an old phosphate-mining lease out in the forest. Nominated as a "project of national importance", it was to be exempted from both environmental controls and scrutiny by the Public Works Committee.

Prison islands have a certain terrible fascination, particularly in the tropics, as places from which escape is impossible. Sharks and drowning are essential parts of the imagery. Howard's camp on Christmas Island was to be part Alcatraz and part Ellis Island: a place of incarceration far from public scrutiny where inmates would be processed for a possible new life in some distant country, almost certainly not Australia. Work began quickly and $60 million had been spent by early 2003 when Canberra called a halt. The project was looking too big and too flimsy.

The boats had stopped. What Howard had done was dirty and dangerous but it worked. Preventing boats from sailing in the first place or forcing them back to Indonesia had killed the trade. So the new island prison didn't have to be so big. But it did need to be more secure. The original idea had been to build another Baxter but in the last days of the year, frustrated detainees at that South Australian detention centre set the place alight. Copycat riots and fires followed at Port Hedland in Western Australia, Woomera in South Australia and Villawood in Sydney. "Touted when it opened three months ago as a state-of-the-art and 'more humane' centre for illegal immigrants, Baxter Detention Centre yesterday resembled the aftermath of a battleground," wrote Catherine Hockley and Daniel Clarke in the *Advertiser* on 30 December 2002. "One entire stretch of units in the compound was little more than a crumpled mess of twisted metal upon a concrete walkway."

Howard might have reassessed the policy of deliberate long detention that had incubated the riots. Instead it was decided that security at North West Point would be increased dramatically. The new plan would involve an escape-proof and riot-proof prison for 400 people or 800 in emergencies. The project would involve building new roads, a new port and a big recreation hall back at Phosphate Hill. As usual, when it came to saving Australia from boat people, the budget was endless. When Baulderstone Hornibrook won the tender and took a closer look at the plans, the budget rose swiftly from $276 million to $336 million and kept rising for another three years. Canberra was discovering all over again that the symbolic value of Christmas Island comes at a mighty cost. Everything out there – except the tax-free booze, cigarettes and second-hand luxury cars from Singapore – is grossly expensive.

Ornithologists were concerned about the fate of one of the world's rarest birds: Abbott's booby, *Papasula abbotti*. *New Scientist* magazine feared the bird, already endangered by mining, might be driven to the edge of extinction by the prison being built so close to its habitat. Later, Malcolm Turnbull as environment minister would try to prevent the mine clearing any more forest, but the bird's fate was not allowed to stand in the way of the prison.

The site was a nightmare. There were limestone pinnacles and "covered caves" that threatened the project with collapse. And then there was the weather. Rick Scott-Murphy of the Department of Finance and Administration told a Senate estimates hearing: "In the period since we have been constructing it we have suffered a near pass with a cyclone, we have had a tsunami and we have had a 6.4 Richter-scale seismic event." The minister for human services, Ian Campbell, piped up: "Building the runway in Antarctica was a lot easier than this, seriously. And cheaper." The completion date kept being pushed back. This out-of-date, over-engineered, hugely expensive building – perhaps *the* building of the Howard era – was still not finished when the Howard government went to its grave.

*

"Basically, my kids have no fathers," says Jennie Collins, a freckle-faced teacher of fierce determination and indeterminate years. A tattoo on one ankle suggests Miss Jennie has seen a bit of life. Today she's teaching eighteen Hazara boys polite English. They are slight kids dressed in the school uniform of the island: black shorts, t-shirts and runners. A few may be in their early twenties but most are about seventeen, the age at which the Taliban begins to take a predatory interest in them, the age when they flee. "Whole villages have clubbed together to get these boys out. Some have mothers and siblings, maybe in camps in Pakistan, but they don't have fathers."

She asks each boy in turn what he would like to be if, *inshallah*, he reaches Australia. It seems we have heading our way three would-be mechanics, two doctors, a poultry farmer, four tailors – already qualified – an engineer, a teacher, an artist, a cook, a software programmer, a social worker and "the top richest man in the world". One kid says he wants to join the navy. "Who remembers the navy rescuing them from their boats?" asks Miss Jennie. "Are they good people?" The boys roar, "Yes!"

They came in five boats. One, with sixty people aboard, was ten days at sea. Another, with seventy-two aboard, was at sea for eight days and leaked all the way. "There was a hole in the bottom. They don't have a water pump to take the water out. They were doing it with a bucket and our hands." They were all seeing the sea for the first time. None could swim. All seem to have travelled via Kuala Lumpur airport, the refugee gateway to Australia. They came the rest of the way by boat. "It is really, really unbelievable that we are alive," says one older detainee, MR. "Unfortunately we lost our way. There is only that much food not to die. That much. There was that much water not to die. The ship was not working. Big waves. The ship was not good. Blue sky and blue water. You can see nothing. It is just like to see a death from your eyes. A big sea. Ocean." Another of the kids adds: "On the way we saw sharks, whales, dolphins, everything."

Now Miss Jennie is teaching them to say sorry. Out of the hub-bub as they practise on each other come "no probs" and "no worries, mate". Thank God they appear not to master "I'll take a raincheck." When do you apologise? she asks each in turn. "When you are late, Miss," one replies. Another says: "When you break someone's heart."

*

Gordon Thomson is a big, pink man from Queensland whose card has two faces. One says he's general secretary of the Union of Christmas Island Workers and the other that he's president of the shire. He hands it over union side up: "This is the side that matters." Swallows dart round us as we sit in a Poon Saan café run by a guy who greets us in loud Malay. "We're in Asia," remarks Thomson, smiling, and sadly the coffee proves his point. Thomson is the successor to Gordon Bennett, the man revered for leading the union's long war with the British Phosphate Commission that ended in the 1980s with decent wages being paid to the indentured labourers – essentially coolies – brought from China, Malaysia and Singapore to work the mine. "BPC" is still slang for overbearing behaviour on the island, says Thomson. "History weighs on this place, absolutely. Abso-fucken-lutely."

The history of the boats is quickly told. The first turned up here in 1992 and for nearly a decade these occasional visitors were greeted by the islanders with hot food and clean clothes before being whisked away to detention on the mainland. The numbers escalated. The government stopped the *Tampa*. Thomson helped bring the European, Chinese and Malay communities together in radical opposition to Canberra's blockade. "We were very upset and angry and had to have a community position." For a few weeks the islanders were feted by the press of the world. Though that image of the island still persists, it was always rose-coloured. Thomson says the island has never been of one mind. "I was attacked by several people in the European community. One was an ex-copper. 'You don't speak for me,' he said. 'They should torpedo those boats.'" The illusory unity of the island splintered further as Canberra began, for the first time, to detain asylum seekers in a temporary camp behind high wire on Phosphate Hill.

These were boat people who could not be delivered into the Pacific Solution. Australia could fiddle its obligations to those intercepted near the 4000 or so reefs and islands "excised" from the nation's "migration zone". But those who slipped through the net of air and sea surveillance to reach the Australian mainland had to be dealt with on Australian soil by Australian tribunals and courts. So in July 2003, when a fishing boat called the *Hao Kiet* almost sailed into Port Hedland, the fifty-three Vietnamese on board were taken by HMAS *Canberra* more than a thousand kilometres east and dumped on Christmas Island where they languished for two years.

"The Vietnamese brought us all together," said Robyn Stephenson, a high-school teacher and a member of the Christmas Island Rural Australians for Refugees. "And then it went on for so damn long. We were buying underwear for the people in detention. Every week I was going up there and they would change the rules. Visitors could be denied entry for any reason at any time." There was a lot of work for decent people to do at a time when even lawyers rarely got out to the island. By July 2005, when the last of the *Hao Kiet* Vietnamese were given their visas and flown to Perth, the island's activists were exhausted.

Six months later, forty-three West Papuans landed on a Queensland beach in an outrigger canoe and were flown by Hercules all the way to Christmas Island. Although they were only held there for two months, the exercise went badly wrong. They were all very black. Some of the families held in the town had never lived in European houses. They were curious and wandered about looking in windows. The night before they were due to fly to Perth, some of the men hit the piss. Then the clouds came down for days and their plane couldn't get away. It was an ugly time that's still not forgotten.

Meanwhile, work was going ahead slowly on the prison out at North West Point. Locals grumbled, but what could they do? This was how Canberra always behaved: imposing grand schemes on them without consultation. Thomson told the press the place was starting to look like Guantanamo Bay. "The government has proven the point that Christmas Island and other places can be excised from the migration zone, and are exempt from other acts of parliament," he said. "It could be a military base, it could be used to detain terrorists, it could be used for anything."

Labor seemed to inherit a white elephant when Rudd came to power in late 2007. No boats were coming. None were expected. North West Point, standing empty, was thought rather a joke. Then in September 2008, a customs vessel intercepted a boat carrying a dozen refugees near Ashmore Reef. A few days later, they were brought ashore at Flying Fish Cove and taken up to the camp on Phosphate Hill. The boats kept coming. The Pacific Solution was no more. All these people were now to be held and processed on the island. Within weeks the camp on the hill behind the town was full. Evans had no choice. A few days before Christmas, the first detainees – including twenty-three Afghans, ten Iraqis and two Iranians – were bussed out to North West Point. Howard's prison was in business.

*

Traffic enters and leaves the Settlement by a roundabout that's flanked by blackboards carrying ads, greetings and reproaches. You bring your own chalk and write: "Lost red dive float and rope. If found please call Johnny." Or: "Stop stealing my granny's orchids. She's just an old lady. We know who you are." And there is one of the world's oddest traffic signs that says which of the island's roads are closed by migrating crabs. Life on Christmas Island is disrupted every November when millions of these famous red crabs (*Gecarcoidea natalis)* make their way to the sea. But all year round, drivers must take care to avoid little red and mighty robber crabs (*Birgus latro)* edging across the roads. When locals sense hazards ahead they say: "I see a few crabs here."

A few reds are on the muddy road to North West Point. Phosphate trucks thunder by. You have to know where you're heading out here because the prison, although it's the biggest building on the island, isn't marked on maps. The road swings round and there it is: sprawling like a vast factory behind high wire fences. The fences are remarkable. The first apparently stops the crabs frying on the second, which is about four metres of mesh topped by half a dozen single strands of wire all, as they say in the prison trade, "energised". Inside lies a perimeter road equipped with microwave probes that are capable of detecting, according to plans leaked to *Crikey* in 2007, the slightest movement. Inside again is another fence – quite friendly, merely man-high – and then the buildings that fill a vast jungle clearing.

It cost $400 million in the end. A jail this size can be built in New South Wales for roughly a tenth of that sum. But everything is so expensive out here. A senior executive of G4S, the company that until this month ran all Australia's detention centres, told me labour costs double on Christmas Island. DIAC foots the bill, of course, and this includes daily food and accommodation allowances of $190 per worker. That's a lot to pay before spending a cent on wages. Oxfam estimates it costs $1600 per day more to hold someone on Christmas Island than the mainland. But Canberra is happy to pay to reassure Australia.

A fortnight before I found myself at these gates, Graeme Innes of the Australian Human Rights Commission had been here inspecting the facilities. The commission is scathing about both the prison and the Christmas Island operation. So is the United Nations High Commissioner for Refugees. "UNHCR does not believe it is an appropriate facility to accommodate asylum seekers except, perhaps, for a very limited few persons whose presence in the future might pose a security threat to the local community."

Evans defends the place: "While it presents from the outside as a prison it's a modern functional detention place and there are many advantages working there in terms of being able to offer recreation to clients, medical treatment, good cooking facilities, all those things." In a way he's right. The electricity doesn't fail out here. The drains work. There are beds. And where else on Christmas Island can you cook a couple of thousand meals a day? If you're going to use Christmas Island, you're going to end up using this place. And now that all the detention centres on the mainland except Villawood are empty or mothballed, North West Point is detention central.

Entry to the detention centre took all the security checks you would expect of a serious prison. Once inside, the place has the feel of a deranged holiday camp. It is all iron, steel and glass. It won't burn, rot or rust. On a stretch of grass worn almost to death, a 25-a-side soccer match between Sri Lanka and Afghanistan is playing itself out. Soon the game will end and both the gym and what they call the "internet café" will close. The 569 single men in the place will then trail back to their yards – where the furniture is bolted to the floor – for a headcount and the evening meal. Keeping an eye on them are 247 cameras.

The detainee I'm visiting is one of the hard cases beginning to queue up on the island. He is waiting to hear how he went at an Independent Merits Review held a couple of weeks earlier. It was his second and last chance. Though gloomy about the outcome, he was not without hope. He has been four months out here. Like so many of the men at North West Point – but how many the department of immigration refuses to say – he is still being held behind the wire despite clearing all his identity, health and security checks. He is taught English for an hour each week. He can find nothing to read in Farsi. He kills time smoking and sleeping.

By the kinder, more civilised rules Labor has laid down for dealing with boat people, he should have been released into the community while he waits. But that's not a policy that can be implemented on Christmas Island. Money can buy a lot of things out here. It can build what it likes. It can house and feed hundreds of detainees and their professional minders. But money has its limits. It can't conjure community out of thin air.

The Settlement is tiny. Vying for beds, cars and food are nineteen Australian Federal Police, ten customs and five quarantine officers, plus twenty-one interpreters who speak nine languages. The Red Cross has a team of six on the island; a Newcastle outfit called Life Without Barriers has nine staff looking after unaccompanied children; and the Forum of Australian Services for Survivors of Torture and Trauma has two representatives on the island. The immigration department has forty-three staff of its own, plus the teams of lawyers and migration agents it hires to represent the detainees. But the biggest employer is the private operator of the detention facilities: until last month G4S but now the Serco Group. Their workforce of about 130 includes medical staff, teachers and even a bunch of happy clappers who lead "dance, art and sport activities" behind the wire. All told, 300 support staff have been brought out here to this rock to deal with 700 detainees, almost doubling the population.

The minister claims the women and children living in workers' dongas in Construction Camp on Phosphate Hill are enjoying a "community environment". One glance tells you that's a lie. A senior medical figure with long experience of the camps told me: "It's as hideous as Baxter or Woomera. There are no facilities for children. They should not be housed there but taken to the mainland." Australian Human Rights Commissioner Graeme Innes told me: "The Construction Camp is not a prison but in some respects it's a worse facility. It's cramped. It doesn't have the facilities of North West Point. The separation detention facility there restricts people to two rows of huts and a boardwalk. People are held there for two weeks at a time. It is not acceptable."

In truth, only about forty detainees are actually living in the community of the Settlement. They include AR and his two young daughters, who came down from Phosphate Hill to a house in Drumsite ten days before I met them. AR is a worried man. The other Hazaras on his boat have all left for Australia. He is waiting to hear how he went in his Merits Review. The other half of his family is in Iran. His wife, who is running out of money, rings to ask what is happening. He doesn't know. He can't say. Apart from his children, AR's existence has come down to this: waiting and worrying.

But now he's in the town he can cook. His Chinese neighbours are polite. He has experienced no rudeness. Like anyone else on the island, he feels stranded without a car. If he knew he was to be here much longer, he would invest in a bike. He has nothing to read. He can find no books in Dari. He prays early, reads the Koran and walks his children round the corner to school. They miss playing with their friends in the Construction Camp and find the house a bit lonely. That morning, he tells me, he kept walking for two hours down the road to the forest and hitched a ride on a truck back home. Later, he rang his migration agent in Sydney again and was told all the paperwork was with DIAC and there was nothing more they could tell him.

On a hot Thursday night, in a garden behind the mosque, I had dinner with Zainal Majid and a few of his friends. Majid is a senior executive at the mine and president of the Islamic Council. I'd wondered why his council was not going in to bat for the detainees. After all, so many of those held in the island camps are Muslim. But here's the wrinkle: the boat people are Shia and the island is Sunni. Majid does not see himself as their spokesman. An offer of help was made by the mosque some time ago but not repeated. He says the detainees are welcome to pray there, "But they don't come."

Opposite me sat the hefty Kamar Ismail, who made a name for himself a few months ago by alerting a Perth shock jock when he saw the navy giving bottled water to asylum seekers as they were brought ashore. "I got so pissed off I rang Howard Sattler," Ismail says. "Two and a half tonnes of water flown up here. Its cost? $26,000. OK?" Tabloid radio made hay with the bottled water story. Ismail speaks for many – perhaps most – islanders when he blames DIAC for rising food prices. "An apple is roughly around two bucks, man!" Later I investigate: at the Poon Saan Supermarket, a small Fuji costs 90 cents, while at the Christmas Island Supermarket and Duty Free in the Settlement, a small Pink Lady is $1.02. But the food argument is as much about passion as price, and the feeling there should be something in this for them.

"We're just a small island," says Ismail. "There are more people to feed since the refugees are here. They're having their special treatment up there – which we think is OK – but we think the government should've looked at providing some kind of subsidy of the freight so all the community can have that same benefit and share it. I know a lot of money's been farmed onto the island but to us there's nothing. We just see how they've been treated. You know, they've been looked after so well sometimes we are thinking we are sitting, maybe, on the wrong side of the fence! We should be in there!"

*

The forest behind the graveyard is alive with the sound of big birds grunting and barking. The air smells of bird shit. Guano is still in production. I've come to visit Gordon Bennett's grave, a kitsch concrete pagoda in the Chinese cemetery. To be buried here is a remarkable honour. In accordance with Taoist custom, booze is left on the headstone to refresh the union hero in the afterlife. All that is left for him this morning are five empty cans of Fosters, a half-drunk Corona and a tiny bottle of Johnny Walker Black Label.

This is an island of graves. Not far off are the graves of Fatimeh and Nurjan Husseini, who drowned in the debacle of the sinking of the *Sumber Lestari* a couple of days before Howard took the country to the polls in 2001. The boat was sabotaged. The navy faced a mass rescue of over 100 people who could not swim. Despite heroic efforts to revive them, two died. After the burial, Fatima's husband, Sayyed, was handcuffed and removed from the island. Attempts to grow trees by the graves have failed. Though the headstones are marble, the inscriptions are nearly obliterated. In the garden of the old administrator's house, the same has happened to the memorial to those who drowned on the SIEV X. The 353 names are all but illegible.

The terrace of the Lucky Ho was alive with rumours on my last night that more boats were on the way. A policeman's wife had told her hairdresser, who told her daughter, who told the other kids at school, who told the teachers eating wahoo in special sauce at the next table, that 150 refugees would arrive in Flying Fish Cove in the morning. It proved to be rubbish, but such rumours can't be wrong for long. The boats will keep coming and, until we're willing to face our fears, we will continue to perform out here this expensive, deeply satisfying, national farce.

LATE 2009

The boats did keep coming. My time on the island would seem, in retrospect, the last manageable weeks of a bizarre regime as Canberra scrambled to hold every single new asylum seeker out on that rock. As the year went on, Malcolm Turnbull intensified his attack on the government for signalling to people smugglers that Australia under Labor was a soft touch. But this tougher stand on the boats would not save the Opposition leader from the deniers of climate change plotting to bring him down.

20.

ABBOTT RISING DECEMBER 2009

Long practice makes Tony Abbott good at confessing. It's in his blood. At his sombre victory conference, he apologised for all his past errors. Details were absent. Contrition was at a minimum. But with a self-effacing smile, he said: "I believe that when you become leader, you make a fresh start." The Liberals' party room was not crowded. A moderate turnout of press was joined by a knot of Abbott supporters. They had the shattered look of people given what they had prayed for. As their new leader pledged to turn the Coalition into "an alternative, not an echo" of the Rudd government, their half-a-dozen voices echoed: "Hear, hear."

Another face will now join the line of black-and-white portraits of Liberal leaders staring down the room. So many hopeful new starts: a dozen leaders from Bob Menzies to Malcolm Turnbull, most of them torn down by their party colleagues. The photographer shouldn't tarry.

The day began quite cheerfully with Kochie's *Sunrise* tent out the front, giving parliament an almost Melbourne Cup feel. Sky News and ABC television staked out corners of the garden. Shade was at a premium. Bronwyn Bishop arrived ready, as always, for her close-up. Bob Ellis arrived predicting an Abbott victory and was scoffed. The press was herded behind ropes. Security guards patrolled the long corridors of parliament. Members of the press gallery passed the time teaching each other Twitter.

Nearby, the Reverend Peter Rose sat all alone reading the Bible in front of a blank television screen. "Did your prayers do us any good?" I asked him afterwards. "There was no rancour in there," the clergyman replied. "That's what I was praying for." Now more than ever parliament was a palace of rancour.

The Liberal whip Alex Somlyay did what he was told, standing on a bright rug showing the floral emblems of all the states just where someone had taped a scrap of paper that read: "Stand here." He announced Abbott's victory without a trace of pleasure. Once the cameras stopped rolling, the press swore, hit the phones, clumped and scattered. Out in the garden, pundits jawed for the cameras. There was little evidence of jubilation in the corridors. Doors were closed.

With shared disbelief, Abbott and the press faced each other forty minutes later. He frankly admitted his surprise: "It is the last thing that I would have expected a week ago." But the boy Churchill of Manly-Warringah never doubted the leadership would be his one day. It's just so soon.

Julie Bishop stood there smiling, smiling. It's a pleasure to reflect that among the few people in that room old enough to remember Dolly Dyer of *Pick-a-Box* are the deputy, the leader and most of his followers up the back. As the voltage of Bishop's smile dimmed, you could see her will it back to life. At times she turned to Abbott with a look of coquettish amusement. But her eyes were dazed.

Malcolm Turnbull had left the building too soon to hear her commend him for the "style and flair and colour" he brought to public debate. Abbott and John Howard were at one in expressing carefully crafted hopes for Turnbull's future in "public life".

There was no mention at all of parliament.

Early in the day I found myself wandering down a corridor behind a National Party senator talking on his mobile phone. "Tony may get up, which personally pleases me," he said. "But even my mother won't vote for him."

21.

CAT AND MOUSE FEBRUARY 2010

From the bridge of HMAS *Childers* on 16 April last year, Lieutenant Commander Brett Westcott watched the sun come up on a scene of great tranquillity. Moving slowly with his ship on a flat sea north of Ashmore Reef was an Indonesian fishing boat crowded with Afghan asylum seekers. "It was a beautiful day," he says. "Conditions were perfect." But with the sun on the horizon, the engines of the fishing boat spluttered and died. Minutes later the military aboard the little boat issued a "high threat" warning. Westcott caught the reek of petrol. "There was a heck of a lot of fuel if you can smell it from sixty yards away."

Westcott sent reinforcements. They took only minutes to arrive. From his vantage on the *Childers* he watched the nine men and women under his command herding reluctant asylum seekers towards the bow of their boat. Then it blew. "I can still hear it," Westcott told Australian Federal Police investigators days later. "I felt it, heard it. There was just bang: huge, deep, real deep, base woof, bang."

The superstructure was shredded. Bodies were flung into the water. The sea around the hull was a mess of debris, bobbing heads and luggage. Blazing figures threw themselves over the side. Others clung for as long as they could to the blazing wreckage. A sack of lifejackets floated uselessly across the water. Calm had turned to utter chaos in twenty minutes. Five Afghans died. Dozens were horribly burnt. Over and again those who examined the events of this morning would say it was a miracle the nine men and women of the navy and RAAF on the boat survived shaken but essentially uninjured. The worst damage was a twisted ankle.

Even as the survivors were being rushed towards Darwin, the explosion set off a political storm. "The refugees spread petrol on their boat," announced Colin Barnett, the premier of Western Australia. The question asked – and exploited – in the children-overboard scandal was in the air again: are these the sort of people we want living in our country?

Almost as quickly, an investigation was afoot. Within hours of the *Childers* and its sister patrol boat HMAS *Albany* tying up next day at Darwin, military personnel were being questioned by detectives from the Northern Territory and Australian Federal Police. First came the interviews, later the counselling. Ten months later, after a huge police investigation, a three-week coronial inquiry that heard evidence from thirty-four witnesses and an internal military review that has recommended fifty-nine changes to practice, a picture has emerged of confusion, heroism, hysteria and appalling mistakes by the military, the refugees – for they have all since been granted refugee status – and the Australian government.

The coroner will apportion praise and blame in his reports to be handed down next month. He is expected to recommend both criminal charges and awards for bravery. But the evidence also discloses the role played in these killings by the brutal domestic politics surrounding boat people. With the enthusiastic backing of the Opposition under Tony Abbott, the Rudd government reserves the right to force any of these boats back to Indonesia. So when they are intercepted, asylum seekers are routinely left in the dark as to their fate for days, even weeks at a time. A baffled senior policeman investigating the explosion, Detective Senior Sergeant Scott Pollock, would ask: "Why is this sort of cat and mouse game played and not telling them where they are going?"

*

At high tide Ashmore Reef barely rises out of the Timor Sea. This tiny patch of Australia lying only a couple of hundred kilometres south of Indonesia is a haunt of illegal fishermen and a natural destination for boats carrying asylum seekers to Australia.

Early the day before the explosion, HMAS *Albany*, under the command of Lieutenant Commander Barry Learoyd, sighted the 25-metre-long green-hulled Indonesian fishing boat heading towards the reef. Several people-smuggling boats were thought to be on their way to the reef that day. This one was dubbed SIEV (suspect illegal entry vessel) 36.

Learoyd, 54, burly and bearded, had spent most of his life in the navy, rising through the ranks to command crews in Operation Resolute patrolling Australia's maritime boundary with Indonesia. Fishing boats are the main business of Resolute. This appears to have been Learoyd's first SIEV. They are a very different business.

Also inexperienced in dealing with boat people was the commander of the boarding party Learoyd sent over to secure the SIEV at 9.43 am. Chief Petty Officer Shane McCallum, 48, had boarded over a hundred fishing vessels but only one SIEV, in 2005. That one was sabotaged.

Despite the domestic political anxiety about boat people, the boat sighted this morning off the reef was only the thirty-sixth to reach Australian waters since SIEV 1, rescued by the *Tampa* nearly a decade ago. On-the-job training in this game is hard to come by.

But the boarding could not have gone more easily. "They looked happy to see us," McCallum says. A man called Humayon Muhamad put up his hand and came forward to answer the call for an interpreter. This key figure – called H. by the boarding party – worked with the Australians all day explaining every direction to the asylum seekers.

The boat was clean and seaworthy. On board were forty-six Afghans, a lone Iraqi and two young Indonesian crewmen. The Australians were pleased to find no women, no children, no elderly, no sick – apart from one toothache and a recent appendectomy – and no apparent troublemakers. Unusually for such boats, the crew and passengers were at peace with each other. McCallum signalled back to the *Albany*: low threat.

But three mistakes had been made. First: smelly diesel engines powered the boat. Diesel does not explode. But there was also a little pump to empty the bilge. For that the Indonesian crew kept a can of fuel handy. Over the next twenty-four hours, most of the military personnel who came and went from SIEV 36 were unaware this pump's motor was petrol-driven.

Second: none of the military entered and searched the forward holds of the boat, where, in normal times, fishermen would store their catch. In that dark space full of food, bags and water was a second undiscovered big can of petrol for the bilge pump. This fuel would rip the boat apart.

Third: cigarette lighters and matches were not confiscated from the refugees. Calm was the imperative. "Taking people's personal pleasures away is one way of getting agitation," Learoyd said. "If a person smokes and he wanted a smoke and he couldn't get one, he was going to get pretty annoyed pretty quickly."

As the boarding party frisked and quizzed the Afghans, Petty Officer McCallum gave one of the crew a notice in English and Bahasa setting out the penalties for people smuggling. The last line of the notice reads: "You should now consider immediately returning to Indonesia with your passengers and not enter Australian territory." Stephen Walsh, QC, counsel assisting the Darwin coroner, would sharply criticise the serving of this "inappropriate" notice and the *Albany*'s commander would express surprise that his chief petty officer had bothered. SIEV 36 had entered Australian territorial waters long ago and was within sight of land. Learoyd said: "It was my expectation that a warning notice would not be issued." But in fact serving such a K-6-4 notice on every arriving SIEV was mandatory under the rules of Operation Resolute.

The asylum seekers would be unaware of this notice until the second day. In the meantime, their efforts to find what was to happen to them were rebuffed. The boarding party, following operational protocol to the letter, would only tell the refugees they were being taken to "Australian authorities" who would decide their fate. Learoyd confirmed: "At no time were they told they were going to Christmas Island." Back in Australia there was no mystery about their destination: the minister for home affairs Bob Debus put out a press release saying SIEV 36 was bound for Christmas Island. And they, too, were Learoyd's orders.

The *Albany*'s commander was in a quandary. He was refused permission to anchor SIEV 36 in the safety of Ashmore lagoon for the federal Department of the Environment feared the boat might pollute the waters of this national park. Learoyd would call this rather tartly "appeasing the environmentalists". But Northern Command (NORCOM) was also refusing to allow him to embark the asylum seekers on the *Albany* and take them to Christmas Island himself. "I was told at this stage that wasn't an option. The long-haul vessel HMAS *Tobruk* would be coming to our position to conduct that move." But the *Tobruk* was at the wharf in Darwin. At first it was said the ship was undergoing vital repairs. But later it would emerge it was simply in a long queue to be refuelled. Either way,

NORCOM was decreeing a holding operation at Ashmore of at least three days.

So with a "steaming party" of six Australian military personnel on board, SIEV 36 spent the day tootling around in the wake of the *Albany*. It was safer, less boring and cooler than leaving the vessel to wallow in calm seas. Every move through the day was signalled to the refugees through H., the ever-present interpreter. At nightfall the boat, now strung with lights, was taken in tow to allow the *Albany* to "maintain a close watch on the vessel and close support". They were still heading nowhere particular. "Up and down," McCallum said. The boarding party reported all on the SIEV "completely calm, very compliant".

*

HMAS *Childers* under Westcott's command first came on this scene just before sunset. His orders were to assist the operation until the *Tobruk* arrived. At a conference on board the *Albany* it was decided the two commanders would take responsibility for the boat day about. Having arranged to return before dawn for the handover, the *Childers* left again for a busy night intercepting fishing boats.

Westcott, a submariner by temperament and training, was also new to this business. "SIEV 36 was my first SIEV," he told the coroner. But he knew that when dealing with people-smuggling boats – unlike fishing boats – sabotage was an ever-present problem. Sabotage compels rescue. In desperate circumstances it is the ticket to freedom. This has been the history of all refugee blockades. Most of the boats the Howard government forced – or attempted to force – back to Indonesia were sabotaged in large ways or small. It is dangerous and even criminal, but it is what happens.

Westcott was troubled next morning. "We were at rendezvous at 6 o'clock, and in hindsight that was an incredibly stupid time to rendezvous," he told police. "It was total darkness. Sunrise wasn't till quarter past 7 and there was a conversation with myself and the [ship's executive officer] going 'Why are we handing over now?'" But his was the junior ship and the briefings given to his people the night before on the *Albany* were reassuring. Westcott assumed there was no petrol on the SIEV and that all matches and lighters had been confiscated. He took it for granted that the boat's forward hold had been thoroughly searched. He was wrong on all counts.

His boarding party under the command of Chief Petty Officer Dean Faunt reached the boat at 6.15 am. A little later *Albany* sent over breakfast – tuna and rice – for the sleeping refugees. With this delivery came the K-6-4 warning notice that McCallum had taken off to be photocopied for his records. It was left in the cabin near the helm. Faunt climbed onto the cabin roof which was his command position for the next hour and a half. Though briefed that there was a co-operative interpreter on board, he never met or used H. From this point, none of the moves made by the *Childers* boarding party were explained to the refugees, who were slowly stirring from sleep.

At 7.02 am the towline was dropped. The plan was to have the SIEV sail once again under its own power. It was growing light. The crew was woken and directed to start the engines at 7.10 am and the SIEV began trailing peacefully east in the wake of the *Childers*. But the refugees were becoming agitated. And something was wrong below. "The engine was struggling," said Faunt. "You could see black smoke coming out." After ten minutes of growing commotion on the foredeck, the engine lost revs, coughed and died – just as the sun rose. Faunt smelt petrol pouring from the bilge into the sea. His eyes were stinging. He thought: "Oh shit, here we go." Word came that the engines had been sabotaged. Up on deck, Afghans were making throat slitting gestures and calling, "No

Indonesia. No Indonesia." Faunt radioed the *Childers* at 7.29 am: "I've got a floating bomb here."

*

The refugees would at first speak frankly to police about the horrors of the next twenty minutes. But a miasma of forgetfulness had overcome their recollections by the time the coronial inquiry began in Darwin last month. Among themselves they had decided not to remember. This account of the explosion draws on early statements which have since been largely disclaimed and denied.

H. had found the warning notice. As soon as he read its vital last paragraph – "In this letter they have advised us that the Australian government will not accept you and you should return back to the place where you have come by this boat" – refugees began crying out. Ibrahim Rezvani told police: "Some of the passengers were saying, 'We have spent all of our savings and we have come this dangerous route, taking all the dangers. How can we go back?' Some of the passengers were screaming and saying 'I have saved my life from the danger in Afghanistan … and then I should go back to danger.'"

Waking on the foredeck shortly after the engine died, a young asylum seeker found petrol spilt on the boards. The men around him were arguing. "One was asking, 'Why did you pour the petrol?' and the other one was answering, 'Oh, I did good. I did it. I did good.'" Two Australians rushed forward to wrestle a cigarette lighter from a thickset man, Arman Ali Brahimi, sitting by the anchor hatch. Another man in a white singlet, Ghulam Mohammadi, was shuffling around the deck on his bum, screaming "No Indonesia" and tearing at the planks. Afghans around him were shouting at both the Indonesian crew and Faunt.

To try to calm the situation, the Australians were at last telling the refugees they were not on their way back to Indonesia. They pointed to the bow: it was not heading north but east into the rising sun. It was too late. Police believe as few as three men were seriously intent on sabotage. But a group of angry refugees was now challenging Faunt at his post on top of the cabin. "They were into me, like yelling at me not to go back to Indonesia." One man was weeping and begging to die: "Please no Indonesia. Shoot me." To the most persistent, Faunt shouted: "You little shit. Shut the fuck up and get up forward." He backed off.

The reinforcements sent from the *Childers* began clambering aboard at 7.44 am. Nine military personnel – men and women, navy and air force – were now on the SIEV. Faunt was, in his own words, "spinning around in circles yelling at everybody". For a minute it seemed the worst was past then: "It just blew us all to the shit house."

*

The *Childers* was hardly more than a swimming pool's length away from the blazing fishing boat. Life rings and life rafts were thrown into the sea. Nets were dropped over the side to help survivors clamber to safety. From the bridge Westcott called through a loud hailer: "Jump clear. Jump clear. Swim to my vessel." But Afghans can't swim. Afghan refugees see the sea for the first time as they cross difficult oceans on bad boats. The survivors continued to cling to the burning hull of SIEV 36 until Leading Seaman Boson Matthew Keogh, the only Australian still standing on the shattered boat, urged and dragged them into the sea.

When I met a dozen survivors of the blast recuperating from their burns last year, they were mute on the circumstances of the explosion, intensely grateful for the airlift and the medical attention they received but still angry that sailors had fought them off in the minutes after the explosion as they tried to clamber into rescue dinghies. The military first save their own. "We did collect ADF personnel first," Able Seaman Quinton Boorman told investigators. "They are our shipmates. We need to get them." Early in the coronial inquiry, counsel assisting wondered if "the strict practice of rescuing ADF members first might justify review". But by the end, Walsh was arguing: "The priority given was appropriate and cannot be criticised."

The RHIB (rigid hull inflatable boat) *Sierra*, which only a couple of minutes earlier had carried the reinforcements to the SIEV, passed an Afghan floating face down as it went to rescue Lance Corporal Sharon Jager. The RAAF medic was winded, heavily equipped and her lifejacket had not inflated. Pulling her aboard proved an ugly business. Able Seaman Adrian Medbury admits making "a kicking motion" to clear an asylum seeker away. Jager watched the kick connect. "From what I saw," she told the inquest, "it was the head." Two Afghans managed to clamber on board. One was probably the kicked man.

The *Sierra* had picked up two more Australians when they heard Keogh shouting from the burning boat: "Medders, get me the fuck off this thing." Boorman navigated past "personnel and debris" to bring the *Sierra* beneath the burning hull to allow Keogh to jump on board. The hunt for further survivors of the boarding party continued. In the end, the *Sierra* would bring back to the *Childers* seven of the nine military caught up in the explosion. By 7.58 Westcott was immensely relieved to know all his people had survived: knocked around but basically OK.

Three other RHIBs were pulling people from the sea. Two bodies were brought to the *Childers* and another to the *Albany*, which had steamed back hurriedly to the scene when the high alert was sounded. Two bodies were never found. Forty-four of the fishing boat's passengers and crew survived. Many were hideously burnt. Jager, bruised from the blast, boarded the *Childers* and went to work. "I've seen Flight Lieutenant Darby who is the doctor already giving somebody oxygen. I've run straight to her and said, 'Where do you want me?' and she's gone, 'Stand back and triage when they come through.'"

Victims were laid out on the quarterdecks of both boats. These men had not been wearing the protective clothing of the Australian Defence Force but light cotton trousers, shorts and t-shirts. Thirty-one needed to be in hospital right away. Half of the worst cases were assessed "primary one", life in jeopardy. The skin was falling away from their faces, arms and legs. Jager and her colleagues worked with dwindling supplies of cling wrap, saline drip, morphine and pethidine. "There was this crying and moaning and the smell of burning skin and everything was – it was incomprehensible."

*

Kevin Rudd told the *Australian* a few days before the 2007 election that a Labor government would be willing to take the ultimate action against refugee boats: force them back to Indonesia. He knows there is a large domestic constituency for such talk, a constituency Tony Abbott addressed in Darwin last week when he declared: "An effective border protection policy requires … being prepared, under the right circumstances, to turn around the boats."

Chief among many factors in stopping the boats under Howard was forcing them back. The navy loathes these operations. They are violent. The usual response of asylum seekers is sabotage. In 2001, the navy was accused of using electric cattle prods to compel returns. Three refugees disappeared into the sea when SIEV 7 was successfully forced back to the island of Roti. A few weeks later, two women drowned when SIEV 10 was sabotaged to prevent its return. The 2001 operation put Australian sailors at terrible risk, cost lives and sent about 650 refugees back to Indonesia. A decade later, the fear of being forced back continues to hover over the refugee boats.

"There is scope under the operation order to do that, even still," Westcott told the investigating police. But it's not up to the military. The fate of the boats is decided in Canberra. "The decision is made certainly no lower than the defence minister. My understanding is prime minister and cabinet." While that happens, military personnel out in the Indian Ocean must maintain an air of deliberate ambiguity. The official protocol reads: "Upon boarding, officers inform potential irregular immigrants that they will be taken to speak with Australian officials, and this may take several days to accomplish." Most boat people only discover they have reached Australia when they arrive under the cliffs of Christmas Island.

Addressing the coroner last Thursday, Walsh argued: "The explosion might well have been avoided if … the passengers were simply and clearly informed that they were not going to be returned to Indonesia and that they would be taken to Australia, and this message was reinforced particularly at the time of handover to HMAS *Childers*."

Operation Resolute will no longer use the inflammatory K-6-4 notice ("You should now consider immediately returning to Indonesia …"), but the fifty-nine recommendations for reform made by the high-level military inquiry into the SIEV 36 debacle do not include scrapping the deliberately ambiguous protocols that keep wide open the option to force boats back to Indonesia. This week the navy was touting the friendliness and clarity of new cards in many languages to be presented in future to crews and boat people when SIEVs are seized. But the key formula is unchanged: "Please remain calm and do as we ask. We will take you to Australian officials who will listen to you. This may take several days. Please be patient."

*

The *Childers* set out for Darwin with the worst burns cases at 9.58 am. The slower *Albany* would spend another hour searching for the bodies that were never found. Facing Westcott was a daunting 725-kilometre voyage at top speed. "I was convinced I was going to lose people." Jager had the same thought. She told the doctor: "Half of them are going to die." But someone at NORCOM was thinking. "That's when it became pretty amazing to be part of the ADF," Westcott said. "I got a phone call to say, 'Righto, there's a ship or offshore gas station, OGI, which has been briefed. If you can get your casualties to her, we can get helos out to her. Check the position.' That was only ninety miles away. So … instead of being twenty-five hours from hope, I was about an hour and a quarter away."

In Perth, Colin Barnett was making hay with the story. "What I think is clear is the refugees spread petrol on their boat," he announced. "Whether they ignited it or it just ignited is unknown at this stage. But clearly that caused a major explosion." All the home affairs minister Bob Debus would say was: "It is clearly a possibility."

At 2.14 pm the *Childers* reached *Front Puffin*, a tanker moored permanently in the Timor Sea. The first casualties were lifted off in a basket at 2.36 pm. Once again the operation was blessed by the weather. "If it was anything other than glassy calm … I would've been trying to work out how the hell to get injured people craned up forty feet of steel." The *Albany* arrived with its casualties. About sunset, the first helicopter appeared with another eight doctors on board. The crane worked into the night. Westcott said: "It just became a long slow process."

Jager was ordered to stop. "I was told that I was fatigued, I was hurt, that I had to sit down. But I wanted to see the end of it. I wanted to make sure that every single one of these last [unauthorised arrivals] got on board a helicopter so they could get some help."

Her work done, she went below for a shower just as the *Childers* was about to pull clear of the rig at eight o'clock. "I can remember being in the shower. You've got no idea how small these showers are. We were still alongside the rig 'cause I could still feel them bashing alongside the rig … I can remember then feeling the calm of taking off. You could feel the engines going …"

MAY 2010

The bravery of Sharon Jager, Matthew Keogh and Dean Faunt was especially commended by the Northern Territory coroner Greg Cavanagh when he delivered an unsparing assessment of the navy's failures: to find and secure thirty or forty litres of petrol on the boat, to confiscate matches and lighters, and to reassure the refugees of their destination. The warning notice – "the catalyst for the unrest" – should never have been served: "Although it may have been mandated, clearly it was inappropriate in the circumstances."

Cavanagh found the passengers and crew had known of a plan that morning to incapacitate the boat. But that's all it was: "I accept that whoever started the fire did not expect that an explosion would occur. What was intended was that a fire be started so that the boat would be crippled and they would be taken off the vessel and taken to Australia." He was unable to find who lit the match, not least because the asylum seekers "colluded with each other and decided as a group to lie to this Inquest". He found the Indonesian crew had also sabotaged the engine by pouring salt into the petrol tank. He remarked on the irony that had the person responsible for the explosion known the engine had been sabotaged, "he may not have set fire to the boat".

Apart from recommending a little "flexibility" in the navy's policy of first saving their own, Cavanagh commended the courage and determination of all the Australian personnel once the boat exploded: "I find that there is nothing about the rescue process which should be criticised in the circumstances of this case." The navy took things a step further: awarding medals to everyone involved in the SIEV 36 operation, including those whose job it was to search the forward hold for petrol. Receiving her Chief of the Defence Force Commendation in May, Jager said: "I have kept to myself as much as I can so I can deal with it within myself. We are all trying to deal with it every day and move on."

All the asylum seekers who survived the explosion were given refugee protection. Many are still dealing with horrific burns. One is facing trial in Darwin: Arman Ali Brahimi was charged with two counts of obstructing the sailors who struggled to seize his lighter in the moments before the explosion. If sentenced to more than twelve months' jail, Brahimi will lose his visa. The two Indonesian crew are serving five years for people smuggling.

22.

MY LOVE OF DRUGS NOVEMBER 2010

"What's wrong with taking drugs?" I asked. "This is a personal question now." I was sitting on the little stage at Gleebooks in Glebe losing my temper with ABC journalist Peter Lloyd. The poor bastard had endured months of imprisonment in Singapore for possessing half a gram of ice and written a fine book about his ordeal. But I felt there was a false note at the heart of *Inside Story*: he wouldn't admit he had enjoyed drugs. Over and again he used the earnest formulation that they were his way of dealing with the stress of covering grisly stories in Asia.

He replied: "I've got to be cautious answering that question in a culture, speaking of Australia, where I've noticed since being back after seven years away there is a very easy step from that question to moral panic. In my case drugs was an opportunity event that satisfied a need in me to be happy. To get happier from a depressed state that had been going on for a long time. It's for others to explain why they do it and I wouldn't want to be the one who jumps in here and does it. You go first."

"Well, I will." I was suddenly furious. This was Sydney, not Singapore. Sure, there was an ABC crew filming our exchange for *Big Ideas*, but weren't we free to speak in this country? Hadn't Peter Lloyd earned the right to be absolutely candid by enduring six unnecessary months in Tanah Merah prison? Yet here he was, as wary of talking as if he were still in the dock. "I've had a lot of fun on drugs," I answered. "I've had a lot of marvellous experiences. I've danced a lot. I've had a great time. I'm not ashamed of it. And I don't see what's wrong with it."

"I look forward to reading this in tomorrow's *Australian*."

"No doubt one day it will be there."

"It won't be too long," Lloyd quipped. "There's a couple of hours till deadline."

I wasn't in the mood for jokes. "This is an experience that I've had and you've had in Singapore, and that is absolutely typical mainstream Australian experience."

Lloyd hinted that the problem was ice. It was easier to talk about ecstasy, cocaine and marijuana. "I'll go back to university and confess I tried very hard at university to smoke marijuana and it made me absolutely puke. I was violently green from the beginning. I just never became friends with it."

I said: "It is a deeply troubling issue of public administration, law and of justice. It's part, in this country, of a failed effort around the world to stop the drug trade. It fails. But why can't we speak frankly about this, frankly from our own experiences, and frankly about the impact on the law and this country of what seems to me to be the utterly failed war on drugs?"

"Take News Limited out of the equation and you probably can talk about it fairly," Lloyd replied. "The *Daily Telegraph* and the rest of that corporation's newspapers are the driving force behind moral panic in this country. Join with them commercial television: Channel 7, Channel 9 and Channel 10. I've worked at two of those places. They drive moral panic and the agenda they have is set by the *Daily Telegraph* and the *Herald Sun* in Melbourne. Take them out of the equation or stop listening to them – if politicians would stop listening to them – then we wouldn't have the moral panic we're talking about."

As I was speaking I knew I'd dealt myself back into a story I hadn't covered for years. When I came back to newspapers in the mid-1990s after a long time away in television and writing books, the war on drugs seemed waiting for me. I reported it for a decade.

1994: On sale around the world, *E is for Ecstasy* is banned in Australia. Why? Because new censorship codes are riddled with the rhetoric of the war on drugs. Books and films can be banned for giving "detailed instruction in drug misuse" or for showing drugs and addiction "in such a way that they offend against the standards of morality, decency and general propriety generally accepted by reasonable adults".

1994 to 1997: Supreme Court judge James Wood's royal commission lays bare systemic corruption of the NSW police force by the drug trade. Sydney laps it up: great characters, earthy dialogue, tears and laughter, hidden cameras, tough arguments for reform and then … drug policy stays much the same. Wood's cautious suggestions for decriminalisation are brushed aside by the NSW premier Bob Carr.

1996: Bill Clinton's chief international drugs enforcer Bob Gelbard flies in to prevent the Australian Capital Territory prescribing heroin to addicts. He threatens Tasmania's legal and lucrative poppy-growing industry should the ACT trial go ahead. His threats are part of an old pattern of US diplomats working around the globe to stymie decriminalisation. The ACT heroin trial never happens.

1999: Cardinal George Pell quashes plans by the Sisters of Charity to open a safe injecting room at St Vincent's Hospital in Darlinghurst, Sydney. "The only appropriate Catholic response," he calls it. "The Catholic Church teaches that taking drugs is wrong because it harms the body, dulls the mind, diminishes self-control, and ultimately it can and does kill."

2001: NSW Director of Public Prosecutions Nicholas Cowdery QC attacks the "law and order auctions" held in every state election campaign. "My view is that the so-called war on drugs is going the way of most other wars. It's costing time, it's costing money, it's costing lives, it's achieving nothing other than creating more crime, which I then have to prosecute."

2001: Fresh powers for the sniffer dogs of Sydney.

2005: Australian-raised Nguyen Tuong Van faces execution in Singapore for running drugs. Our hearts are hard. Talkback is loud in its admiration for Singapore. A couple of nights before the kid's death, Roy Morgan Research finds 47 per cent of us believe he should hang. Women, the young and Labor voters are not so keen, but a great swathe of the nation wants Nguyen to die for trying to smuggle half a kilo of heroin to Melbourne.

*

America began its crusade to rid the world of opiates after its conquest of the Philippines in 1898 and the discovery that opium smuggling was rife in the islands. A passionate fear of opium had grown up in the US after the Californian gold rushes and this was mixed up with distaste for the Chinese who smoked the stuff. Race was, and remains, a potent element in this enduring moral panic. In the first years of the new century America set out on a mission to rid the world, especially the white world, of the scourge of opium. Not much might have come of this but a few years later Britain elected its first anti-opium government. After centuries of protecting the trade – and recently fighting a war to force the drug into China – Britain was now keen to see the trade brought under control. At a conference called by America in Shanghai in 1909, a number of powers signed up to the crusade. Every treaty since has, in a sense, been a forlorn attempt to make that Shanghai strategy work.

Australia was locked into the system after World War One by the Treaty of Versailles. In Geneva a few years later we joined the rest of the world in putting cannabis – the oldest continuously used drug on earth – on the banned list. Once available over the counter here as Cigares de Joy, cannabis had just about disappeared from our streets by the time we signed this Geneva convention. Perversely, the fact that the drug problem didn't seem to affect Australia much made us even happier to sign these treaties. In *From Mr Sin to Mr Big*, the academic lawyer Desmond Manderson wrote: "Australia was blown along by the winds of international opinion without genuine commitment or thought."

The United Nations took over from the League of Nations but America continued to drive the cause of drug eradication. As the conventions grew tougher, Australia kept signing them. We pushed back only once. After World War Two, the United States was determined to wipe out opium's powerful derivative heroin by banning its use even as medicine. At the time, heroin was a standard ingredient in cough medicine and the best painkiller available. Australian doctors resisted but were brought into line by Canberra. In Britain, a powerful counterattack by the medical profession preserved their right to prescribe heroin to addicts. That practice survives – heavily circumscribed – even today.

Australia still had no heroin problem of its own. Then the Vietnam War started winding down and the American Drug Enforcement Agency very successfully stopped heroin following the troops home. "The DEA in effect compelled the syndicates to sell heroin originally produced for American addicts in alternative markets," wrote Alfred McCoy in *Drug Traffic: Narcotics and Organized Crime in Australia*. "In short, the DEA simply diverted South-East Asian heroin from the US into European and Australian markets, evidence for what we have called the iron law of the international drug trade." Heroin washed into Australia and the cycle began of crime, corruption, addiction and death. The treaties we had entered into did little to inhibit supply and left us unable to take any radical initiative to cope with the unfolding disaster. Yet in 1992 we ratified another of these Shanghai-style agreements, the United Nations Convention Against Illicit Traffic in Narcotic Drugs and Psychotropic Substances, which made the most sweeping promises yet to work towards the complete and unqualified prohibition of drugs.

It's not going well. Here's a snapshot courtesy of the 2011 *World Drug Report* of the UN Office on Drugs and Crime: the tonnage of cannabis being grown is unmeasurable; opium production was sharply down in 2010 to about 5000 tonnes because of disease in the Afghanistan poppy fields; plantings in Myanmar are picking up the slack; 375 tonnes of heroin hit the markets generating about US$70 billion revenue for traffickers; the area under coca has declined a little to about 150,000 hectares producing 800 tonnes of cocaine; the global manufacture of ecstasy, amphetamines and ice is increasing despite huge seizures of precursor chemicals. The world isn't losing its taste for drugs: "The overall number of drug users appears to have increased over the last decade, from 180 to some 210 million people."

More than 7 million of those live, work and love in Australia. We know that because the Australian Institute of Health and Welfare conducts a huge survey of our drug habits every three years. The latest results are based on fat questionnaires completed by 26,000 households in the middle of 2010. The bad news here for the UN is that illicit drug use is on the rise once again in this country. Marijuana is by far the most popular drug: over 7 million Australians have tried it at some point in their lifetime. Ecstasy is our number two drug of choice: 2 million of us have given it a go and another half a million of us have used the dance drugs GHB and ketamine. By the time Australians turn twenty, 37 per cent of us have already tried illicit drugs and that figure rises to a shade under 60 per cent by the time we turn forty. That's mainstream. The questionnaires reveal that in any given week, a million of us are smoking, popping or shooting up. The authors warn these figures are almost certainly too low: "It is known from past studies of alcohol and tobacco consumption that respondents tend to underestimate actual consumption levels."

We have a taste for the stuff. "Privately, we are a nation of drunks, junkies and pill-poppers, and we always have been," argues Craig Fry of Melbourne University. Yet our enthusiasm for drugs does not translate into fervour for reform. "Publicly, the dominant community attitude on drugs in Australia is disapproval and fear, and this feeling seems to be growing." The figures in the latest institute survey bear Fry out. They show us implacably hostile to dealers and suppliers: 80 per cent of us would like even harsher punishment for those caught pushing heroin, cocaine, amphetamines and ecstasy. Support for legalising those drugs doesn't reach double figures. Even though we are far more relaxed about marijuana, only 25 per cent of us actually want to see it legalised. And for a nation that consumes drugs so eagerly, we remain surprisingly keen to see drug users punished. Half the community believes ecstasy and heroin users should still be sent to jail or fined or made to do community service. Again we are more relaxed about dope smokers – two-thirds of us want them hit with no more than a caution or an education program – but the default position of the nation remains: drugs are criminal.

It might seem a mystery in the face of such figures that we have softened as much as we have the old hard line on drugs. But change was driven from above, not below, by AIDS and the crippling cost of prisons. For a while we were at the forefront of developing harm minimisation strategies: needle exchanges, methadone, drug courts, allowing smokers to grow a few plants, and a safe injection room in Sydney. Then the drive for reform stalled in the face of relentless opposition from the Coalition, some churches and News Limited. Between them they have pulled off a triumph of fear over fact. Scientists, police, lawyers and directors of public prosecution can write reports and plead for change but public debate on the subject remains as primitive as ever. The slope is slippery; the flood is coming; peril is everywhere. After all these years we are still dealing with the basics – over and over again. That's no accident. It's what panic does. It traps us in kindergarten.

*

Only the Greens have had, for a time, the courage to campaign for drug reform. But the rhetoric of their 2001 "Drugs and Addiction" platform was frankly bizarre:

> In a democratic society in which diversity is accepted, each person has the opportunity to achieve personal fulfilment. It is understood that the means and aims of fulfilment may vary between people at different stages of their lives and may, for some people at particular times, involve the use of drugs.

The party pledged to work towards the decriminalisation of drugs. All drugs would be reclassified according to their "known health effects". A pilot program would test the effectiveness of prescribing heroin to addicts. Cannabis and perhaps ecstasy would be made available at "appropriate venues" under strict regulation:

> The Australian Greens believe that softer, less addictive drugs should be more freely available as in the Netherlands model, as

research shows that such availability mitigates against the use of hard drugs.

The policy caused no stir. For a couple of years the press regarded it as rather daffy and had almost nothing to say about the Greens' hopes for drug reform. Then came the 2003 NSW election campaign. In that dull contest, the only remotely interesting question was whether the Greens might for the first time win a seat in the state's lower house. News Limited appeared determined to prevent this happening and on the weekend of Mardi Gras the *Sunday Telegraph* fired a page-one broadside: "Ecstasy Over the Counter – Revealed: The Greens' Hidden Policy". That the "hidden" policy was on the party's website and had been relaunched only a few days before by its co-author, upper house MP Lee Rhiannon, were details the paper missed in its determination to scare New South Wales.

A barrage of fear followed from all sides. "I am deeply opposed to the greater ongoing use by Australians of amphetamines and ecstasy," declared the premier Bob Carr. "I don't want us to be a pill-popping society with youngsters boiling their brains on amphetamines and marijuana." John Howard denounced the Greens' policy as irresponsible. The Liberals assailed Labor as well as the Greens for being "soft" on drugs, a strategy designed to target a dozen marginal seats with numbers of either Greens or One Nation voters. Greens candidate Jamie Parker lost on polling day and the party purity of the Legislative Assembly of New South Wales was preserved for another eight years.

From this point, their drugs policy dogged the Greens. It wasn't like trying to save the Franklin: the party had no sheltering support from a mass movement demanding change. No one marched in the streets for dope cafes and heroin prescription. There were no blockades to keep the cause alive. Supporters were invisible and opponents were everywhere, recasting the party's high hopes in the most frightening terms. As the Melbourne *Herald Sun* showed in the early stages of the 2004 federal election campaign, a lot of damage could be done with a few adjectives:

> Ecstasy and other illegal drugs would be supplied over the counter to young users in a radical policy framed by Senator Bob Brown's Greens. The Greens manifesto backs official supply of the dangerous drug ecstasy as well as state-sanctioned heroin and marijuana sales at what it calls appropriate venues.

Next day, Brown engaged in heated exchanges with News Limited journalists. "Do you think we should not be investigating alternatives to the existing policy, which has led to the death of fifteen young Australians?" he asked. "I don't back illegal drug traders. I don't back open slather, over-the-counter ecstasy promotion." Brown compelled the Christian lobby group Family First to withdraw a "false, defamatory and misleading" television campaign which claimed the Greens wanted to legalise all hard drugs. Behind this relentless focus on drugs was a much-feared possibility that the elections would deliver the Greens the balance of power in the Senate. Control of the upper house passed, in the end, to Howard. The Greens would have to wait another six years.

The party couldn't take the pain. The Greens' national conference in Hobart in early 2006 saw "a fight for the party's soul" between the ideologues of New South Wales led by Rhiannon and the pragmatists of Tasmania led by Brown. The pragmatists won and the "Drugs and Addiction" policy was stripped of its fuzzy New Age rhetoric and its most controversial provisions: there would now be no decriminalisation and no Amsterdam-style cafes. Brown announced: "The contentious past proposals to investigate options for the regulated supply of marijuana and ecstasy have gone." But the party continued to stand by its policy of giving counselling and treatment rather than fines and jail terms to drug users. It also remained policy to hold "a rigorous scientific trial" of heroin prescription.

Retreat earned the party no favours. The Victorian state elections later that year saw attacks from Labor, the Coalition and News Limited continuing unabated. "Greens new policy would mean … Addicts get free drugs" was the *Herald Sun's* opening salvo:

> Hardcore heroin addicts would be given taxpayer-funded drugs under a controversial policy unveiled by the Greens … the party that could win the balance of power in the Upper House on November 25 …

The *Australian* attacked on a broader front, denouncing the whole "short-sighted" policy of harm minimisation and especially the plans to follow Sydney's lead and open a safe injecting room in central Melbourne:

> If there is one positive to the Victorian Greens' drugs proposal, it is this: the party, smelling success at the next election, has become cocky enough to reveal its real agenda to voters. Come November, it will be interesting to see how inner-city voters sympathetic to the Greens feel about the party now that its policies threaten to land, quite literally, on their doorsteps. The problem of drug abuse requires co-ordinated efforts of law enforcement and mental health authorities and rehabilitation centres, not policies that will lock addicts in their own taxpayer-funded hells.

Labor and the Coalition both pledged to stay tough on drugs but this time the strategy to box in the Greens didn't entirely succeed. The party ended up with the balance of power in the new Legislative Council, yet the worst fears of its opponents went unrealised: there was no drug reform dividend. Even now Victoria has no safe injecting room.

These days the Greens also hold the balance of power in Canberra but the party long ago lost its enthusiasm for drug reform. It's too hard, too damaging. Julia Gillard did not have to promise heroin trials to win the Greens' support for her government. And if drugs are mentioned anymore by the party's detractors, they come way down the list of terrifying changes these renegades are accused of trying to force on Australia – somewhere after the carbon tax, same-sex marriage, death duties, ending mandatory detention for boat people and banning junk food advertising on television. On all sides of the political divide these days, drug reform is dead.

*

As I wandered out of Gleebooks that night, leaving Peter Lloyd upstairs signing copies of *Inside Story*, I was counting off in my mind the politicians who have confessed, as I had, to taking drugs. Bill Clinton in 1992 was not the first but remains the funniest: "I didn't inhale and I didn't try it again." It takes a spoilsport like Christopher Hitchens to write of his fellow Oxford student:

> He has always been allergic to smoke and he preferred, like many another marijuana enthusiast, to take his dope in the form of large handfuls of cookies and brownies.

Barack Obama inhaled: "Frequently. That was the point." And in his memoirs he confessed to using a little "blow" as a young man.

That these confessions failed, even in moralising America, to bring down the roof is due only in part to the worldly good sense of an intelligent republic. More important, perhaps, is the fact that drugs cross the party divide. Republican former Speaker Newt Gingrich and presidential candidate John McCain have had to make the requisite admissions. George W. Bush confessed without specifying what was rumoured to be a long list of substances: "When I was young and irresponsible, I was young and irresponsible." Then he found Christ.

The honour of being the first Australian politician to come clean appears to go to Natasha Stott Despoja. Answering her party's "Youthpoll 97", the Democrat senator admitted smoking marijuana but declined to say if she had ever tried ecstasy or speed. "She didn't want to upset her mother with the answer," reported the Sydney *Daily Telegraph.* None of the many Australian politicians who have since made these ritual confessions have upset their mothers. The rules appear to be: neither admit you enjoyed what you did nor own up to anything but dope. "Never a drug heavier than marijuana," said Mark Latham while leading the Opposition. "I don't think it has done any harm. It was not a habit." Tony Abbott owned to puffing without inhaling. "In this matter, Bill Clinton and I have something in common." By 2004 the self-confessed dabblers among politicians included the Victorian premier Steve Bracks, the chief minister of the Northern Territory Clare Martin and the foreign affairs minister Alexander Downer. Fearing perhaps that all this coming out about drugs might make them seem somehow normal, the *Australian* urged its readers not to lose focus:

Soon there won't be a politician who grew up in the era of flares and sideburns whose recreational habits back then haven't been exposed … What makes all this even more trivial and pointless is that there is a marijuana problem we need to be focusing on in the Australia of 2004, not 1974 … So let's concentrate on the real drug issues now, and drop the national audit of who inhaled what 30 years ago. Besides, aren't some of the tabloid journalists who rush to ask the marijuana question also children of the last days of disco? They should pause before casting the first stone, in case they end up getting stoned themselves.

This was in the midst of ugly brawls over drugs in the 2004 Victorian state election. Bob Brown had by this time come out with his own rather bare confession: "When I was in London back in 1970, I did sit in a circle with some Eritrean students and puff on some marijuana, and I did inhale. But I haven't since."

So much and so little changed when John Howard made way for Kevin Rudd. No change on drugs. "I've always had a very tough line on this stuff – really, really hard line," the Labor leader said. "I'm in John Howard's camp on this one. We have a unity ticket." But Wayne Swan confessed to what the *Sunday Telegraph* called a "wild youth of sex and drugs". The new treasurer himself was more modest: "Like many people around that time I had partaken." Malcolm Turnbull was ready to answer the question the moment he became leader of the Opposition: "Smoked dope? Well, yes, I have." That made him the first Liberal Party leader to come clean, though of course he deplored the stuff: "I think it is a very serious drug and it is a drug we should strongly discourage." Turnbull flushed out Gillard next day. She was to become the nation's first prime minister to have admitted knowing the scalding, slightly nauseating taste of dope: "At university, tried it, didn't like it. I think probably many Australian adults would be able to make the same statement, so I don't think it matters one way or the other."

The *Sunday Telegraph* took a while to find my chat with Peter Lloyd on the ABC's website. The paper was alerted, it seems, by a mischievous inquiry from *Crikey*. I've no complaints: they gave me the lightest tickle on page three. Under the headline "My love of drugs" and a fuzzy snap of me looking heavenwards – perhaps in a state of bliss and perhaps in delusion – the paper reported:

> Journalist and author David Marr has advocated illegal drug use, saying taking illicit substances was "marvellous" and a "typical mainstream Australian experience". Marr, a Fairfax writer and former host of ABC TV's *Media Watch*, revealed his illegal drug use, adding: "I don't see what's wrong with it."

A week later they published this brief letter from me:

> The *Sunday Telegraph* made me sound as though I'm calling for an open slather on drugs. I'm not. I'm calling for an open debate on drug policy, a debate that draws on the experience – pro and con – of the six or seven million Australians who have tried recreational drugs.

23.

BELLING THE CAT 10 DECEMBER 2010

I know it's hard. I know it goes against the grain. But unless human rights advocates are willing to have an open brawl with their most effective opponents the hopes of a national charter – let alone a bill of rights – in Australia are doomed. It's time we were less polite; it's time to name the enemies of rights and identify their motives. It's time, as Cardinal George Pell is so fond of saying, to bell the cat.

"No reasonable person can object to the protection of rights," the academic Helen Irving suggested recently. "Those who question the bill of rights agenda are rarely contemptuous of rights … most are concerned, rather, about the best *means* of protecting rights." I have no doubt that's her position. But this long struggle is not driven by such abstract disputes. Opponents of bills and charters are tramping the corridors of Canberra and polishing opinion pieces for the *Australian* because most *do* object to the effective protection of rights. That is the point. It is time we said so. This is not a contest about ways and means but about outcomes.

Australia's failures to protect rights are now so many over so many years that the failure itself becomes a grimly interesting subject. We are a unique species: a people without national guarantees of free speech and freedom of assembly and due process. And after the failure of Frank Brennan's great national consultation on human rights, it seems we're going to stay that way for a long time. It makes us a species worth studying.

At every election for the last fifty years, Labor in Opposition has been promising a human rights act. But every new Labor government lets Australia down without a fight. Lionel Murphy's bill for which there were such high hopes died with the parliament in 1974. Gareth Evans's bill never made it to parliament. At least Lionel Bowen's bill was debated twenty-five years ago – probably the last full-scale human rights debate in the national parliament – but like all the others it was allowed to die. The modest proposals of the 1988 referendum were all lost. Today's attorney-general Robert McClelland set Brennan's team off on its national journey of exploration but Kevin Rudd ditched their recommendations in April without meeting their author and without a word of explanation.

This is national failure of a particularly interesting order. Elsewhere in the world in those fifty years, Britain, New Zealand and South Africa all signed up to rights regimes. God bless and preserve Canada: she signed up twice. That a charter is on the way in Tasmania, is secure in the ACT and shelters Victorians – at least for the time being – is entirely welcome. But despite all the hopes and campaigns of the last half-century, Australians remain uniquely exposed to rough treatment by bureaucrats and government. The polls say we want our rights better protected but failures on this front provoke little concern round the kitchen tables of the nation. We muddle through, hoping and trusting. It's the Australian way.

Post Brennan, the human rights bandwagon is going to have to stay under tarps in the garage for quite a while. A few useful ideas he proposed look like seeing the light of day. But an exercise of the Brennan kind, on that scale, can't be repeated for years. My advice – speaking as someone who did nothing useful during the Brennan process – is to use the time to make an unflinching appraisal of how these campaigns have been fought and should be fought. And we must begin by identifying our opponents: Liberal politicians, News Limited newspapers and the churches. The churches are crucial. One of the most highly placed human rights observers in this country told me: "If you could turn church leaders around, you'd turn the debate around. They give credibility to opposition."

Not all churches are the same, not all preachers and not all bishops. It makes no more sense to lump all Christians together than lump all nations into a single bloc. Some of the great human rights leaders of history were driven by the example of Christ to fight the slave trade, to lead the early trade union movement, to put their lives on the line for the civil liberties of American blacks and to agitate for the rights of refugees. Even Christian leaders who throw every argument they can muster at bills and charters see themselves as heirs to this great tradition. They can talk about human rights so beautifully they move us to tears. But in their book this should never allow the courts to trump the churches – or mosques and synagogues for that matter – on issues dear to conservative faiths.

The lists of issues are quite ecumenical. Brigadier (ret.) Jim Wallace of the Australian Christian Lobby deplores the prospect of courts deciding matters of life, sex, death and – here he shows his Protestant colours – pleasure. Wallace mocks the Bill of Rights: "In America, it has been successfully argued that naked dancing in bars is protected by the outer limits of the First Amendment because it is a form of sexual expression." Cardinal Pell has a somewhat longer list and his language is more elevated. He fears allowing "the secularist mindset" to call the shots on matters of "life, family, freedom of religion, discrimination and equality". They are issues better left to cardinals. Stripped of its gorgeous rhetoric and philosophical gravity, this is what used to be called a demarcation dispute.

Pell is keenly aware of the limits of rights protection in today's Australia. We are, he says, a pragmatic, moderate and politically sophisticated people with a bedrock commitment to the idea of a fair go. But in his 2008 essay "Four Fictions: An argument against a charter of rights" he acknowledges this isn't fail proof. "The asylum seeker issue highlights where the limits of the ethic of the fair-go among the majority can be encountered. I wonder about the consequences for Australian democracy if we were to suffer a major terrorist attack on our own soil ..." Yet he is not persuaded that fundamental guarantees are needed. In the end he is willing to see *all* rights exposed to uncertain protection rather than risk "what can happen when a charter of rights is interpreted from the premises of the secular mindset".

On democracy, these warriors of the collar can be as moving as they are on the subject of rights. Their big pitch to secular Australia is the need to protect the mainstream from unscrupulous moral minorities. Pell goes further. He detects a "suspicion of majority" among rights advocates that encourages contempt for democracy itself and contempt for the feelings of decent Australians. He writes: "It helps to understand the game that is afoot in the push for a charter of rights to consider the way 'the tyranny of the majority' is used to browbeat majority scepticism about minority agendas."

Statements like this are everywhere in the pages of the *Australian* and submissions to Brennan. Conservative politicians have been warning us about tyrannous minorities forever. It takes my mind back to the dark forebodings of One Nation in its heyday that by 2005 Australia would be ruled by lesbian robots of Chinese extraction with names like Poona Li Hung. But rights advocates bring some of this on themselves by too often talking only about protecting minorities. They matter of course: they are vulnerable and need protection. But the key to the worst excesses of government are the mad passions, the panics, that strip us all of rights. What is done to box in terrorists, defeat paedophiles and save us from invading hordes in little boats sailing down from the north is done to us all.

Pell couldn't have chosen a poorer example: same-sex marriage. "A minority of the homosexual minority," he writes, "are actively seeking to impose their redefinition of marriage on the rest of the population through spurious rights-claims and judicial fiat." Not so, George. Polls show conservative Christian teaching on contraception, abortion, cloning, chastity, divorce, homosexuality, euthanasia and gay marriage are all now – and most have been for some time – minority positions. Last month's Nielsen poll found only 37 per cent support for the Pell–Wallace position on same-sex marriage, with 6 per cent undecided and 57 per cent of us backing the right of blokes to marry each other. Let's bell this cat: conservative Christians do not want courts protecting rights because lobbying and influence offer their best hope of defending beliefs that are becoming increasingly distasteful to the Australian people.

There is a sharp focus to all of this. Ever since anti-discrimination laws first appeared in Australia thirty or forty years ago, the faiths have won exemptions to allow them to sack – or refuse to hire – adulterers, homosexuals, lesbians, single mothers and transsexuals. It is not a boutique issue. The faiths are big employers. Indeed, the Catholic Church is one of the biggest private employers in Australia and claims the right to vet the sexual morals even of the gardeners in hospital grounds. Across the schools, hospitals and welfare agencies of the faithful, applications are rebuffed, promotions are blocked, individuals are picked off and jobs are lost.

This privilege to punish sinners is by world standards remarkably broad and jealously guarded. It has survived challenges at something like a dozen inquiries over the past five or six years from human rights advocates, peak law bodies, gay and lesbian advocates and a handful of brave politicians. Church leaders make no secret of the fact that they oppose bills and charters of rights because they fear they will undermine the privileges they enjoy to hire and fire by light of virtue alone.

"There is no doubt about that," Jim Wallace told me. "This is an extremely important issue." The Anglicans agree: "We are concerned about the human rights and anti-discrimination lobby intruding too deeply into our organisations," spokesman Bishop Rob Forsyth explained. "That's why we react." The Catholics are of the same mind. Pell says: "There is no doubt that if Australia gets a charter of rights, upfront or by stealth, it will be used against religious schools, hospitals and charities by other people who don't like religious freedom and think it shouldn't be a human right … the target will be the protection in anti-discrimination laws that allow religious schools to exercise a preference in employment for people who share their faith."

None of that is hard to grasp: awful and comic, but not hard to understand. The churches and mosques and synagogues are fighting for their corner and enlisting the backing of conservative politicians on both sides of politics: politicians who agree with them, and politicians who don't have the stamina to stand up to them. This is an issue that spooks politicians. Grappling with preachers and imams complaining about threats to religious freedom is about the most distasteful contest a government can imagine. Rudd's wasn't even going to try.

But what's in it for a newspaper like the *Australian* to campaign against bills and charters of rights? Over in America there are calls this week for Julian Assange to be hunted down as if he were a terrorist. His supposed source, Corporal Bradley Manning, is being held, manacled and naked, in an isolation cell. The United States government is using its muscle to cut off money to Assange and has bludgeoned Amazon and other sites to cut their links to Wikileaks. But the *New York Times* goes on publishing the leaked documents because it has the First Amendment on its side. And despite the angry grandstanding of the Obama administration the *Times* can go on doing this by my estimate – for there are 250,000 documents in the pile – for the next twenty years.

Yet there are newspapers in this country which – like politicians and churchmen – would prefer to work in the world of lobbying, influence and back-room deals rather than have rights that can be enforced in court. So extraordinary. "Freedom of speech, already limited in Australia by hundreds of secrecy provisions, could be further threatened under a charter of rights," the *Australian* declared in one of its many editorials implacably hostile to the Brennan process. Pell is quoted with approval. The rise of Pauline Hanson is blamed on "a reaction to the rights agenda that flourished during the Fraser, Hawke and Keating years, fuelled by lawyers and urban elites". The key problem identified by the paper is the transfer of democratic responsibilities from politicians to judges:

> The logic of the charter lobby is that ordinary Australians sometimes make the wrong decisions when choosing their lawmakers. Instead of remedying these mistakes at the polls, the charter lobby would prefer to hand real power to wise, all-knowing judges who are far removed from the grubbiness of the political process. The arrogance of such an approach is exceeded only by its naivety …

And some big claims are made for the foresight of the delegates of the colonies who drafted the constitution:

As shadow Attorney-General Mr McClelland offered a one-word explanation for the decision by the founders not to include a bill of rights in the Constitution: bigotry. But the founders also had faith in the common law and its political culture. These are living legacies which have served the nation well.

The *Australian* is incontestably right on one point:

> Bill of rights advocates have suffered one defeat after another. They have executed a series of tactical retreats. After the political disasters and popular rejections of the 1980s most advocates gave up as too hard the notion of a constitutional bill of rights. What remains is a campaign for a statutory bill of rights.

The proposals in 1988 were so modest. As Helen Irving would ask: what reasonable person could object to such rights? Yet all three proposals – to extend trial by jury, confirm freedom of religion and make state governments pay fair compensation for properties they acquire – were lost overwhelmingly.

You know the score now: forty-four failures from fifty-two attempts to change the constitution. It's a result to make us look at ourselves. The lesson we are supposed to draw from all of those defeats is that Australians hate change, or at least hate to change the constitution. That's not untrue. But the deeper lesson is that contrary to our larrikin myths we have a deep respect for authority. Much that is wonderful about life in this country is wrapped up in the contradiction between who we think we are and who we really are: a tractable, law-abiding people who may loathe politicians but respect authority. So when it comes to changing the constitution – or any of our institutions – we rarely move unless our leaders speak as one and reassure us it's time to change. This isn't evidence we love the constitution so much as deeply trust authority.

The unremarkable proposals of 1988 went down in flames because the Coalition campaigned against them. Not long afterwards I found myself spending a pleasant day at leisure in South Africa in the company of one of Howard's shadow cabinet, Michael Wooldridge. I was still a bit narky about the outcome of the referendums and over lunch asked him why Howard had also opposed a constitutional change that would rid Australia forever of gerrymanders, a curse that had so often worked against the Liberal Party. We couldn't support that, Wooldridge explained, because it would mean losing our majority in the upper house of Western Australia. Our leaders divided and Australia delivered a 62 per cent "no" vote.

As someone who still hopes for constitutionally embedded rights along American lines, I was disappointed that Brennan was only allowed to look at the pros and cons of a statutory charter: a law directing judges to give proper weight to human rights but without the power to strike down laws that violate those rights. If this pre-emptive buckle was designed to disarm critics, it didn't work. Churchmen, politicians and News Limited mastheads simply ignored the distinction between bills and charters. They stayed angry and they carried on.

But hobbling Brennan did acknowledge, perhaps wisely, that the times are not right for the huge struggle it would take to bolt rights into the constitution. No one should doubt how hard that exercise is. History tells us such guarantees are only made after national upheavals we would not wish on this country. Look at the list: the US First Amendment after a war of independence; The Declaration of the Rights of Man after the French revolution (and that one didn't last); the European Convention on Human Rights after the slaughter of World War Two; and South Africa's Bill of Rights after the long nightmare of Apartheid.

Australia's best opportunity for securing bedrock rights in the constitution came and went one day in February 1898. Whether we know it or not, rights advocates are still picking around in the wreckage of that single day in the life of the Australasian Federal Convention. Apart from anything, it was staggeringly hot: forty degrees in the shade when the overdressed delegates gathered in the Legislative Assembly of the Victorian parliament. As fires raged through the Grampians and smoke obscured the sun, Australia's best hopes of a bill of rights were burnt to a crisp.

According to the legend, this is the point at which an emerging Australia rejected American ways and stuck to its British guns, turning its back on the allure of constitutional rights in order to express what the *Australian* called "faith in the common law and its political culture". Sir Owen Dixon and Sir Robert Menzies sang this song particularly when lecturing Americans on the drawbacks of their own constitution. In his rough, democratic accent Michael McHugh belted out the same refrain in *Australian Capital Television v. The Commonwealth*:

> The makers of the Constitution … rejected the United States example of a Bill of Rights to protect the people of the Commonwealth against the abuse of governmental power … because they believed in the efficacy of the two institutions which formed the basis of the Constitution of Great Britain and the Australian colonies – representative government and responsible government …

But this is an invention. Read the transcript of that day's debates and you find no such high-flown considerations in the air. No hymns were sung to British ways. Not even the most conservative delegate – stand up if you can after a long lunch, Sir George Reid – attacked the theory of allowing courts to set limits to the exercise of government power. Something else entirely was in the air.

A bit of history: at earlier conventions the idea had been put forward of incorporating into our constitution something along the lines of America's Fourteenth Amendment that guarantees due process and equal protection of the laws to all people in the United States. The idea had caused little controversy at first but its enemies, led by Isaac Isaacs, were waiting to pounce in Melbourne. It's a strange reflection that the leaders of the contest that day – in whose shadows we still work – were both Australian sons of persecuted peoples: Isaacs the brilliant, tedious, dogmatic child of a Polish tailor and Richard O'Connor the charming son of an Irish librarian. Isaacs couldn't abide the idea proposed but O'Connor begged the delegates to put into the constitution they were drafting, "a guarantee for all time for the citizens of the Commonwealth that they shall be treated according to what we recognise to be the principles of justice and equality".

The forty-two delegates growled and sniped for an hour, broke for lunch and came back – clearly in a foul mood – to shred that rights initiative in less than twenty minutes. First went the notion that "a state shall not make or enforce any law abridging any privilege or immunity of citizens of the Commonwealth" and then hacked down were the words "nor shall a state deprive any person of life, liberty, or property without due process of law" and finally, by twenty-three votes to nineteen, the delegates ditched the formula "or deny to any person within its jurisdiction the equal protection of its laws".

This was not a contest in the abstract but the particular. The delegates were not voting against a constitution that contained rights but a constitution that contained *these* rights. Why? Because, as Isaacs put it so bluntly, their original object in America was "to protect the blacks", and in Australia they would "protect Chinamen in the same way". The delegates' vote was not about preserving British values down under, but the birth of a white man's Federation. Sir John Forrest belled that cat during that day's debate:

> It is of no use for us to shut our eyes to the fact that there is a great feeling all over Australia against the introduction of coloured persons. It goes without saying that we do not like to talk about it, but still it is so.

In fact, as the heat rose and lunch sat heavily the delegates became less and less inhibited. With the point-by-point endorsement of Isaacs, John Cockburn of South Australia spoke with the passion of a planter stripped of his slaves as he condemned the proposed guarantees as vindictive abroad and unnecessary at home:

> They were introduced, as an amendment, simply as a punishment to the Southern States for their attitude during the Civil War ... to inflict the grossest outrage which could be inflicted upon the Southern planters, by saying: "You shall not forbid the negro inhabitants to vote. We insist on their being placed on an equal footing in regard to the exercise of the franchise with yourselves." I do not believe that this amendment was ever legally carried ... it was simply forced on a recalcitrant people as a punishment for the part they took in the Civil War. We are not going to have a civil war here over a racial question.

So astonishingly racist was the temper of the discussion that day that no delegates even mentioned Aborigines. The guarantees they were shredding would have given citizenship, the vote and the equal protection of the law to Aborigines in perpetuity. But Aborigines were not in the delegates' minds. They were fighting these guarantees of rights in order to keep Chinese off the West Australian goldfields and out of the furniture factories of Victoria. Isaacs had the US case law at his fingertips: the Supreme Court in *Yick Wo v. Hopkins* had called on the "equal protection" provisions of the Fourteenth Amendment to strike down a San Francisco city ordinance designed to put out of business all the Chinese laundries in the city. Isaacs did not object to the validity of that ordinance being decided by the Supreme Court of the United States. His target was not an unelected judiciary. He just didn't want the same protection extended to the Chinese in Australia.

What's the point of this excursion into history? To bell yet another cat: opposition to judges safeguarding human rights is not in the DNA of this nation. That is an invention. The fight for entrenched rights is worth continuing. Success is still possible. Alas, what *is* in our DNA is a marked reluctance to extend rights to "coloured persons". Not for the last time we chose between race and rights in 1898 and the price we have all paid since is high. The politics of rights protection continues to be – and I seek the polite word – complicated by the fact that those who most obviously need protection in Australia these days aren't named McClelland or Evans or Ruddock but Haneef and al-Kateb and ul-Haque.

You have all heard of Murphy's Law: if something can go wrong it will go wrong. But scholars of the subject know there are many Murphy Laws and one of them – my favourite – is this: Whenever you want to do something, you have to do something else first. If we want effective national rights protection in this country we have to tackle two challenges: dealing with race and confronting the churches. Both are hard.

Isaac Isaacs lived a very long time: long enough to be our first native-born governor-general; long enough to watch the anti-German panic that swept Australia in World War One; long enough to watch civilised Germany descend into the Holocaust; and to witness Australia's appalling response in the late 1930s to Jewish refugees who wished to come here. Indeed, he lived long enough to see Allied victory in World War Two. I wonder if at any time in his late life he reflected on O'Connor's wise words on that afternoon in 1898 about the role the law might play in protecting us all – not minorities, but all – from the madness that sweeps nations from time to time. O'Connor said:

> We are making a constitution to endure, practically speaking, for all time. We do not know when some wave of popular feeling may lead a majority in the Parliament of a state to commit an injustice by passing a law that would deprive citizens of life, liberty, or property without due process of law. If no state does anything of the kind there will be no harm in this provision, but it is only right that this protection should be given to every citizen of the Commonwealth.

It wasn't. It still hasn't. And we still need it.

24.

THE DARK MATERIALS OCTOBER 2011

The Magi didn't linger. After presenting their gifts of gold, frankincense and myrrh they fled Bethlehem. Joseph was urged to do likewise by an angel appearing in a dream: "Arise and take the young child and his mother, and flee into Egypt, and be thou there until I bring thee word: for Herod will seek the young child to destroy him." Only Matthew tells this story and the details are sketchy but Christians regard the flight into Egypt as much a part of Christ's life as his birth, his teachings and his death. It's a subject of the oldest Christian art. Giotto paints the mother and child on a donkey, the father on foot, an angel hovering overhead, as the family heads south through the desert to safety.

I don't believe any of this: there were no Magi, no Christ and no flight from Herod. But it is the bedrock belief of the faithful that it was thanks to the generous refugee policies of Egypt that Christ survived to do his work on earth. So churches tend to be good on refugees while the record of Christian politicians is patchy. Between faith and action, they falter. This was to prove true of Tony Abbott, who found himself leader of the Opposition in the last weeks of 2009.

"I would be appalled," he says, "absolutely appalled, to think religion drove anyone's politics in a secular democracy like ours." Yet in the last half-century, no Australian political leader has so professed a Christian mission in public life as Tony Abbott. His guiding light is B.A. Santamaria, the trade union warrior who tore Labor apart in the 1950s in a hopeless quest to build a peasant, Christian society Down Under. Abbott told Paul Kelly years ago that this man and John Howard were his political mentors. Santa lived in a lather of panic about the end of the West, a looming catastrophe only God could reverse. Abbott put it a little differently: "Santa really saw politics as a religious vocation. He saw politics as a way of giving glory to God in the human world and I mean, without being preachy or anything like that, I think frankly that is important."

Abbott won the leadership after leading a backwoods revolt against an emissions trading scheme his own party had been about to ease through the Senate. He stopped it in its tracks. That day he began chanting his "giant big new tax on everything" mantra that would become so numbingly familiar as he threw himself body and soul into destroying Labor's efforts to combat global warming. First he would intimidate Rudd into taking his scheme off the table. Then, when the time came, he would relentlessly attack Julia Gillard's great big new carbon tax threatening to impoverish households, ruin industry and bankrupt the nation. He thrived on contradiction and was unembarrassed by his own wild exaggerations. To the business of inciting alarm he brought a certain earthy charm.

But how would he respond to the refugees? The fifty-first and fifty-second boats of the year were intercepted in Australian waters the week he seized the leadership of his party. Tamils were fleeing the bloody aftermath of the civil war in Sri Lanka. Violence continued to rage in Afghanistan and Iraq. Asylum seekers were heading for Australia in numbers not seen since John Howard stopped the *Tampa*. Though Christmas Island was overflowing, the immigration minister Chris Evans was still holding out against transferring any-one to the mainland. Tents were being pitched in the compounds of North West Point and seventy construction dongas were on their way from Alice Springs. Tamils and Afghans were recovering from injuries sustained in a short, wild brawl at North West Point. Seventy-eight Tamils had finally left the Australian customs vessel *Oceanic Viking* at the island of Bintan after a long and embarrassing standoff. Still unresolved was the fate of 250 more Tamils in the port of Merak sitting on a boat intercepted, on its way to Christmas Island, after a direct request by Kevin Rudd to President Susilo Bambang Yudhoyono. What might have been the start of a new era of co-operation between the countries had soured so badly that the president postponed a state visit to Australia. Despite all this, Rudd bestrode the politics of the nation. Polls in November 2009 put his approval rating at 68 per cent and though the boats had taken a little shine off that high figure, the damage was small.

So what would Abbott do? The drab efforts of his predecessor Malcolm Turnbull to take political advantage of the boats had produced a poor political dividend. Perhaps after thirty-five years of both sides of politics demonising refugees who make their way here by boat it was time for an entirely new approach. From the start there has been a constituency for dealing with these people decently. But if our leaders choose to bore down into the artesian basin of fear that lies under us, they can anytime. There have always been votes there. The choice is theirs.

*

Our leaders knew in the 1960s and 1970s they had to dismantle the White Australia policy or risk their country becoming a pariah state. Both sides knew they had to do the work carefully. What Harold Holt began, Gough Whitlam finished. Neither Labor nor the Liberals would take advantage of the deep hostility to this great change: as late as 1984, a McNair Anderson poll found 27 per cent of us wanted no immigrants from Asia. An Opposition can do a great deal of damage to a government by playing on the fears of a quarter of the electorate. But a truce was struck and it still holds fifty years later. When John Howard called for Asian immigration to be slowed in 1988, he lost the leadership of the Opposition. For a time it seemed his career was finished. It remains unthinkable today for a mainstream politician to call for a return to White Australia.

But at sunset on 26 April 1976 the battered *Kien Giang* anchored off the Darwin suburb of Nightcliff. The skipper had a little speech ready when an immigration officer came aboard next morning: "Welcome to my boat. My name is Lam Binh and these are my friends from South Vietnam and we would like permission to stay in Australia." The ditch had been crossed. That Lam Binh and his five crew had chosen to come here of their own accord violated the notion that once White Australia was gone the new people coming here would be chosen carefully: there would not be too many of them; they would be as much like us as possible; and they would fit in. Fifty-five boats over the next few years would bring a couple of thousand Vietnamese all the way down to Australia. Their refugee claims were impeccable and numbers tiny but their impact was profound. "They had not been processed thousands of kilometres away by skilful immigration officials," wrote the former diplomat Bruce Grant. "Reflecting population pressures and political turmoil near at hand, they simply turned up, uninvited, asking for refuge. For Australia, history and geography had merged, causing a shiver of apprehension."

Another truce was struck between the parties, this time a dark truce: not to contest but appease the fears the boats aroused. Politics didn't have to be played to the fearful. During this first wave of boats from 1976 to 1979, Morgan Gallup polls showed arresting levels of hostility: 20 per cent rising to 32 per cent of us wanted all boat people barred from Australia. But the same polls in the same years showed more than twice that number wanted at least some of these new and unwelcome arrivals to be allowed to settle here. The politicians and the parties had a choice, and they chose to play to the smaller constituency of fear. Whatever their differences, Labor and the Coalition have shared a common objective since 1976 of belittling boat people and working to stop their boats.

The language of "queue jumpers" and "illegals" and "coming in by the backdoor" was fashioned in the late 1970s. Instead of attempting to reconcile Australia to this novel but hardly unusual development, both sides of politics reinforced the vague but profound sense that for refugees to turn up in this way was a violation of the true order of things. It was by far the easier political path to take, and if they took it together they protected each other's flanks. So these first boat people were abused as interlopers. Vast holding camps were established in Malaysia. The navy fought what was called a "war on smugglers" out in the Indian Ocean. Malcolm Fraser bravely resettled nearly 100,000 Vietnamese here but he did all he possibly could to stop their boats reaching our shores.

I was a young journalist working on the *Bulletin* then and recognised the fears the boats provoked. I was taught as a kid that the sea protects us from the hordes to the north. In my mind's eye I see a canvas map on a classroom wall with pink for the empire and blue for those protective oceans around Australia. It was taken for granted that the poor people up there would want to live down here. They would not be led by armies and navies for they didn't have much in the way of military forces. They would invade, Dunkirk fashion, in little boats. Mine was not the last generation that could see a couple of hundred Afghans in a fishing boat as the advance party of unimaginable numbers: the vanguard of our destruction. It's a fear we've carried with us from the childhood of the nation.

In 1992, Labor made another bad decision. The boats had reappeared after nearly a decade's absence: one in 1989, two the following year and six each for the next two years. The numbers were tiny but so poisonous was the politics that Paul Keating's government bowed to an old ambition of the Department of Immigration to put into law the incarcerating of all boat people until either they are granted a visa or thrown out of the country. The truce with the Coalition held fast: they backed the plan. Gerry Hand was minister and his cabinet colleague Neal Blewett recorded in his diary: "Hand supported his proposals with his usual blend of vivid anecdotes about the wickedness of the boat people, their sinister manipulators (Chinese tongs this time) and attacks on the self righteous attitudes of churches and the do-gooders." Liberal dissenter Petro Georgiou says: "It was on the basis of such arguments that Australia, alone amongst democratic nations, established a mandatory detention system."

Expensive, cumbersome and damaging, mandatory detention has remained ever since as the politically reassuring face of a system built on fear which works, day in and day out, to reinforce those fears. That these "detention centres" are immigration prisons makes boat people look more than ever like criminals. That they overflow so quickly makes it seem Australia itself can't cope with refugee arrivals. That they empty so slowly leads, inevitably, to illness, riots, self-harm and suicide. As we watch television reports of camps in the desert burning, we ask ourselves: are these really the sort of people we want living among us?

"What was to unfold was a moral panic," says Georgiou, "a heightened, disproportionate concern with refugees and their targeting for increased hostility by sensational headlines and political demagogues." This second wave of boats found us markedly more hostile. Though by September 1993 a mere 2794 boat people had made their way to Australia, 44 per cent of us wanted every one of them "sent straight back where they come from despite what they say may happen to them". There were no political leaders urging calm; no calls for compassion except from lawyers and churches; no hope that the politics of the boats could focus on the better instincts of the somewhat more welcoming 46 per cent of us who wanted Australia to "detain and assess" these refugees crossing by boat.

Uncontested fears flourished first under Keating and then under Howard. A term of the truce between the parties seemed to be that neither party would move towards a more sympathetic under-standing of the boats. The pact that began by each party protecting the other now locked them together in common hostility. Through the 1990s, politicians across the spectrum joined in the persistent, low-level abuse of boat people as "queue jumpers" for not waiting in the camps and "illegals" for arriving without proper papers. Already Australians were wildly overestimating their numbers: an AGB McNair survey in June 1997 found the "best estimate" of three-quarters of us was an exaggeration, often a gross exaggera-tion, of the true figure: about 300 a year.

Then in 1999 boats began reaching Australia in truly large numbers: eighty-six of them carrying 3721 refugees. They would find no political allies of any consequence at the far end of their dangerous little journey. The dazzling redhead Pauline Hanson had formed her own One Nation Party and was clawing votes from the Coalition. But Howard must take most of the credit for what followed. He was unafraid to use race for political advantage. The most fearful Australians were his people and he was one of them. The ugly culture wars of this time were, more than anything, about winning the right to exploit race free of the constraints of "political correctness". So this immensely professional politician suddenly confronted with thousands of refugees arriving here by boat had no compunction about drawing on the deep fears of his country.

First he ramped up the language. To the old vocabulary he added a term plucked from the world of tariff reform. "Border protection" powerfully fused race fear with anxiety about the nation's security. Howard didn't invent the link between race and invasion: this is what focus groups, particularly on the fringes of big cities, were telling his people. Howard's genius was to find the language to accuse disorganised, exhausted people arriving in dribs and drabs at islands far out in the Indian Ocean of being a threat to the security of a heavily defended modern nation. Legislation in 1999 to give the navy fresh powers to stop and search refugee boats on the high seas was called the Border Protection Legislation Amendment Bill. Many "border protection" bills, task forces and commands would follow over the dozen years since. This overblown language of national defence remains fixed in law.

On a Saturday in April 1999, a boat carrying sixty Chinese from Fujian province beached at Scotts Head on the NSW north coast. They wandered out of the scrub, conspicuous figures in suits and ties to be rounded up swiftly by the local police. There being no pretence they were seeking refugee protection, all were deported to China within weeks. Though farcical, this episode marks a stage in the evolution of the abuse of boat people. After Scotts Head, the term "people smugglers" hitherto attached to scams that delivered dodgy asylum seekers to airports became attached to the crooks who delivered the real thing to Australia by boat. The man who did that work was the minister for immigration Philip Ruddock, who raged against the smugglers as sophisticated, obnoxious, unacceptable and the perpetrators of a "gruesome trade in human beings". He was not entirely wrong but he took no account of a long history of refugees being forced to pay criminals to escape persecution. Labor backed legislation rushed through parliament on 1 July to punish the smugglers savagely and severely limit the access of the smuggled to lawyers and the courts.

Ruddock set about stoking Australia's fears. When 1245 Iraqis and Afghans turned up in November 1999, he insisted another 10,000 from the Middle East were about to "assault" the nation's borders: "Whole villages are packing up and there is a pipeline. If it was a national emergency several weeks ago, it's gone up something like ten points on the Richter scale since then." He ridiculed the refugees: "When they arrive … they even have the audacity to ask for Pert 2-in-1 shampoo. They even have the audacity to say, 'We know we're entitled to medical care, gee look, the kids need orthodontic treatment now, can you effect it?'" In fact, the Howard government had moved by this time to strip boat people of most of the entitlements granted to refugees. This was a key policy of Hanson's One Nation Party: only temporary protection and no family reunions for boat people. Labor condemned this for a time but then fell quietly into line.

Panic forbids retreat. If there had been a political contest about the boats, measures which were merely punitive and doing nothing to stem the flow might have been done away with. Only the small voices of the Greens and Democrats questioned mandatory detention's purpose, barbarities and expense. But the boats kept coming, fuelling calls for yet tougher measures. Hanson, fresh from a triumph in Western Australia she was about to repeat in Queensland, launched her party's campaign in early 2001 with a call to push the boats back out to sea: "We go out, we meet them, we fill them up with fuel, fill them up with food, give them medical supplies and we say, 'Go that way.'" Six months later that was government policy. When the *Tampa* refused to sail away with the asylum seekers she had rescued from the Indian Ocean, Howard sent the SAS to occupy the ship and from this time directed the navy to try to force all refugee boats back to Indonesia. Australia was locked into a dangerous and hugely popular military operation against the refugees. Treating them as invaders made them look like invaders.

The language Howard and Ruddock used in these weeks was deliberate, outrageous and effective. Their hyperbole was questioned by human rights organisations and commentators, but those calls for calm had little traction. This was pure panic. People were seized by a perverse exhilaration in the face of exaggerated danger. There was, as in all panics, something real here: concern for the security of the nation. But the link between borders and boats was always bogus. When the World Trade Center was destroyed a fortnight into the operation, Howard and his defence minister Peter Reith linked the boats to terrorism. Howard: "Australia had no way to be certain terrorists, or people with terrorist links, were not among the asylum seekers trying to enter the country by boat from Indonesia." He had nothing to back this. His most senior security adviser, ASIO chief Dennis Richardson, would later describe the likelihood of terrorists coming by sea in this way as extremely remote. John Howard was deliberately inflaming fear, a fear we have yet to shake off.

The point of all this was to cause terrible damage to Labor. The party was split right down the middle: on one side were the progressives who found Howard's policies towards the boats abhorrent and on the other conservatives who saw them as a mark of core Australian values. This was a split the party had never addressed, hoping, it seemed, that time would see it fade away. Not so. And having sung the same tune as the Coalition for so long, Labor was in no position to find new policies to take to an election now only weeks away. So it could only protest at the government's more extreme language and propose, rather woefully, a coastguard be set up to patrol the north. When Labor's leader Kim Beazley rejected an early version of a new Border Protection Bill – which aimed to validate all that had been done to the *Tampa* and its cargo of refugees – Howard attacked him and his party viciously for failing the national interest. Labor took a huge hit in its working-class heartland where the Liberals handed out leaflets with a hard message: "The Howard Government is rock solid on protecting Australia's borders. Labor is soft on illegal immigrants."

Tampa time saw Australia in the grip of a classic panic. So hostile were we to boat people in those weeks that the constituency for turning back all their boats – last measured at 44 per cent in 1993 – rose as high as 77 per cent. Support for allowing at least some of the refugees ashore shrank in that same ACNielsen poll to a mere 18 per cent. All the polls showed Howard's handling of the crisis he created had Australia's overwhelming support: in the high 70 per cents. But once the panic passed, so did our confidence that all had been handled well in the heady weeks of late 2001. Three years down the track, Newspoll found support for Howard's *Tampa* strategy had more than halved to 35 per cent. The nation had second thoughts.

*

Who worries about the boats? The most hostile have always insisted their fears have nothing to do with race. Howard claimed Australia would be just as keen to turn back boats full of "white or Japanese, or North American" refugees. "It is a question of protecting our borders." The *Australian*'s Janet Albrechtsen takes the argument a few steps further. In a column in August 2011 she suggested talking race in this context is a "trick" the politically correct use to bully their opponents: "To close down discussion about, say, immigration or border control, you call your opponents racists and point to xenophobia in the community. Opponents are not just wrong, they're evil. Their views should not be aired in a civilised society."

That line requires some deliberate forgetting and a resolute lack of curiosity. It overlooks the deep history of White Australia, ignores the impact of Pauline Hanson and Howard's courting of her constituency and disregards findings by political analysts going back decades of xenophobia in marginal electorates. Mainstream Australia appears willing to admit what commentators find inadmissible: after the 2005 Cronulla riots, a Nielsen poll found 75 per cent of us willing to agree "there is underlying racism in Australia". Political scientists Murray Goot and Tim Sowerbutts have no doubt race fears lie behind our hostility to the boats: "We are certain it would have been very different had the asylum seekers been 'white.'" But, crunching figures from the 2001 Australian Election Study, they conclude that more than race is at work here. They identified two constituencies driving the hostility: those who see boat people as rule breakers – "queue jumpers" and "illegals" – and those who are hostile to their ethnicity: "The popular rejection of asylum seekers is a product of both sets of values: for the most part, opposition to immigration, especially from the Middle East, and opposition to Aboriginal land rights; but also a concern about crime and the need for harsher punishments, including the re-introduction of the death penalty."

This is about race and the manipulation of the fears of a minority of us – perhaps a third – who are older and not so well educated and tend to live on the fringes of big cities, who vote for both Labor and for the Coalition but whose hostility is such that they may switch their votes to the party offering more vigorous policing of immigrants and refugees. Their fears focus on the boats. Poll after poll has demonstrated this over the years. The Scanlon Foundation's latest social cohesion survey taken in mid-2011 found 73 per cent of us feel "positive or very positive" towards refugees we select and bring here from abroad. That figure is about as good as it gets in the world. We're almost as happy to bring these "good" refugees in as we are to welcome skilled immigrants to our shores. By contrast, only 22 per cent of us believe boat people should ever be allowed to settle in Australia. This is about the fear of dusky people coming here uninvited by boat. And though these fears are associated with old Australia, there is no evidence that they are dying out.

*

Kevin Rudd could promise reform in 2007 because the boats had all but disappeared and the detention system was mired in scandal. The most damaging of these outrages was the discovery of deeply disturbed Cornelia Rau – German by birth but a permanent resident of Australia since childhood – held illegally in Baxter Detention Centre while in desperate need of medical attention. A Nielsen poll taken in the aftermath of her release found 42 per cent of us thought detention too harsh. The following year polls showed a similarly strong – though minority – constituency for ending the Pacific Solution: 40 per cent of us opposed the transfer of boat people "to offshore centres such as Nauru or Christmas Island while their claims are assessed". These were figures Rudd might have built on had he the courage to reshape the system. Instead, he played to both sides of his deeply divided party: he would speed up processing, abolish temporary protection visas and end the Pacific Solution. Any new boats and refugees would be dealt with far away on Christmas Island. As so often the case with Rudd, the aim was to skate through, rather than address, the fundamental problem: mandatory detention.

Peace reigned for a few months. Compassion was in vogue. The Coalition under Brendan Nelson signed up to Labor's reforms. But in September 2008 the first of half a dozen boats appeared and by December the new Liberal leader Malcolm Turnbull was talking about a "real problem" with border protection. Once again, the Coalition was using the boats as a political weapon against Labor. As arrivals picked up pace in 2009, Turnbull intensified his attacks on reforms now entirely disowned by the Opposition: "There is no doubt that the impression has been created that we are more accommodating or taking a less hard line towards people smuggling than we had in the past." SIEV 36 blew itself to smithereens in April and old warriors of the Howard years, galvanised by the disaster, began banging on once more about tougher border protection. But Australia wasn't too perturbed. Pollsters in the field that weekend found little support for tougher measures and not much optimism that they would work: Newspoll found approval and disapproval of the government's handling of the boats was evenly balanced and 57 per cent of those quizzed thought tighter immigration laws would make little difference to boat arrivals.

As the boats came back that year in numbers not seen since Howard's time, Turnbull was facing criticism inside the party for failing to "cut through" on the issue. Rudd was talking tough, denouncing the smugglers and still managing to quarantine the problem out on Christmas Island. In October Paul Maley analysed the ructions inside the Coalition in the *Australian*:

Pressure is building within the Liberal party to toughen the Coalition's line on asylum-seekers. Partly this pressure is ideologically driven. But it is also tactical. The Coalition see illegal immigration as a rich political environment, but only if a clear point of difference between itself and the government can be established.

Senior Coalition figures are alive to the risk that Labor could outflank them on border protection if they are slow to move. The trajectory is ominous: Rudd is ramping up the rhetoric. His policy response will follow.

If Rudd were to stem the flow of boats, the result could be catastrophic for the Coalition. Rudd's response to the global financial crisis has usurped the Liberals' credentials as the party of sound economic management. If Rudd can stop the boats, the Coalition's border security credentials will also be shredded.

The American embassy in Canberra had been keeping a quizzical eye on the boats issue, alert to its history and curious to see how it might play out. "In terms of overall migration, the surge in asylum seekers is a drop in the ocean," an embassy officer told Washington in October. "But Rudd is not mentioning this, or lauding his government's more humane approach to asylum seekers. Given his dominance in the polls, some on the Left may be disappointed Rudd has not tried to create a new paradigm of debate on this issue." The embassy thought Rudd strangely cautious and Turnbull, "a social Liberal, doesn't appear comfortable pursuing this issue, but is way behind in the polls and needs an issue to try to erode Rudd's formidable poll numbers". The embassy rated Turnbull's leadership "beleaguered". In mid-November, an unnamed "key Liberal Party strategist" who called at the embassy talked enthusiastically about the boats. "The issue was 'fantastic'," he said. "And 'the more boats that come the better'." But they had yet to make the issue work in their favour: "His research indicated only a 'slight trend' towards the Coalition."

Almost the same day, Turnbull announced a Coalition government would restore temporary protection visas. For this he was attacked by members of his own back bench, refugee lawyers and human rights groups quick to remind the public that all the visas did the last time was fill the boats with women and children denied reunion with their men. These visas only ever impressed Australian voters, and Turnbull was talking tough for them. But it didn't save his leadership, white-anted by climate change sceptics and crippled by the bizarre Godwin Grech affair. On 1 December, Tony Abbott slipped through the party's ranks to become Leader of the Opposition.

"When Winston Churchill drove to Buckingham Palace in the dark days of 1940 to accept the king's commission, he felt that his whole life had been but a preparation for this moment," Abbott wrote ten days later in the *Australian*. "This is not wartime Britain. And I am certainly not Churchill. Still, I feel well equipped to take on the leadership of the party in what are testing times for the conservative side of politics."

*

And what would he do about the boats? He didn't hesitate. The new leader would exploit our race fears for his party's advantage. Santamaria was not his mentor now. He would be guided by John Howard's superb handling of the dark materials of our past and present. It was a case for absolutely secular Abbott. Asked on *Q&A* one night what Jesus would do about asylum seekers, he parried:

ABBOTT: Well, Jesus wouldn't have put his hand up to lead the Liberal Party, I suspect, or the Labor Party for that matter.
TONY JONES: But someone who believes in principles that he espoused did do that, so it's a legitimate question.

ABBOTT: Yeah. Don't forget Jesus drove the traders from the temple as well.

JONES: What's the point of that?

ABBOTT: The point is that Jesus didn't say yes to everyone. I mean Jesus knew that there was a place for everything and it is not necessarily everyone's place to come to Australia.

Abbott cast himself as a hero in the battle of the boats. He would do what it took to stop them. This was not a promise but a guarantee. No irksome details would stand in his way. Labor's soft policies were a magnet for boat people. The man he labelled "Mr Compassionate" was outsourcing migrant selection to people smugglers; was blackmailed by the Tamils on the *Oceanic Viking*; and was being weak, muddled and manifestly ineffective in the face of a "form of peaceful invasion" by a "small armada" of boats. "The problem is that we do not control our own borders." He would pull in the welcome mat. He would buy three $100 million Global Hawke surveillance drones to track the boats. He would take the toughest course despite the risk of sabotage and death: "You've got to be prepared to turn boats around." This was the way Australia sent a powerful message last time: "The fact that it was prepared to do it, I think let people in these countries know that trying to come to Australia illegally was a pretty risky business." There must be long mandatory prison terms for people smugglers. The Pacific Solution must be restored. "On day one of a Coalition government, I'd pick up the phone to the President of Nauru to reopen the Australian-built and Australian-funded off-shore processing centre – because ladies and gentlemen, the people smugglers need to know that their game is up." And the boats would stop. "We've done it before, we will do it again. Stop the boats we must, stop the boats we will." His election pledge in

August 2010 was "to end the waste, pay back the debt, stop the big new taxes, stop the boats …"

Abbott had a great deal to work with. Boats were arriving in numbers never seen before: nearly 7000 asylum seekers would come by sea in 2010. Yet even at that rate they would yield a tiny fraction – 2 or 3 per cent – of the immigrants Australia took in that year. Most years the boats bring less than 1 per cent. These figures aren't secret but have no impact. Poll after poll shows Australians wildly over-estimating the raw numbers of boat people who come. The five men on the *Kien Giang* have been followed by less than 30,000 in the years since, thirty-five years in which Australia has taken in three and a half million immigrants. But facts don't stick in panics and Abbott was fanning this old panic with ruthless skill as Christmas Island became a transit camp and new detention centres were found in desolate corners of mainland Australia. To appease hardliners, the government ceased processing Tamils and Hazaras for months. Hunger strikes, suicides and unrest followed. Rudd now began trying to dispel the myths, to put the boat arrivals in the perspective of history and refugee movements around the world. But no one was listening. Labor's explanations were about thirty-five years late.

The national mood darkened in 2010. In the space of a year those of us "very concerned" about boats and boat people had risen from 43 to 52 per cent. Another 26 per cent of us were "concerned", making eight out of ten Australians anxious about the issue. Those who thought Labor was "too soft" on boat people rose from 55 per cent to 63 per cent in almost the same months. Those who thought Labor's policies too harsh could barely be measured: hovering between 4 and 7 per cent. Abbott's plans for reintroducing the Pacific Solution won the immediate backing of nearly two-thirds of the nation. So did suspending the processing of the Tamils and Hazaras. A wide gap was opening between the parties: twice as many Australians – 39 to 20 per cent – thought the Coalition rather than Labor best represented their views on refugees and asylum seekers. Abbott had found the clear point of difference party strategists had been looking for. Hostility to refugees who arrive by water was rising to levels last seen at *Tampa* time: over half of us wanted to send all the boats back.

On a morning of wild weather a few days before Christmas, a boat turned up at the foot of the cliffs of Christmas Island at first light. That stretch of cliff is the dress circle of the island and early risers in the big houses along its edge heard the boat's motor spluttering and saw it was in trouble. They rang the navy, customs and the police but no help came before the boat was smashed to pieces on the rocks. The islanders had their cameras with them. Within hours, the carnage was on every television station in Australia in all its appalling detail. As many as fifty drowned that morning and within a couple of days Abbott was playing the politics as hard as he could, calling for an urgent return to the policies of the Howard era: "The sad truth is that as long as the people-smuggling trade exists, as long as the boats keep coming, the risk of disaster remains."

Panic-mongers need what the espionage world calls plausible deniability. Abbott nearly came to grief over the wreck because it became so obvious – and a matter of open contention in his party – that he and his immigration spokesman Scott Morrison were using the catastrophe to fan race fears and contempt for the government. On the morning a number of the dead were buried, Morrison complained on radio about the cost of flying survivors to Sydney for the funerals. Abbott backed him: "I'm also curious as to why rellies are being flown around the country. I mean, look, a terrible tragedy and I think everyone shares the grief of people who have lost loved ones particularly in these horrible circumstances, but, you're right, it does seem a bit unusual that the government is flying people to funerals."

Liberals were aghast. Shadow Treasurer Joe Hockey publicly rebuked his leader and Morrison: "No matter what the colour of your skin, no matter what the nature of your faith, if your child has died or a father has died, you want to be there for the ceremony to say goodbye, and I totally understand the importance of this to those families." Several senior Liberals appalled at what was happening told the *Sydney Morning Herald*'s Lenore Taylor that at a recent shadow cabinet Morrison had urged them "to capitalise on the electorate's growing concerns about 'Muslim immigration' and Muslims' 'inability' to integrate". The paper's political editor Peter Hartcher was told: "He put it on the table like a dead cat." Hartcher reported the events of this week under the headline: "Ugly game of race baiting." In the open party warfare that flared after the leaks and the funerals there was talk of Abbott's leadership being at risk. He survived. There was also talk that the Coalition might now stop beating up on boat people. It was not to be. One Liberal MP told the *Courier Mail*: "It works incredibly well for us in outer metropolitan electorates."

But the battle over the boats is having a "direct negative impact" on the social cohesion of Australia according to the 2011 Scanlon Foundation survey: "It is an issue that fuels disillusionment with government and heightens division within the population." The survey finds us growing distrustful of one another, gloomy about the future and in a slough of despond about government. "What goes on in Canberra doesn't stay in Canberra," says the survey's author, Andrew Markus of Monash University. He blames political brawling over the boats: "The combative style of saying about these complex problems there is a simple solution, why doesn't the government just *do* it? You say that today and you say it tomorrow.

That style of politics is having ramifications in the outside community. People are being told the government is so stupid it can't even solve the simplest problems."

*

Julia Gillard had gone to the polls in August 2010 indulging the fearful: "My view is many in the community should feel anxious when they see asylum seeker boats, and obviously we as a government want to manage our borders. For people to say they're anxious about border security doesn't make them intolerant, it certainly doesn't make them a racist, it means that they are expressing a genuine view that they are anxious about our border security." During the campaign she had touted a plan for processing boats in East Timor. Canberra was dreaming a dream that went back to Fraser's day of building holding camps up there for refugees heading down here. Fraser had Malaysia. Howard had Nauru and Manus Island. Rudd had Christmas Island. East Timor was a fizzer but in May 2011 Gillard announced a strategic swap of asylum seekers with Malaysia.

Her rhetoric was focus-group perfect: "As Prime Minister, I won't tolerate people smugglers attempting to bend and break the will of the Government to protect our borders and also our will to do the right thing as a country and to provide safe haven for those in need ... if someone seeks to come to Australia, they are at risk of going to Malaysia and going to the back of the queue." Abbott, who was pushing for the reopening of Nauru, damned the Malaysia plan as inhumane and a "lousy deal for Australia". Human rights bodies condemned both schemes in chorus. Australians were uneasy. A Nielsen poll taken in mid-August showed only 28 per cent of us backed Canberra's bipartisan determination to send all boat people away to be assessed. Despite the nation's profound reservations about these irregular arrivals, 53 per cent of us wanted them processed in Australia. Then the High Court stopped the Malaysia plan in its tracks.

Six of the court's seven judges decided Australia could only send these asylum seekers to countries that offered the protections set out in the Refugee Convention: to be safe from arbitrary detention, to be allowed to work, to be able to educate their children, to practise their religion and not to be re-exported to countries where they might once again face persecution or death. Australia's deal with Malaysia covered many of these points but the deal was not binding. Asylum seekers could do nothing to protect themselves once they were dumped in Kuala Lumpur. The court decided this was not good enough: protection must mean enforceable protection in law. Malaysia was out.

Abbott's response was merciless. "I think this is a Government which this morning is almost dying of shame at its own incompetence." Cabinet met hours after the court's decision. This might have been the moment to bravely change course, to shelter behind a decent decision of the court and continue processing asylum seekers onshore as they had been for thirty of the past thirty-five years. But the government's message for months had been that without Malaysia, Australia would be swamped. It was politically impossible to admit that all we had on our hands here was a manageable problem, not an invasion. Under attack from Abbott for her "great big" carbon tax and her failure to stop the boats, the prime minister's approval rating had sunk to 23 per cent and her party's primary vote was stuck at a catastrophic 27 per cent. What mattered in the aftermath of the court's decision was not the spirit of the country, its treaty obligations or the fate of asylum seekers already on the high seas heading for Christmas Island, but the authority of the Gillard government. The decision was taken to do whatever was necessary to resurrect the Malaysia deal. Labor would play to the panic.

"Nobody should doubt our resolve to break the people smugglers' business model," Gillard announced solemnly next day. "Nobody should doubt our resolve to implement this agreement." Over the next few days, the government produced two versions of amendments to the Migration Act which would achieve the same purpose: strip away human rights protections and allow Australia to send boat people – including young unaccompanied children – to whatever country it liked. The minister would never have to answer to the courts. Constitutional authority George Williams called the bill: "An affront to the basic principles of the rule of law. It also shreds any pretence of Australia remaining compliant with the 1951 Refugee Convention."

Abbott had to choose: support an unscrupulous plan that might stop the boats, or continue to undermine Julia Gillard. His genius from the start had been to present the boats as an issue of competence. Labor had foolishly come to accept his terms. So every group of Afghans reaching Christmas Island was seen as a failure of government. After the court's verdict, Abbott raged against this untrustworthy, shambolic, hopelessly incompetent, proud, stubborn government which had completely lost control of the nation's borders. Gillard needed Coalition votes to pass her amendments. Abbott refused to help. His faux objection to her strategy was that Malaysia, unlike Nauru, had not signed the Refugee Convention – the convention both sides of politics were now hoping to ditch. This stubbornness in the face of Gillard's requests for help came after nearly two years of insisting Canberra stop the boats. The naive were puzzled. But as that key Liberal Party strategist told those American diplomats in 2009: "The more boats that come the better."

Andrew Metcalfe was despatched by his masters to brief journalists and try to persuade the Opposition leader. The secretary of the immigration department is one of Canberra's most senior bureaucrats. He goes way back on the boats. He was the man who threatened the *Tampa*'s captain Arne Rinnan all those years ago with prosecution as a people smuggler if he didn't take his shipwrecked refugees away. The Malaysia plan has Metcalfe's fingerprints all over it: determined and cunning. On 7 September he spoke with unprecedented frankness to journalists in his office. He told them "off the record" that mandatory detention is patently not a deterrent; long-term detention is almost inevitably violent and very difficult to manage; temporary protection visas fill boats with women and children; towing boats back was highly effective in its day but Indonesia will not allow it to happen again; Nauru would not work a second time around; the Malaysia strategy is a game changer and the law can easily be amended to allow it to proceed.

What would happen, one journalist asked, if Malaysia fell through? Lurid versions of Metcalfe's answer in newspapers next day suggested he offered a stark choice between offshore processing and riots in Australian cities. Though more nuanced than that, Metcalfe was voicing his department's oldest imperative: absolute border control. Without Malaysia, he said, boat arrivals would return to the 600 plus every month of 2010; long-term detention would become unviable; large numbers of asylum seekers would be released into the community; support for the immigration system and multiculturalism would break down over time – decades perhaps – and lead to civil disorder. If we can't control our borders, he said, we will end up with the difficulties of London and Paris. He mentioned riots. The High Court's Malaysia decision, he remarked, might turn out to be more influential than *Mabo* or *Wik*.

On Wednesday 12 October, Gillard enjoyed a great parliamentary triumph: the House of Representatives passed the carbon tax. She had faced this panic, and won. But next day, all her lobbying efforts having failed, she abandoned the bill to resurrect the Malaysia deal. The weeks between the High Court decision and this tactical retreat marked one of the lowest points in the long history in this country of demonising boat people. This cage fight in Canberra saw each contender lashing the other for opening the nation to invasion. The press played along. Melbourne's *Herald Sun* the day after the court's decision carried not much more on its front page than a picture of a crammed refugee boat and a huge headline: "HERE THEY COME." That boat arrivals in 2011 were running at less than half the rate of the previous year was a fact without traction in these brawling weeks. Abbott now railed against the prime minister as if the fate of governments should turn on saving the nation from refugees: "She lacks the numbers in the parliament to do the most vital function of any government – to protect the borders of this nation. I say a party with no policy on border protection is a party with no right to be in government."

*

Where we are now is simply put: old fears and poor leadership have left us despising these wretched people who turn up on our shores in little boats wanting refugee protection. We continue to wildly overestimate their numbers. The 2011 Lowy poll shows 62 per cent of us still call them queue jumpers; 61 per cent of us believe they pose a threat to the security of the nation; and only 30 per cent of us believe they are really fleeing war and conflict back home. Australians are deeply suspicious not only of their motives and characters but their cleanliness. The Ipsos Mackay report of June 2011 found less than a third of us are confident these people are not bringing diseases into the country. These measures of disdain are not, of course, backed by fact. But as we know: in panics, what counts is fear.

At an event in Melbourne marking the tenth anniversary of the landmark – but unsuccessful – fight in the Federal Court to bring the asylum seekers on the *Tampa* ashore, there was talk among the lawyers of a new mood of generosity sweeping the nation. I urged caution. It is true that there survives a solid constituency for dealing decently with boat people once they reach our shores. And the 2011 Scanlon Foundation's survey shows a quickening sympathy for their plight: we are more likely than we were a year ago to believe they really *are* refugees. But the absolutely hostile – those Australians who simply want to send all refugee boats and their cargoes back out to sea – have not been budged by decades of humanitarian pleading. An Essential poll in September 2011 showed 28 per cent of us still want all the boats turned around – nothing much has changed there since the late 1970s – and 74 per cent of us rate as important or very important stopping the boats altogether. That is the constituency Abbott and Gillard are brawling over. But the most confronting figures I presented to the lawyers were these: between April 2009 and November 2010 eight polls asked if Australia was being too soft or too harsh on boat people. This is the bottom line. The figures jump about from poll to poll but the pattern is clear: about half of us want even harsher measures taken, about a quarter of us think what's done to boat people now is about right and only 10 per cent find Australia's distinctive policies too harsh. It's a tiny constituency for change.

"Our civilisation is inconceivable without the influence of Christian faith," Tony Abbott told the bishops and pastors and Salvation Army colonels gathered to vet the nation's leaders at Old Parliament House before the last election. Even grave George Pell had turned up to eye the contenders. Abbott was angling for more than the sectarian vote: "I want to stress that I am a Christian in politics, not a Christian politician and I am not asking Christians to vote for me because I am of like mind." But this street fighter sold his principles hard, first and foremost his dedication to the two rules of Christ: to love God and love our neighbours. The Christian worthies asked him no testing questions. Alas, they stuck to politics instead of investigating his theology. I wish one had challenged him to square his refugee policies with Matthew's account of the flight into Egypt. A bishop might make headway there. I've tried once or twice but boyish Tony laughs the question away.

Notes

Erik Jensen my colleague at the *Sydney Morning Herald* was hired as a researcher for this project and became critic, proofreader and goad. I owe his sharp eyes a great deal.

1: Fear itself
"It is in the plainest": the *Sydney Morning Herald,* 15 October 1975, p. 1. "Thousands of Australians": *The Wolf,* William Heinemann Australia, Melbourne, 2009, p. 124. "Australia has exceeded": the *Sydney Morning Herald,* News Review, 10 September 2011, p. 22. Carr, "I think it is": the *Sydney Morning Herald,* News Review, 23 July 2011, p. 1. Jones, "I can't get": the *Sydney Morning Herald,* 18 November 1999, p. 11.

2: Beyond the pale with Pauline
This is a considerably reworked version of the original which appeared in the *Sydney Morning Herald* on 12 May 1997.

3: Primal fear
This is a lightly edited version of the original which appeared in the *Sydney Morning Herald* on 31 May 1997, p. 1.

The 1996 poll: Jeannette Johnson, "Unfinished Business, Australians and Reconciliation", Commonwealth of Australia, 1996, http://www.austlii.edu.au/au/other/IndigLRes/car/1996/3/unfinished.html?stem=0&synonyms=0&query=Brian%20Sweeney%20and%20Associates.

4: Pictures from *Wik*
"Backyards in Peril" appeared in the *Sydney Morning Herald* on 4 December 1997, p. 2, "Harradine's Sandwich" on 6 December, p. 2 and "Save the Bees" in the same issue on p. 41.

5: The faithful gather

One of the most extraordinary scenes I've witnessed in my life. This first account appeared in the *Sydney Morning Herald*, 29 October 2001, p. 7. I gave a more detailed account in *Dark Victory* at pp. 244–6.

6: On the nose

This originally appeared in the *Sydney Morning Herald*, 22 December 2001, p. 20.

The NSW Ombudsman's review: *Review of the* Police Powers (Drug Detection Dogs' Act 2001, http://www.ombo.nsw.gov.au/publication/ PDF/Other%20Reports/executive%20summary.pdf.

7: The shape of the argument

This is part of the *Overland* Lecture I delivered in September 2004. The full lecture appeared about the same time in issue 176 of the magazine. On 14 October 2004 the *Australian* accused me in an editorial of comparing here "the ascendency of Howard to the rise of Hitler". Go figure.

My first account of this meeting with Harradine appeared on p. 1 of the "Spectrum" section of the *Sydney Morning Herald* on 1 February 1997. Howard, "without being accused": *Dark Victory*, p. 176. Attitudes to the death penalty: *Capital Punishment*, Australian Institute of Criminology, Trends & Issues, No. 3, February 1987; Bolt's attacks on *Media Watch* came by the dozen but this was the *Herald Sun*, 25 June 2004, p. 21.

8: Saving the nation

This is an edited version of the 2004 Allen Missen Lecture delivered to Liberty Victoria. Lost in the editing is all mention of Missen. My apologies to a fine man's memory.

The remarks of the High Court justices can be found in *Al-Kateb v. Godwin*: http://www.austlii.edu.au/au/cases/cth/HCA/2004/37.html. Admiral Ritchie, "We are talking": evidence to Senate Inquiry into a Certain Maritime Incident, 4 April 2002, p. 405. Those first newspaper reports of the court's decision: the *Sydney Morning Herald*, 7 August 2004, p. 5; the *Age*, 7 August 2004, p. 1, followed by an editorial, 9 August, p. 12; Barns, the *Herald Sun*, 11 August 2004, p. 18; Lawrence, the *Age*, 12 August 2004;

Henderson, the *Sydney Morning Herald*, 17 August 2004, p. 11 and the *Age* p. 11; ABC Radio National *Law Report*, 31 August 2004; Ackland, the *Sydney Morning Herald*, 17 September 2004, p. 15. Malouf, "Passionately evangelical": Quarterly Essay 12, *Made in England*, p. 46. Bush, "I believe in the transformational": the *Washington Post*, 3 September 2004, from p. A24. Howard, "will let them get on": Liberal Party website, 26 September 2004, http://www.liberal.org.au. Roxon, "to lead a debate": "The Great Legal Debate", NSW Parliament House, 21 September 2004.

9: The hero of Cronulla

A boast: I was the first to report Jones's role in the riot in the *Sydney Morning Herald*, 13 December 2005, p. 6. This is an expanded version of that original story. Jones, "If ever there was a clear example": broadcast 28 April 2005, see *Trad v. Jones (No. 3)* [2009] NSWADT 318. Jones: "What kind of grubs": broadcast 5 December 2005.

Update: ACMA, "likely to encourage": http://www.acma.gov.au/WEB/STANDARD/pc=PC_310133. Howard, "I think Alan Jones": the *Sydney Morning Herald*, 12 April 2007, p. 2.

10: Pick and stick

This originally appeared in the *Monthly,* November 2006.

11: A dawn sweep through Sydney

This was originally part of Quarterly Essay 26, *His Master's Voice: The Corruption of Public Debate Under Howard.* It has been lightly reworked.

Menon, "serious knocking" etc: interview, 4 April 2007. Robins, "the police are trashing" etc: interview, 5 April 2007. Davis-Frank, "My father answered" etc: interview, 4 April 2007; "on the night of November 18": *Green Left Weekly,* 28 March 2007, p. 9. Ryan, "I've shouted a lot" etc: interview, 4 April 2007. Carr, "street fighting fascism": the *Australian,* 12 September 2000, p. 1. Jamieson, "minimal": the *Age,* 18 November 2006, p. 8; "our streets" etc., the *Age,* 19 November 2006, p. 1. Various accounts of the melee on 19 November: the *Age,* 20 November 2006, p. 5; the *Sunday Age,* 19 November 2006, p. 1; the *Sunday Herald Sun* same day, p. 2; the *Herald Sun,* 20 November 2006, p. 1; and the *Age,* 7 December 2006,

p. 3. The *Age* report of Boljevic: 20 November 2006, p. 5. Rudd on Sydney demonstrators: the *Telegraph*, 24 February 2007, p. 4. Daniel Jones, "a very broad rally": interview, 5 April 2007. Hinman, "it was quite clear": the *Telegraph*, 24 February 2007, p. 4.

Update: Stary, "I've never seen": to me. Robins, "I never directed": the *Herald Sun*, 11 November 2008, p. 8. Parsons, "not … great force": County Court of Victoria, 24 November 2008, paragraph 16. Heilpern, "Australia has a long": the *Sydney Morning Herald*, 11 July 2007, p. 6.

12: Cowboys and Indians

The account of Haneef's life is taken from the transcripts of his interrogation: http://pandora.nla.gov.au/pan/84427/20090121-0022/www.haneef-caseinquiry.gov.au/www/inquiry/haneefcaseinquiry.nsf/Page/RWP14628B2902A7E152CA2574810022BC01.html. Keelty, "There is a lot of confusion": the *Sydney Morning Herald*, 29 July 2007, p. 11. Keelty, "connected to a terrorist group": *7.30 Report*, ABC TV, 3 July 2007. Beattie, "model citizen": the *Herald Sun*, 4 July 2007, p. 1. Keelty, "links to the UK": the *Sydney Morning Herald*, 7 July 2007, p. 1. Russo, "do you mind": the *Australian*, 12 July 2007, p. 4. Keelty, "there is something": *AM*, ABC radio, 10 July 2007. Ruddock, "I am told": the *Age*, 9 July 2007, p. 1. Keim, "That's not natural": *Lateline*, ABC TV, 18 July 2007. The *Guardian*, "Those who have": 20 August 2007. Bugg, "This decision was made": statement, 27 July 2007. Rudd, "these are tough": the *Australian*, 25 July 2007, p. 2. Howard, "whoever has been": the *Courier Mail*, 19 July 2007, p. 5. Ruddock, "inappropriate, highly unethical": *PM*, ABC radio, 18 July 2007. Keelty, "It's undermined": *AM*, ABC radio, 18 July 2007. Keelty, "until such time": the *Sydney Morning Herald*, 28 July 2007, p. 1. Howard, "all of this": the *Age*, 27 July 2007, p. 11.

Update: Kafeel's jihad note: the *Telegraph*, 16 December 2008, http://www.telegraph.co.uk/news/uknews/3689301/Glasgow-bomb-plot-Wills-to-families-left-by-airport-terrorists.html. Calvert-Smith, "no sign": the *Australian*, 12 April 2008, p. 16. Clarke, location of the SIM card: *Report of the Inquiry into the Case of Dr Mohamed Haneef*, November 2008, Vol. One, p. 92; Jabbour's failings: pp. x–xi; the caution of Simms and Thompson: pp. 48 and 144; "I could find no evidence": p. vii.

13: Scenes from a city under siege

Scene One originally appeared in the *Sydney Morning Herald,* 4 September 2007, p. 10. Scene Two: 5 September, p. 10. Scene Three: 6 September, p. 9. Scene Four: 7 September, p. 7.

14: Home free

This originally appeared in the *Sydney Morning Herald,* 27 October 2007, p. 28.

Update: Manne, "These people are stuck": the *Sydney Morning Herald,* 14 January 2010, p. 4.

15: Trust me

This originally appeared in the *Sydney Morning Herald,* 17 April 2008, p. 11.

16: Naked as the day

This is an edited version of the opening chapters of *The Henson Case* published by Text Publishing, Melbourne, in October 2008.

Update: most of this material can also be found in the book: Bush at p. 56; Turnbull at p. 86; the verdict of the Classification Board at pp. 117–18. But the Smith material is taken from a number of press reports: for the forgery see the *Daily Telegraph,* 11 July 1995, p. 2; for the 1998 flashing incident see Amanda Meade in the *Australian,* 3 November 1998, p. 3; and for his confession after the 2009 Christmas party groping see the *Sunday Telegraph,* 13 December 2009, p. 3.

17: The wash-up

This first appeared in the *Monthly,* December 2008.

Update: Henson, "I think you": the *Sydney Morning Herald,* 8 March 2011, p. 5. "Class groups view" and Baillieu quotes: the *Herald Sun,* 1 April 2011, p. 3. Conroy, "correctly reflects": the *Sydney Morning Herald* online, 9 July 2011; "we will be": Senate *Hansard,* 26 May 2011, p. 57.

18: One hot night forty years ago

The *Sydney Morning Herald:* 27 June 2009, Spectrum p. 12.

Update: ACMA complaint 2431: http://www.acma.gov.au/webwr/_

assets/main/lib312032/atn7_report_2431.pdf. Devine, "As a Catholic":
the *Sunday Telegraph*, 14 August 2011, p. 43. "Don't Meddle with Marriage": http://www.family.org.au/index.php?option=com_content&view=
article&id=419&Itemid=94. Katter: "Nobody has the right": the *Canberra
Times*, 17 August 2011, p. 7. Hagelin, "It won't stop at homosexual marriage": http://family.org.au/index.php?option=com_content&view=articl
e&id=425&Itemid=94.

19: Time on the island

This is an edited version of "The Indian Ocean Solution", the *Monthly*,
September 2009, p. 18.

Turnbull, "There cannot be": the *Sydney Morning Herald*, 6 May 2009,
p. 1. Chris Evans, "Labor's new regime": "New Directions in Detention",
http://law.anu.edu.au/Cipl/Lectures%26Seminars/2008/Evans_paper.pdf.
Hockley etc., "Touted when it": the *Advertiser*, 30 December 2002, p. 4.
Rick Scott, "In the period": http://parlinfo.aph.gov.au/parlInfo/search/
display/display.w3p;query=(Dataset%3Acommsen,commrep,commjnt,es
timate,commbill%20SearchCategory_Phrase%3A%22committees%22)
%20Department_Phrase%3A%22department%20of%20finance%20
and%20administration%22;rec=4. UNHCR, "UNHCR does not": Sub-
mission to the Joint Standing Committee on Migration Inquiry into
Immigration Detention in Australia, September 2008, paragraph 78.

20: Abbott rising

The *Sydney Morning Herald*, 2 December 2009, p. 4.

21: Cat and mouse

This is a fresh version of a piece that first appeared in the *Sydney Morning
Herald*, 20 February 2010, News Review, p. 4 under a joint by line with
my Darwin colleague Lindsay Murdoch. He was covering the coronial
inquiry in Darwin and provided me with advice, guidance and a cache of
documents. I was the writer.

All of the quotes from ADF personnel come from submissions and
evidence to the coronial inquiry. Rudd to the *Australian* a few days before
2007 elections: 24 November, p. 1.

Update: Cavanagh's findings: Inquest into the death of Mohammed Hassan Ayubi, Muzafar Ali Sefarali, Mohammed Amen Zamen, Awar Nadar, Baquer Husani [2010] NTMC 14 (17 March 2010), http://www.austlii.edu.au/au/cases/nt/NTMC/2010/14.html. For the navy's medals and its self-serving account of the operation: http://www.defence.gov.au/SIEV36/honourroll.htm. Jager, "I have kept": the *Sydney Morning Herald*, 5 May 2010, p. 5.

22: My love of drugs

E is for Ecstasy: the *Sydney Morning Herald*, 4 December 1996, p.12. Gelbard's visit was reported by me and Bernie Lagan in the *Sydney Morning Herald*, 19 July 1997, Spectrum, p. 1. Pell, "The only appropriate": the *Sydney Morning Herald*, 28 March 2001, p. 15. Cowdery, "My view is": the *Sydney Morning Herald*, 16 February 2001, p. 11. Morgan poll on Nguyen execution: the *Age*, Insight, 3 December 2005, p. 1. Manderson, *From Mr Sin to Mr Big, A History of Australian Drug Laws*, Melbourne: Oxford University Press, 1993, p. 173. McCoy: *Drug Traffic: Narcotics and Organised Crime in Australia*, Harper & Row, Sydney, 1980, p. 348. *2011 World Drug Report*: opium production, figure 2, p. 20; heroin on the markets, p. 45; coca cultivation, figure 1, p. 19; cocaine tonnage, p. 21; rising ATS manufacture, p. 20; and "The overall number": p. 22. Australian Institute of Health and Welfare National Drug Strategy Household Survey 2010: drug use figures, table 5.1; age of drug use, table 5.2; "It is known": p. 255. Fry, "Privately we are": the *Age* online, 30 November 2010, http://www.theage.com.au/opinion/politics/drug-policy-stalls-in-lawandorder-gear-20101129-18dkq.html. AIHW survey: punishment for drug dealers, table 13.15; support for decriminalisation, table 13.14; punishment for drug users, table 13.17. Greens' 2001 drugs policy: http://parlinfo.aph.gov.au/parlInfo/download/library/partypol/INMD6/upload_binary/inmd62.pdf;fileType=application/pdf#search=%22greens%20drugs%20and%20addiction%202001%20principles%22. "Ecstasy Over the Counter": the *Sunday Telegraph*, 2 March 2003, p. 1. Carr, "I am deeply": the *Sydney Morning Herald*, 3 March, p. 9. "Ecstasy and other": the *Herald Sun*, 31 August 2004, p. 3. Brown, "Do you think": the *Australian*, 1 September 2004, p. 6. "A fight for the party's soul": the *Sunday Age*, 8 August 2010,

p. 10. Brown, "The contentious past": the *Herald Sun*, 26 January 2006, p. 2. "Hardcore heroin addicts": the *Herald Sun*, 18 July 2006, p. 5. "If there is one": the *Australian*, 19 July 2006, p. 15. Confessions: Clinton: the *New York Times*, 30 March 1992, http://www.nytimes.com/1992/03/30/us/the-1992-campaign-new-york-clinton-admits-experiment-with-marijuana-in-1960-s.html?pagewanted=all&src=pm. Hitchens: *Hitch 22, A memoir*, Twelve, New York, 2010, p. 123. Obama: *New York Times*, 24 October 2006, http://www.nytimes.com/2006/10/24/world/americas/24iht-dems.3272493.html. Bush: http://news.bbc.co.uk/2/hi/in_depth/americas/2000/us_elections/profiles/576504.stm. Natasha Stott Despoja and "She didn't want": the *Telegraph*, 28 January 1997, p. 13. Latham: *Herald Sun*, 7 December 2003, p. 5. Bracks, Martin, Downer and "soon there won't": *Australian*, 26 July 2004, p. 8. Rudd: the *Herald Sun*, 12 July 2007, p. 2. Swan: *Sunday Telegraph*, 2 March 2008, p. 11. Turnbull: the *Age*, 26 September 2008, p. 9. Gillard: *Advertiser*, 27 September 2008, p. 2. "Journalist and author David": 7 November 2010, p. 3. "The Sunday Telegraph makes me": 14 November 2010, p. 110.

23: Belling the cat

This piece began life as the tenth Human Rights Oration for the Victorian Equal Opportunity and Human Rights Commission delivered on 10 December 2010 at Zinc in Federation Square. But I have incorporated some paragraphs from a story I wrote for the *Sydney Morning Herald* in February 2011 showing how church opposition to bills and charters of rights is driven by fear of losing their anti-discrimination exemptions.

Helen Irving, "no reasonable person": in *Don't Leave Us with the Bill: The Case Against an Australian Bill of Rights*, edited by Julian Leeser and Ryan Haddrick, Menzies Research Centre, Canberra, 2009, p. 170; Wallace, "In America": p. 257. Pell, "secularist mindset" etc: http://www.cam.org.au/perspectives/four-fictions-an-argument-against-a-charter-of-rights.html. Wallace, "there is no doubt" and Forsyth, "we are concerned": the *Sydney Morning Herald*, News Review, 12 February 2011, p. 6. Pell, "there is no doubt": http://www.cathnews.com/article.aspx?aeid=17252. The *Australian*'s leaders: "freedom of speech" and "a reaction to the rights", 11 December 2008, p. 13; "logic of the charter", 4 December 2008,

p. 15; "as shadow Attorney-General" and "Bill of rights advocates", 3 October 2008, p. 13. McHugh in *Australian Capital Television v. The Commonwealth* (1992) 177 CLR 106 at pp. 228–9. O'Connor: "a guarantee for all time", *4 Convention Debates*, 8 February 1898, p. 689; Forrest, "It is of no use": p. 666; Cockburn, "they were introduced": p. 685; O'Connor, "we are making": p. 688.

24: The dark materials
I have many debts to acknowledge here to the lawyers who have guided me over the years through the labyrinth of migration law particularly Mary Crock, Debbie Mortimer, Claire O'Connor and David Manne; to the activist Jack Smit who has become a historian of this long panic; and to Professor Murray Goot of Macquarie University and John Stirton of Nielsen for guiding me through the endless polling material.

The flight into Egypt: Matthew 2:1–23. Abbott, "I would be appalled": the *Daily Telegraph,* 20 February 2010, p. 36, and "Santa really saw": the *Australian*, 13 December 2003, p. 18. Abbott, "giant big new tax": the *Australian,* 2 December 2009, p. 4. He had plucked the expression from Barnaby Joyce and given it at least one trial run in October when Turnbull was negotiating changes to the ETS which, if not accepted, said Abbott, would make the scheme a "jobs destroying stealth tax on everything": the *Australian,* 19 October 2009, p. 14. Poll showing Rudd's approval rating at 68 per cent: Nielsen, the *Sydney Morning Herald,* 9 November 2009, p. 1. Poll on no migrants from Asia: http://www.immi.gov.au/media/publications/multicultural/nmac/statistics.pdf, p. 34. Lam Binh, "welcome to my boat" and Grant, "they had not been": *The Boat People: An Age Investigation*, Penguin Books, Ringwood, Victoria, 1979, p. 179.

No boat people in Australia, 1977 to 1979: "Boatpeople and Public Opinion in Australia", *People and Place*, Vol. 9, No. 4, 2001, p. 40. For "queue jumpers", "illegals" etc. and Fraser's response to the boat people: Jack Smit, "Malcolm Fraser's response to 'commercial' refugee voyages", *Journal of International Relations,* University of Dhaka, Bangladesh, Vol. 8, No. 2, 2010, pp. 76–103. Neal Blewett: *A Cabinet Diary: A Personal Record of the First Keating Government 1991–93*, Wakefield Press, Adelaide,

1999, p. 106. Georgiou, "It was on the basis": "Principles and Refugees", lecture delivered for the Cranlana Programme, 14 April 2010. Poll for sending boats back, September 1993: Irving Saulwick, the *Age*, 11 October 1993, pp. 1 and 4. Poll on estimating boat numbers: AGB McNair, June 1997; T. Vinson, M. Leech & E. Lester, "The number of boat people: fact and fiction", *Uniya Brief Research Report*, No. 1, 1997. Ruddock, "gruesome trade in human beings": the *Advertiser*, 28 May 1999, p. 3. "Assault": the *Sydney Morning Herald*, 19 November 1999, p. 2. "Whole villages": the *Age*, 18 November 1999, p. 1. "When they arrive": the *Age*, 21 November 1999, p. 14. Hanson, "We go out": the *Australian*, 15 February 2001, p. 4. "Australia had no way": the *Courier Mail*, 7 November 2001, p. 1. Leaflets, "The Howard Government": Marr & Wilkinson, *Dark Victory*, p. 237. Poll on pushing boats back during *Tampa* time: ACNielsen, Issues Report, 11 October 2001. Lower figures were reported by Morgan (68 per cent) and Newspoll (56 per cent). These are set out in Goot's excellent "Neither entirely comfortable nor wholly relaxed: public opinion, electoral politics, and foreign policy", published in James Cotton & John Ravenhill (eds), *Trading on Alliance Security: Australia in World Affairs: 2001–2005*, tables 13.3, p. 256. Poll showing collapse in support for Howard: Goot, table 13.2 at p. 56. Howard, "white or Japanese": the *Herald Sun*, 9 November 2001, p. 1. Albrechtsen, "to close down": 3 August 2011, p. 12. Poll on underlying racism: *Age*, 20 December 2005, p. 1. Goot & Sowerbutts: "Dog whistles and death penalties: the ideological structuring of Australian attitudes to asylum seekers", Australasian Political Studies Association Conference, Adelaide, September 30 – October 1 2004, pp. 1 and 14. Poll: Scanlon Foundation, *Mapping Social Cohesion 2011*, figures 20 and 22: http://www.arts.monash.edu.au/mapping-population/--documents/mapping-social-cohesion-summary-report-2011.pdf. Poll on mandatory detention: the *Age*, 15 February 2005, p. 1. Poll on Pacific Solution: National Opinion Report, 23 April 2006. Turnbull, "real problem": the *Australian*, 8 December 2008, p. 1. "There is no doubt": the *Age*, 10 April 2009, p. 9. Poll on whether tougher measures would have any impact on boat arrivals: the *Australian*, 21 April 2009, p. 1. Maley: the *Australian*, 17 October 2009, p. 11. American embassy reports: Wikileaks cables, 16 October 2009, http://wikileaks.org/

cable/2009/10/09CANBERRA934.html; 21 April, http://wikileaks.org/cable/2009/04/09CANBERRA398.htm; and 13 November 2009 reported in the *Sydney Morning Herald*, 18 December 2010, p. 6. Abbott, "When Winston Churchill": 12 December 2009, p. 3. Q&A: ABC TV, 5 April 2010. Abbott on the boats, "doing what it takes": the *Canberra Times*, 28 May 2010, p. 13; "magnet": the *Australian Financial Review*, 28 July 2010, p. 19; "Mr Compassionate": the *Mercury*, 2 January 2010, p. 25; "Outsourced": address to the Menzies Research Centre, 4 May 2010; "blackmailed": the *Australian*, 31 December 2009, pp. 1 and 2; "peaceful invasion" and "small armada": *AM*, ABC radio, 7 July 2010; "The problem is that": the *Australian*, 3 April 2010, p. 9; "drones", the *Canberra Times*, 17 August 2010, p. 4; "You've got to be" and "The fact that Australia": the *Australian*, 31 December 2009, pp. 1 and 2; "idyllic" and "a picture postcard": the *Advertiser*, 4 November 2010, p. 15; "On day one of a Coalition": campaign launch, 8 August 2010; "We've done it before": the *Canberra Times*, 28 May 2010, p. 13. Poll, level of anxiety about the boats: The Lowy Institute's *Australia and the World, Public Opinion and Foreign Policy*, 2011, p. 14. Poll, too soft or too harsh: Essential online polls for April–May 2009 and October 2010. Poll, backing to reintroduce Pacific Solution: Nielsen, the *Age*, 7 June 2010, p. 2. Poll, suspension of processing: Nielsen, the *Sydney Morning Herald*, 19 April 2010, p. 7. Polls, differences between the parties and sending the boats back: AES analysis in I. McAllister et al., *Australian Election Study, 2010*, Australian Social Science Data Archive, Australian National University, Canberra, 2011. Abbott, "the sad truth": the *Mercury*, 20 December 2010, p. 10. Abbott, "I'm also curious": the *Age*, 16 February 2011, p. 1. Hockey, "No matter what": the *Sydney Morning Herald*, 16 February 2011, p. 2. Morrison on Muslims: the *Sydney Morning Herald*, 18 February 2011, p. 1. Hartcher, "Ugly game" and "dead cat": the *Sydney Morning Herald*, News Review, 19 February 2011, p. 9. Liberal MP, "It works incredibly": the *Courier Mail*, 24 February 2011. Scanlon 2011 Poll, "direct negative impact": p. 37. Markus, "What goes on": to me. Gillard, "My view is": the *Australian Financial Review*, 5 July 2010, p. 1. Gillard, "as prime minister" and Abbott, "lousy deal": the *Sunday Telegraph*, 8 May 2011, p. 4. Poll, Nielsen on push backs and assessment in Australia: the *Sydney Morning Herald*, 16 August 2011, p. 1.

High Court decision: *Plaintiff M70/2011 v. Minister for Immigration and Citizenship; Plaintiff M106 of 2011 v. Minister for Immigration and Citizenship* [2011] HCA 32 (31 August 2011). Abbott, "I think this": the *Australian*, 2 September 2011, p. 1. Newspoll on standing of Gillard and Labor: the *Herald Sun*, 6 September 2011, p. 2. Gillard, "nobody should doubt": the *Age*, 1 September 2011, p. 7. Williams, "an affront": the *Sydney Morning Herald*, 11 October 2011, p. 11. Metcalfe's briefing: various sources to me. "Here they come", *Herald Sun*: 1 September 2011, p. 1. Hansard, 14 October 2011, p. 51. Poll on queue jumpers etc: The Lowy Institute Poll 2011, figure 20, p. 14. Poll on disease: Ipsos Mackay, June 2011, figure 1, p. 3, http://media.sbs.com.au/home/upload_media/site_20_rand_556105992_sbs_immigration_nation_summary_for_gbt-wycf.pdf. Scanlon 2011: table 17. Poll on turning back the boats: Essential, September 2011, http://www.essentialmedia.com.au/category/essential-report-110926-26th-september-2011. Eight polls: Goot, "Population, immigration and asylum seekers: patterns in Australian public opinion", table 5, p. 34. Abbott, "our civilisation": http://www.tonyabbott.com.au/LatestNews/Speeches/tabid/88/articleType/ArticleView/articleId/7435/Address-to-the-Australian-Christian-Lobby-Old-Parliament-House.aspx.